# SLAVE NATION

## How Slavery United the Colonies & Sparked the American Revolution

Alfred W. Blumrosen and Ruth G. Blumrosen

Introduction by Eleanor Holmes Norton

SOURCEBOOKS, INC.
NAPERVILLE, ILLINOIS

Copyright © 2005 by Alfred W. Blumrosen
Cover and internal design © 2005 by Sourcebooks, Inc.
Cover image © Corbis Images
Sourcebooks and the colophon are registered trademarks of
Sourcebooks, Inc.

Published by Sourcebooks, Inc.
P.O. Box 4410, Naperville, Illinois 60567-4410
(630) 961-3900
FAX: (630) 961-2168
www.sourcebooks.com

Library of Congress Cataloging-in-Publication Data
Blumrosen, Alfred W.
   Slave nation : how slavery united the colonies and sparked
the American Revolution / Alfred W. Blumrosen and Ruth G.
Blumrosen.
      p. cm.
   Includes bibliographical references and index.
   1.  Slavery--United States--History--18th century. 2.  United
States--History--Revolution, 1775-1783--Causes. 3.   African
Americans--History--To 1863.   I. Blumrosen, Ruth G. II.
Title.

   E446.B58 2005
   973.3'11--dc22

2004027271

Printed and bound in the United States of America
            QW   10 9 8 7 6 5 4 3 2 1

To Ruth
For our lives together

To Erica, Charlotte, and Victoria
Our granddaughters

For their lives in a better world

# TABLE OF CONTENTS

# Acknowledgments

We must first acknowledge the two universities—the University of Michigan and Rutgers University Law School—that have been our base for most of our lives. At Michigan we met and married; learned journalism at the Michigan Daily; and studied history, economics, political science, and, of course, law. One of our near classmates, Ted St. Antoine, long-time dean of the Michigan Law School, encouraged our book project at a time when we needed support.

We continued to study and learn from the Rutgers law faculty when we came to the law school in 1955. Most memorable were Tom Cowan, Gerry Moran, Bob Knowlton, and Clyde Ferguson. A succession of deans supported our activities in labor relations, civil rights, and employment discrimination law: Lehan Tunks, Willard Heckel, Jim Paul, Peter Simmons, Roger Abrams, and now Stuart Detsch. We inflicted our evolving ideas about slavery and the Revolution on those faculty members who would listen, particularly Greg Marks and Mark Weiner.

Our second acknowledgment is to the work of generations of historians, many of whom we rely on in this book. Although we criticize those who believe that slavery played no role in the beginning of the Revolutionary era, we recognize that we are standing on their collective shoulders in order to reach our conclusions to the contrary. Particularly, we have built on Staughton Lynd's *Class Conflict, Slavery, and the United States.* Lynd's underlying principle—that slavery was an important element in the beginning of our national existence—resonated with our own thinking about that topic. Lynd did not get it all right, but he first saw that slavery had to be more central in the analysis of our Revolution than the "conventional wisdom" recognized. We built upon his essay, "The Compromise of 1787," to better understand the relation between the Constitution and the Northwest Ordinance. Since Lynd wrote, nearly forty years ago, others, including John Hope Franklin, Paul Finkelman, Gary Nash, Don Fehrenbacher, Duncan McLood, and Don Robinson, have examined the role of slavery in our history. They rarely focused on the summer of 1772, when an English judge denounced slavery as "so odious" that a master could not recapture a slave in England. Nor did they make the connection between the Continental Congress and the deadlock at the Constitutional Convention in 1787.

Third, we have a debt of gratitude to the repositories of information that were unfailingly helpful: the law libraries at Rutgers, Newark; Columbia University; Fordham University; the Butler Library at Columbia; the New York Historical Society; the British Museum; the British Anti Slavery Society in London; the library of Colonial Williamsburg, Virginia; and the Library of Congress.

Fourth, we have received support over the years that expanded our understanding of the breadth of legal culture, commencing in 1957 with a grant from the Russell Sage Foundation to examine the relationship between law and sociology. In 1993 we had Fulbright Scholarships to South Africa to examine whether the U. S. experience with equal employment opportunity would be useful there as South Africans embarked on the peaceful dismantling of apartheid. This was followed by a month's residency at the Rockefeller Study Center in Bellagio, Italy. Beginning in 1998, the Ford Foundation enabled our statistical study of intentional job discrimination that is relevant to the closing chapter of this book. All of these institutions—meaning the people in them—have helped us to understand the problems we have addressed in this book.

During the civil rights era, it was often said that "if we could go to the moon, we could surely end discrimination at home." These last forty years have demolished that prediction. Going to the moon involved an environment of known or knowable forces; discrimination involves complexities of human behavior that defy the certainties of natural science.

We learned much about these complexities working with those involved in civil rights activities. We were privileged to know workers who were male and female, black, white, Hispanic, and Asian Pacific, as well as employers, unions, and civil rights organizations. We saw government, both as participants in its activities and as litigants against it. Eleanor Holmes Norton, with whom we worked during her years as chair of the New York Commission on Human Rights and the Federal Equal Employment Opportunity Commission, has always been a tower of strength, critical judgment, and warm friendship.

Most of all, we admired those men and women of the 1960s who had faith that a government that had ignored them for so long would help bring justice into the realities of their workplaces. They came to the then-new Equal Employment Opportunity Commission at great personal risk, in the hopes of influencing those workplace realities they had long endured. The example of their courage has sustained us through difficult times.

To our agent, Ron Goldfarb, who had confidence in the book, and to our editor Hillel "LeGree" Black, his assistant Sarah Tucker, and our distant editor Michelle Schoob, we are indebted for critical and supportive commentary, and the publication of this book.

Our sons, Steven and Alex, read, reviewed, criticized, and encouraged multiple versions of the book as they evolved through the years, along with lots of conversation and not a little argument. They have been patient and helpful at every turn. Alex usually gave advice, counsel, and criticism from Paris where he practices law. Steven has been more closely involved in recent years, in editing, advising, revising, and researching text and images; in solving computer problems; and in countless other ways supporting our efforts. His daughter Erica alphabetized our growing library and helped with the bibliography and footnotes. Frederica Wechsler fine-tuned the final version of our text.

# Introduction

This fascinating and readable book about the conundrum of black slavery and the birth of a free nation is an exacting history by two remarkable scholars who have distinguished themselves as lawyers and intellectuals. Although the Blumrosens are not professional historians, the history of slavery and discrimination has had an important place in their personal and professional lives. Living with the consequences of this history in our country fueled their lifelong dedication to racial justice and their work as civil rights lawyers. Their strong professional bonds nurtured their remarkable, loving marriage as well. They worked together as lawyers, scholars, and professors, sometimes on the same subjects, but often not. Theirs was a lifelong partnership of parallel interests, professions, scholarship, and now this final collaboration.

The Blumrosens' work to eliminate discrimination based on race, sex, religion, and national origin has been rooted in the nation's racial history. They were among a small band of lawyers who developed path-breaking legal theory and converted it to judicial doctrine. History assumed pragmatic importance in the search for the first effective remedies for discrimination, often becoming the predicate for the new remedies that finally emerged.

As legal pioneers in the field of equal employment law, the Blumrosens could not afford to be strangers to history. Understanding the history of slavery and discrimination has been essential to the remedies they helped fashion in race and sex discrimination law. Three centuries of the cumulative consequences of discrimination required strong remedies, but they could be justified only by unusual circumstances. Those circumstances were found in our nation's unusual history.

*Slave Nation* is a logical if unpredictable product of the interest of these two lawyers in the close relationship between American law and America's racial history. In this book, the Blumrosens have gone beyond the uses of history to grapple with history itself.

The Blumrosens are fascinated by contradiction and irony. The historical contradictions between slavery and freedom in America find parallels in the law they know best. American law was the guardian and the guarantor of slavery. The legal system rationalized and enforced slavery and discrimination. Yet, the law that guaranteed and fostered legal subjugation became an instrument of liberation with the 1954 school desegregation cases and the wide-ranging jurisprudence that has developed since. The Blumrosens are part of the generation of lawyers who changed American law. They also changed America.

The authors investigate the sources of the old contradiction between slavery and freedom and find it in full form before the American Revolution. They reconstruct the straight line between slavery and our national origins. They show that the slavery question did not simply arise at the writing of the Constitution when the future of black slavery and its place in the new nation had to be publicly faced because it could no longer be avoided. The security of slavery had to be settled before the Revolution or the cause of independence and nationhood would have been stillborn.

The Blumrosens bring fresh eyes to the problematic national emergence of slavery as an issue in the pre-Revolutionary period. Of course, slavery was a native institution originally present in all the colonies and ultimately shaped the South and its economy. For more than a century slavery flourished, increasingly favoring the South, which regarded slavery as indispensable to the products of its agricultural economy. However, black slavery was more than geographical. In the South, the practice hardened into an institution bolted into economic and cultural life, affecting everything it touched. Black slavery was not as useful to northern commerce and antislavery sentiment grew, but northern entanglement with slavery was deep and unavoidable. Although two nations were taking shape long before revolution was in the air, slavery quickly became a national issue once the idea of an independent nation began to take shape. The South insisted on slavery, but as the Blumrosens show, the North not only tolerated southern slavery, but early agreed to its permanence in the new nation.

Although the issue grew to divide the country, slavery did not have to be squarely faced while the colonies were part of a mother country that tolerated it, allowing North and South each to go its own way. However, for the slave-centered South, even the possibility of this change was enough to light the spark for the coming revolution. The spark came with the *Somerset* decision in England that freed a slave brought to London by a colonist and raised a question as to slavery's legitimacy in the Empire. Although this decision did not overturn slavery in the colonies, its logic was not lost on southerners. The Blumrosens take us from *Somerset* to the Revolution. They show that England had accommodated tax grievances in the past and might have compromised that issue further. However, for the South, compromise on slavery was unthinkable. Independence was the only solution.

In *Slave Nation*, the Blumrosens go down seldom explored paths that lead to the pro-slavery compromise that was sewn into the national fabric well before the Revolution. The Revolutionary patriots in the North did not speak openly about maintaining slavery but made it clear to the South that slavery would not be disturbed. There would have been no revolution to create one nation if John Adams, the Massachusetts antislavery stalwart and other northerners had not accepted southern prerogatives on slavery. There would have been no union if both the Northwest Ordinance and the Constitution had not guaranteed the continuation of slavery in the southern territories and the entitlement of owners even to their slaves that escaped to the North. The price of freedom from England was bondage for African slaves in America. America would be a slave nation.

North and South made their way to the same barricades with the same national slogans and for many of the same reasons. The committees of correspondence spread revolutionary ardor to increasingly receptive colonies, and British intransigence to greater autonomy and equal rights between England and the colonists congealed.

Beneath the unity of revolution lurked a compromise that could not endure and would lead to civil war in the next century. The Constitution and the Northwest Ordinance memorialized the bargain that had been struck to allow the Revolution to go forward and create a slave nation. The Blumrosens write compellingly from the evidence. The riches are in their research and documentation. They leave us without illusions about how we became one nation. *Slave Nation* will surprise many readers about the central role of slavery in our nation's Revolutionary history, but this book should deepen their appreciation about the distance we have had to travel and for the nation we are becoming today.

*EHN 11-30-04*

Eleanor Holmes Norton, Congresswoman for the District of Columbia, Professor, Georgetown University Law School.

# Chapter I

# Somerset's Journey Sparks the American Revolution

On June 22, 1772, nearly a century before the slaves were freed in America, a British judge, with a single decision, brought about the conditions that would end slavery in England. His decision would have monumental consequences in the American colonies, leading up to the American Revolution, the Civil War, and beyond. Because of that ruling, history would be forever changed. This book is about that decision and the role of slavery in the founding of the United States.

The story of that British court decision begins with the kidnapping of a nine-year-old boy who was growing up in a West African village. He joined the river of slaves that sailed the infamous Middle Passage to America, arriving in Virginia in March, 1749.[1] Along the way he was given his slave name—Somerset. He was healthy and quickly picked up English. These qualities caught the eye of a Scottish born, up-and-coming, twenty-four-year-old merchant and slave trader named Charles Stewart. Stewart's office and storehouse were in Norfolk, Virginia, a town where many of the Scottish merchants drawn to the tobacco industry had settled.

Stewart purchased Somerset on August 1, 1749, and trained him as his personal servant. Somerset was given better clothing than Stewart's other slaves and taken to meetings with Stewart's friends and business associates. Somerset was a personable young man with both white and black friends. Correspondence to Stewart included compliments about "able Somerset Stewart" from Nathaniel Coffin, an important Quaker from Boston, along with the terms of the highest friendship from "Sapho and Tambo," presumably black slaves or workers for Coffin.[2]

The lives of Somerset and Stewart would not now be remembered except for an act of courage and tact by Stewart in 1762 during the French and Indian war. A ship carrying Spanish soldiers, who had surrendered to the British and were being repatriated, floundered off the coast near Norfolk. The ship was under repair when a mob of Virginians attacked the soldiers, killing two and wounding several. Stewart intervened, quieted the mob, and saved the remaining Spaniards. Britain was grateful for his intervention, and rewarded him with a position of authority over customs collectors from Quebec to Virginia. Somerset traveled with Stewart as he enforced the customs laws and met Stewart's friends and associates.

Stewart rose in the customs service, becoming paymaster general of the American Board of Customs. In October, 1769, Stewart sailed to England with Somerset to help raise his sister Cecilia's children after the death of her husband. They settled in London. Somerset, with new household duties, familiarized himself with the city and found a black community of thousands of former slaves and free persons, mainly from the British West Indian colonies.[3]

The large number of former slaves proved unsettling to Sir John Fielding, the man who had modernized the London police force. In 1762, he published a book of extracts from the statutes that governed merchants and artisans of London, hoping that doing so would improve their understanding of the laws. In this, he anticipated modern administrative regulation of business.[4]

In his book, he tried to discourage colonials from bringing their slaves to England. He explained that when slaves were brought to London, "They put themselves on a footing with other servants, become intoxicated with liberty, grow refractory, and...begin to expect wages."

Fielding warned colonials that there were "a great number of black men and women who...make it their business to corrupt and dissatisfy the mind of every fresh black servant that comes to England; ...makes it not only difficult but dangerous to the proprietor of their slaves to recover the possession of them, when once they are spirited away."

In his final argument against bringing slaves to England Fielding declared that the slaves would be useless —and dangerous—when they returned to the colonies:

> The sweets of liberty and the conversation with free men and Christians, enlarge their minds and enable them...to form such comparisons of the different situations, as only serve...to embitter their state of slavery, to make them restless, prompt to conceive, and

alert to execute the blackest conspiracies against their governors and masters.

Some London blacks were free. Some, like Somerset, were slaves to colonials living in London. Some had been freed by their masters. Some worked; some were beggars known as the "St. Giles Blackbirds." Some were popular artists and singers. Others were seamen or servants.[5] Some had been runaways whose owners had given up looking for them because, according to Fielding, "the mob [was] on their side." The "mob" was "the working people of London, the preindustrial craftsmen and laborers who poured into the streets of the capital in their thousands to demonstrate for 'Wilkes and Liberty.'"[6] John Wilkes was a colorful character in the East End of London in the 1760s and 1770s. He was elected to parliament, but having incurred George III's displeasure was denied his seat repeatedly and was often arrested, only to be freed by the mob shouting "Wilkes and Liberty."

Somerset met many blacks on the streets while running errands for his master, in the stores, and along the docks where he looked longingly at ships that might take him to freedom in a friendly climate. He also became acquainted with some white persons, possibly those with whom Stewart was friendly or had business connections. His pleasant personality, noted in connection with his activities in the colonies, generated friendships in England as well. His conversations with "free men and Christians," as Fielding suggested, may have led to his decision to leave Stewart.

In August of 1771, he was baptized in the Church of St. Andrew, Holborn. He probably took his first name, James, at that time. His godparents were Thomas Walkin, Elizabeth Cade, and John Morrow. Some thought that baptism—becoming a Christian—would either ensure freedom for a slave, which was not true, or would be a positive element in any litigation concerning his status. Some five or six cases seeking freedom for black slaves were brought before English courts after 1769. This litigation had been inspired by Granville Sharp.

Sharp, a thin, short man with intense features, had illustrious religious ancestors; he was grandson of the archbishop of York, and son of an archdeacon. He disdained the ministry and applied his fine mind to a variety of intellectual matters while working as a government clerk in the ordinance department. He was an intellectual dilettante until he stumbled onto the problem of slavery. He had befriended Jonathan Strong, a young black slave whose master had beaten him nearly to death. Sharp assisted in Strong's recovery and helped him get a job after he recovered. Two years later, Strong's "owner" saw him and had him detained to be shipped to Jamaica to be sold.

Sharp secured Strong's release. He was appalled by Strong's owner's actions and could not believe they were permitted under the laws of England.[7] Although he was not a lawyer, Sharp thoroughly researched the confusing precedents on the subject. In 1769 he wrote a powerful tract in support of his views,[8] and helped secure the freedom of five or six runaway slaves who had been recaptured by their masters.

Somerset left Stewart's home on October 1, 1771, and did not return. Stewart was not only dismayed at Somerset's action, but felt Somerset had betrayed him and "insulted his person." He posted notices and may have hired slave catchers.[9] Somerset was caught, and on November 26 was delivered to Captain Knowles aboard the *Ann and Mary*, a ship preparing to sail to Jamaica. Knowles was to sell him there. Knowles's sailors dragged Somerset into the hold and put chains on him; chains that Somerset must have thought would never come off.

But they did come off. His godparents acted quickly. On December 3, a week after he had been captured, they petitioned the Court of King's Bench for a writ of habeas corpus, with affidavits stating that Somerset was being held against his will aboard ship by Captain Knowles. Lord Mansfield, the chief justice of the court, issued a writ requiring Knowles to explain to the court the reason for Somerset's detention.[10]

King's Bench was the oldest and highest common law court in England; it was so named because in earlier years, the king himself sat in judgment in that court. In 1772, it consisted of a chief justice and four associate justices. One was William Blackstone, the author of the *Commentaries on the Law of England*, which were well known to colonial lawyers. In 1765, he had written his interpretation of the confused English precedents concerning slavery:

> And this spirit of liberty is so deeply implanted in our constitution, and rooted even in our very soil, that a slave or a Negro, the moment he lands in England, falls under the protection of the laws and so far becomes a freeman.[11]

Lord Mansfield was a former attorney general, a cabinet minister, and a firm upholder of the powers of Parliament over the king and the colonies.[12] No radical abolitionist, Mansfield was a powerful jurist and parliamentarian who dominated the Court of King's Bench. His major fame as a jurist was in rationalizing British law to facilitate commerce. He was careful to include in his opinion on Somerset's case that "Contract for the sale of a slave is good here; the sale is a matter to which the law properly and readily attaches."[13] Mansfield was speaking only to the commerce in slaves relating to the colonies, not to the authority of a master in England.

On December 9, Captain Knowles appeared in King's Bench with Somerset and a written explanation of why he had been holding Somerset. His reason was simple: Stewart had delivered his slave Somerset to Captain Knowles so that Knowles could take the slave to be sold in Jamaica. Somerset's lawyer, William Davy, asked for more time to prepare. Mansfield released Somerset, with sureties, until the hearing. Somerset remained in London, and appeared at the final hearing in his case, which took place on June 22, 1772.

After Somerset was released by Mansfield, he went to meet Granville Sharp. Sharp had secured freedom for other slaves, following the same approach that Somerset had used—obtaining affidavits of white witnesses alleging that the runaway slave was held against his will. These affidavits were submitted to Lord Mansfield, who required the person imprisoning the slave to explain his authority.

In Sharp's previous cases involving slaves brought to England, Lord Mansfield had persuaded the slave owner to free the slave, thus enabling the chief justice to avoid what for him was a complex legal and social problem of liberty versus property. In 1771, Mansfield had told a lawyer for another escaped slave:

> Perhaps it is much better that [the legality of slavery] should never be discussed or settled. I don't know what the consequences may be, if the masters were to lose their property by accidentally bringing their slaves to England. I hope it never will be finally discussed; for I would have all masters think them free, and all Negroes think they were not, because then they would both behave better.[14]

Mansfield had a personal interest in the situation of people of color. He was especially fond of his grandniece Dido Elizabeth Lindsey, who was the daughter of Sir John Lindsey, Mansfield's nephew. Dido's mother had been aboard a Spanish ship that Lindsey had captured. He acknowledged his paternity in his will.[15] Dido, in a painting with her cousin Elizabeth Murray, appeared to be a light-skinned black woman. She lived with Mansfield's family and had grown up close to Mansfield's grandnieces— her cousins—and she was accepted socially. She wrote letters for Mansfield when he was too ill to write. In his will he confirmed her freedom, left her £500 plus £100 per annum for life, and the life use of a painting of himself "to put her in mind of one she knew from her infancy and always honored with uninterrupted confidence and friendship."[16]

Mansfield released Somerset temporarily, but he was not a free man yet. The case dragged on while Mansfield tried to persuade Stewart to free Somerset. Mansfield did not want to decide on the legality of slavery in England. But the West Indian planters wanted a decision upholding slavery in Britain because the uncertainty was affecting the price of their "property." They financed Stewart's defense. Stewart promised them not to cave in to Mansfield's urging. Mansfield even tried to persuade Elizabeth Cade, the "poor widow" who had paid for the writ of habeas corpus that freed Somerset, to purchase Somerset herself and set him free. She replied that this would acknowledge that Stewart "had a right to assault and imprison a poor innocent man in this kingdom, and that she would never be guilty of setting so bad an example."[17]

Mansfield was exasperated with the planters. He warned them in a preliminary hearing that they were likely to lose. He may have resolved the conflicting precedents in his own mind, or may have used this pressure to achieve a settlement. He told them that the case was so clear that it was unnecessary to convene the full court; he had succeeded in five or six cases in settling the matter by the owner agreeing to free the slave. He recommended that Stewart free Somerset, but: "if the parties will have judgment, whatever the consequences, *fiat justitia, ruat coelum* (let justice be done though the Heavens fall)."

Stewart's lawyer had argued that freeing the fourteen or fifteen thousand slaves in England would produce profound disruption, and that the owners would suffer a loss of £700,000, or an average of £50 per slave. To this, Mansfield responded, "£50 a head may not be a high price."

To Stewart's claim that the uncertainty on the issue was already disturbing the commercial world, Mansfield told the slave owners that they had come to the wrong place to get the issue settled: "An application to Parliament, if the merchants think the question of great commercial concern, is the best, and perhaps the only method of set- tling the point for the future."[18] His approach echoed Mansfield's attachment to the principle of parliamentary supremacy over the colonies that was emphasized in the Declaratory Act of 1766. Having warned the merchants that they might lose, he postponed the decision so that they might reflect on his warning. The merchants tried, but were unable even to secure a hearing on a proposed bill despite their influence in Parliament.[19] No reason was given, but we may assume that the members were content to let the matter rest while it was before the court.

In late May, a London newspaper speculated on the consequences of Mansfield's decision:

> The West-India merchants have, we hear, obtained a promise from Mr. Stewart not to accommodate the Negro cause, but to have the point solemnly determined; since, if the laws of England do not confirm the colony laws with respect to property in slaves, no man of common sense will, for the future, lay out his money in so precar- ious a commodity. The consequences of which will be inevitable ruin to the British West Indies.[20]

On June 22, Somerset prepared for his final judgment. Many of his friends and interested blacks attended court that day. Granville Sharp was not in court. Sharp had pressed Mansfield to decide on the legality of slavery for several years. Mansfield had avoided the issue, but now appeared prepared to face it. Sharp's presence, some believed, might have antagonized Mansfield.

Bewigged, Lord Mansfield mounted the bench while the clerk called the case of "James Somerset, a Negro, on Habeas Corpus." Mansfield recited the facts, discussed the law briefly and concluded:

> The state of slavery is of such a nature, that it is incapable of being introduced on any reasons, moral or political; but only by positive law, which preserves its force long after the reasons, occasion, and time itself from whence it was created, is erased from memory; it's so odious, that nothing can be suffered to support it but positive law. Whatever inconveniences, therefore, may follow from the decision, I cannot say this case is allowed or approved by the law of England; and therefore the black must be discharged.[21]

Black members of the audience rose and bowed to the court. Somerset basked in the pleasure of being a hero in the black community. He was the guest of honor at a party of nearly two hundred blacks. The community celebrated not only his victory, but freedom for all black slaves in

England. Sharp told him that Lord Mansfield had decided that a slave could not be held captive by his master. This, he said, would effectively abolish slavery in England.

That was the interpretation of the *Somerset* decision in both Britain and in the colonies.[22] The London papers took note. The *Public Advertiser*, June 27, 1772, wrote:

> On Monday near two hundred blacks with their ladies had an entertainment at a public-house in Westminster, to celebrate the triumph which their brother Somerset had obtained over Mr. Stuart [sic], his master. Lord Mansfield's health was echoed round the room; and the evening was concluded with a ball. The tickets for admission to this black assembly were 5s. each.

Parliament never took issue with Mansfield's decision. There would have been little enthusiasm in Britain for encouraging colonials to bring their slaves to England, as Sir John Fielding made clear in his 1762 book.[23] The idea of introducing slavery into the law of England would have little or no support among the common people.[24]

Benjamin Franklin, then in London, was unimpressed. He minimized the *Somerset* decision at the time it was published.

> It is said that some generous humane persons subscribed to the expense of obtaining the liberty by law for Somerset the Negro....It is to be wished that the same

humanity may extend itself among numbers;
if not to the procuring liberty for those that
remain in our colonies, at least to obtain a
law for abolishing the African commerce in
slaves, and declaring the children of present
slaves free after they become of age....
—Pharisaical Britain! to pride thyself in setting free a single slave that happens to land
on thy coasts, while thy merchants in all thy
ports are encouraged by thy laws to continue
a commerce whereby so many hundreds of
thousands are dragged into a slavery that
can scarce be said to end with their lives,
since it is entailed on their posterity![25]

The decision in Somerset's case meant more than
Franklin suggested. If a master could not use force to
restrain a runaway slave, the slave could liberate himself.
On July 10, 1772, a little more than two weeks after the
*Somerset* decision, Charles Stewart, Somerset's "owner,"
received a letter from an acquaintance named John Riddell
who lived in Bristol Wells:

I am disappointed by Mr. Dubin who has
run away. He told the servants that he had
rec'd a letter from his Uncle Somerset
acquainting him that Lord Mansfield had
given them their freedom and he was determined to leave me as soon as I returned from
London which he did without even speaking
to me. I don't find that he has gone off with

anything of mine. Only carried off all his own cloths which I don't know whether he had any right to do so. I believe I shall not give my self any trouble to look after the ungrateful villain. But his leaving me just at this time rather proves inconvenient.[26]

"Uncle Somerset" probably hoped he had many such nephews and nieces. Over time, many black slaves in Britain freed themselves, as had Mr. Dubin, by walking away from their masters, who, like Mr. Riddell, decided not to seek them out.[27] Sharp's antislavery society gained in size and influence. Slavery was abolished in the British colonies in 1833.

In the end, James Somerset merged into the black community of London, but his case lived on. And Mansfield's description of slavery as "so odious" echoed through the Anglo-American world and gave the impression that he had abolished slavery in Britain: "News of the case echoed through American drawing rooms—the first repudiation of forced work by the mother country."[28]

Somerset never knew that his private quest for freedom was the spark that helped start the American Revolution and that has haunted the nation down to the present day.

# Chapter 2

---

# The Tinderbox

---

Beginning in the early spring and continuing until late fall of 1772, published reports of Lord Mansfield's decision trickled into the colonies through weekly newspapers. There were at least forty-three stories about *Somerset* in at least twenty newspapers, all of which made clear in different ways that black slaves in England had been freed by that decision.[1] The vast majority of these reports appeared in northern newspapers—Massachusetts, Pennsylvania, Rhode Island, New York, and New Hampshire. There were accounts published in two of the slave states, Virginia and South Carolina, where fewer newspapers existed. Two of the papers were in Rhode Island where many slave owners from South Carolina and Georgia had summer homes.

The *Virginia Gazette* had six stories, starting on May 7, with reports of several preliminary hearings. On November 12, 1772, it also published a critique of the decision that had been circulated in England.[2] This critique, signed "A West Indian Planter," marshaled the arguments against the release of Somerset which had been submitted in Somerset's case. The critique argued that Somerset's case had been wrongly decided and would have disastrous consequences.

The *South Carolina Gazette* had one major report on August 13. Another on September 15 reported "the substance of Lord Mansfield's speech on the Negro cause," under a dateline of June 24. The report included the following:

> The state of slavery is of such a nature, that it is incapable of being now introduced by courts of justice upon mere reasoning or inferences from any principles, natural or political....And in a case so odious as the condition of slaves must be taken strictly, the power claimed by this return was never in use here; no master was ever allowed here to take a slave by force to be sold abroad because he had deserted from his service, or for any other reason whatever; we cannot say the cause set forth by this return is allowed or approved of by the laws of this kingdom, therefore the man must be discharged.[3]

The next week, the *Gazette* reported on the party in London attended by two hundred "blacks and their ladies" that celebrated the decision.[4]

These publications warned southern slave holders that if the *Somerset* principle became the law in the colonies, their society would be at risk. These risks included greater supervision of colonial action, perhaps taxation of slavery that had now been declared "so odious" that it could not exist in England, and possibly direct parliamentary control of colonial slavery.

Decisions about slavery could be made by Parliament, or the courts, or perhaps even the king, without consultation with the colonists themselves. If Britain hesitated to free slaves in the colonies because of the incomes the slaves produced, the government still might impose taxes on the sale or purchase of slaves and control the export of products they produced, providing needed revenues for the mother country's treasury.

This was a serious worry. The *Somerset* decision reached the colonies in the second year of a thaw in the strained relations with Britain stemming from the taxation issues of the 1760s. Every colony had been established by a document from the king that authorized a colonial legislature to enact laws for the colony so long as they were "not repugnant to the laws of England."[5] Thus the British government retained a kind of superintending power over the colony's behavior. This was well known in the colonies.[6] This power was exercised by the Privy Council, an organization of senior advisors to the crown. The Privy Council acted through its Board of Trade and Plantations. The power to invalidate colonial legislation had been exercised against three colonial acts in the years immediately preceding 1772 when the *Somerset* case was decided.[7]

Colonial suspicions that Britain was trying to "milk" the colonies of their hard earned incomes by taxation had been exacerbated by British actions beginning in 1763, the year in which the French and Indian war ended. The British promptly established a "proclamation line" to prevent colonials from seeking to settle west of the Allegheny mountains for fear of inciting further conflict with Native Americans. In 1765, the British imposed the Stamp Act, requiring the colonists to buy stamps that taxed common paper goods like playing cards and writing paper, as well as deeds, wills, and lawsuits. The British imposed the tax assuming that the colonists would be grateful for the British efforts during the French and Indian war. They were not. Every level of society was directly affected by this tax. The colonial reaction against "taxation without representation" was spearheaded by Massachusetts; it was spontaneous among the colonies and it was effective. In every colony people refused to use stamps and reduced their purchase of British goods.

Colonial lawyers like John Adams in Boston and Thomas Jefferson in Virginia pressed the view that the colonists should not be taxed because they were not represented in Parliament. Samuel Adams, more a man of the streets and back rooms than his cousin John, occasionally invoked mob action to "encourage" merchants to boycott British goods. The same scenes were played out from Boston to Virginia. Those individuals who had prepared to sell the stamps were vigorously persuaded to withdraw.

The fury of the people caught at least two of the founding fathers off guard: Benjamin Franklin, then in London, and Richard Henry Lee in Virginia, one of Jefferson's aspiring political companions. Franklin had sought the position of stamp commissioner for a friend, whose house was nearly destroyed by a mob in Philadelphia that also had threatened Franklin's wife and home.[8] In Virginia, Lee had initially applied for the commissioner's job before he felt the temper of the community and withdrew.[9] The temper was furious. A mob of property owners and merchants coerced George Mercer to resign as stamp distributor for Virginia and threatened to tar and feather a ship owner who publicly stated he would obey the Stamp Act.[10] In Boston, Governor Hutchinson's house was torn down by an angry mob, leading to the stationing of British troops there.[11]

Under pressure from British merchants who lost business because of the boycott, Parliament repealed the taxes in 1766. At the same time it adopted the Declaratory Act asserting that Parliament had authority to govern the colonies, "in all cases whatsoever."[12] Most of the colonists did not worry about the abstract claim that Parliament had unlimited power over them. The claim appeared to be merely a face-saving device to cover up the failure of the Stamp Act. The boycott was abandoned, the mobs went home, and life in the colonies and among the merchants and the citizens returned to normal, except that the seeds of distrust of Britain had been planted in the colonists. They would sprout in 1767 when the British tried once again to tax the colonies with taxes devised by British chancellor of the exchequer, Charles Townshend. These were taxes on paper, glass, paint, and tea imported into the colonies.[13] These "indirect" taxes aroused another storm of protest and boycott, once more spearheaded by Massachusetts. The state assembly issued a "circular let-ter" to all the colonies to harmonize the protests against the tax. London overreacted, and required governors to dissolve or refuse to call colonial assemblies unless they rejected the Massachusetts letter. The colonial assemblies resisted this call, and once again the British retreated. In March of 1770 they repealed all the Townshend taxes except a small tax on tea to preserve the principle of parliamentary supremacy in the Declaratory Act. The colonists who normally drank smuggled tea anyway ignored the tea tax.

As before, the boycott faded away and matters returned to normal.[14] Even the Boston Massacre of that year, where

British troops fired on a crowd that was taunting them and killed five men, including Crispus Attucks, did not revive revolutionary fervor.[15] John Adams defended the troops and their captain in court on grounds of self-defense against a mob of "saucy boys, Negroes and mulattoes, Irish teagues, and outlandish jacktars."[16] Boston juries acquitted the British soldiers and the streets remained calm.

The thrust toward independence had ended, except for a few who could not convince their countrymen that the British claim to control the colonies was serious.[17] These repeated efforts at taxation did increase the atmosphere of distrust between Britain and the colonies, as the British increasingly believed the colonies were bent on independence, and the colonists increasingly believed the British intended to exploit them by either taxation or repression. John Dickinson, a Philadelphia landowner and political figure, had pressed the "no taxation without representation" issue in 1768 in his widely published articles entitled "Letters from a Farmer in Pennsylvania."[18]

But these mutual resentments subsided after the Townshend taxes were repealed in 1770. Business between the colonies and Britain resumed. The period from 1770 to 1773 is described by historians as a "calm," a "pause," an "uneasy truce," or "the quiet years," in the movement toward revolution.[19] It is difficult to realize that what is now called a pause looked like peace at the time. The *Somerset* case, arriving as it did against a background of efforts by the British government to tax and otherwise interfere with colonial governments between 1763 and 1770, gave the southern colonists yet another reason to be concerned with British meddling in their affairs.

The "repugnancy clauses" in colonial charters authorizing only legislation that was not contrary to British laws, and the Declaratory Act claiming parliamentary power over "all cases whatsoever" in the colonies combined to make thoughtful southern leaders exceedingly nervous.[20] Once Lord Mansfield had pronounced slavery "so odious" that "it is not allowed or approved by the Law of England," the prospect that the repugnancy clause might be used in the future to challenge colonial slavery became a serious risk. As historian Richard Hildreth asked in 1846:

> How, then, were those [colonial] assemblies competent to legalize a condition, many of the consequences of which are pronounced by Mansfield "absolutely contrary" to English law?[21]

While these complex details of British colonial relations may not seem to be the stuff of which revolutions are made, the fact is that much of the political leadership in the colonies consisted of lawyers, and in the southern colonies these lawyers were often also planters, slave owners, and land speculators.[22]

Historian Jack Greene has analyzed the occupations of the one hundred ten leaders in the Virginia House of Burgesses between 1720 and 1776:

> Most of the one hundred ten leaders of the house were, of course, planters. Indeed, at least ninety-one were directly involved in planting and raising tobacco, although a

third of these engaged in planting only as secondary occupation. The lawyers—most of whom were planters on the side—were the next most numerous professional or occupational group. Thirty-nine of the one hundred ten were practicing lawyers, but they were far more significant than their numbers would indicate....They had precisely those talents required in framing legislation and carrying on the business of the Burgesses, and throughout the period under consideration they were conspicuous by their presence at the top level of power. Of the four men who served as speaker, John Holloway, Sir John Randolph, and Peyton Randolph—were lawyers.

Nearly all the leaders of the house had secondary economic interests....Their most important secondary occupation was land speculation. Over two-fifths, and perhaps more, speculated in western lands—a profitable avocation.[23]

These lawyer-planter-slave-owner-speculator-political-leaders would view events through the lawyer's lens—"How will this event affect my clients?"

Henry Laurens of South Carolina, a wealthy former slave trader turned plantation owner who would later become president of the Continental Congress, was in London when Lord Mansfield announced his decision in *Somerset*. After the decision, Laurens, writing to a friend, was critical of the argument of John Dunning, who was counsel to Somerset's owner, Charles Stewart:

> I will not say a word of Lord Mansfield's judgment in the case of *Stuart v. Somerset* [sic] until we meet, save only that his lordship's administration was suitable to the times. The able Dunning set out on the defendant's [slave owner's] part by declaring that he was no advocate for slavery, and in my humble opinion he was not an advocate for his clients nor was there a word said to the purpose on either side.[24]

Why was Laurens so cautious in expressing his view about the *Somerset* decision? Mail was insecure and Laurens was already a major political force in South Carolina. Perhaps he believed that the best course was to blame the lawyer. Laurens's letter implies that the decision was the result of poor advocacy by Dunning, the slave owner's lawyer. Laurens's negative attitude toward the decision was consistent with his reliance on slave labor as the basis for his two fortunes as slave trader and planter.[25] He was also consistent in the protection of slavery whenever he had an opportunity.

In 1777, as president of the Continental Congress, Laurens presided over an amendment to the Articles of Confederation that prevented the *Somerset* decision from being applied anywhere in the new states.[26] In 1783, his major contribution as a United States representative in Paris at the treaty of peace with Britain was to insist on a provision in the treaty requiring Britain to return Negroes who had joined them during the war.[27] Laurens did not further commit his views on the *Somerset* decision to writing. However, he wrote three letters relating to arrangements to send a slave named Cato to Charleston from England in 1772. The editors of Laurens's papers suggest that Cato had been brought to England by Laurens's former partner and was being sent back post haste to "avoid the difficulties that arose in the case of James Somerset."[28]

Charles Stewart, Somerset's owner, held the same view of Dunning's argument: "Dunning was dull and languid, and would have made a much better figure on the other side."[29]

Not only were the slave masters concerned about the *Somerset* decision, the slaves learned of it too. Some of them ran away to find a ship that would take them to England and freedom because they heard about the *Somerset* case. One advertisement for the return of a runaway in 1774 read:

> Run away the 16th instant, from the Subscriber, a Negro man named BACCHUS, About 30 Years of Age, five feet six or seven inches high, strong and well made...He was seen a few Days before he went off with a Purse of Dollars, and had just before changed a five Pound Bill; Most, or all of which, I suppose he must have robbed me of, which he might easily have done, I having trusted him much after what I thought had proved his Fidelity. He will probably endeavour to pass

for a Freeman by the Name of John Christian,
and attempt to get on Board some Vessel
bound for Great Britain, from the Knowledge
he has of the late Determination of Somerset's
Case. Whoever takes up the said Slave shall
have 5£ Reward, on his Delivery to
GABRIEL JONES.[30]

The possibility of a British rejection of slavery anywhere in the empire appalled the plantation owners and
their representatives because slavery was a necessary
underpinning of their prosperity.[31] Slavery was the foundation of the economic and social environment that their
leaders represented and protected.

The riches that flowed from slave ownership were
threefold: the value of the slaves themselves, both as capital and as security for loans; the value of the product they
produced, including more slaves; and the value of the land
that they cleared and planted.[32] Slavery in the southern
colonies made white slave owners the wealthiest group on
the mainland, as economist James A. Henretta has
described:

> The average free wealth holder in the South
> had total physical resources of £395 in 1774
> as compared to £161 for those in New
> England and £187 for the Middle
> Colonies....Yet the economy of the South
> was not more productive than the economies
> of other regions....Per capita wealth—land,
> livestock, producer and consumer goods

—was almost exactly the same in 1774 in
every region of the country. White southerners
had more wealth than white northerners only
because black southerners had none.[33]

The importance of slavery to the southern colonists had
its roots in the pre-Revolutionary period. As a result of a
rebellion by poor whites in 1676, Virginia shifted its labor
force from a mix of black slaves and white indentured servants to slaves alone.[34] Most whites owned one or two
slaves, not the much larger numbers owned by the major
planters. But these few slaves were crucial to their masters
in easing the daily labor necessary for an agricultural existence. For example, owning slaves enabled white children
to have some schooling, or enabled ill or disabled family
members to bear lighter loads. In addition, the existence of
black slaves provided the poor white slave owner with a
status that connected him with his betters and distinguished him from those destined to labor forever. These
conditions gave most poor whites an incentive to protect
slavery that was equivalent to or exceeded the more obvious interests of those who held a greater number of slaves.[35]

Planters were constantly in debt to their merchants as
long as tobacco was the primary crop, and slaves could
not only be sold, they could be mortgaged or pledged.
Tobacco depleted the soil, requiring the clearing of new
land; cultivation of the crop demanded the use of slaves.[36]
The result was an economic spiral in which most slave
owners were compelled to continue to invest in more
slaves, consuming capital which, in the North, had begun
to flow into industrial and commercial activities.

Although northern states possessed fewer slaves, the slave trade supported their shipbuilding and commercial activities.

All of these considerations combined to make southern political lawyers anxious about their property in slaves that was threatened by the *Somerset* decision.[37] Taxation may have taken some of their property; *Somerset* threatened to take it all.

The colonial upset over British taxation had ebbed with the withdrawal of all taxes except that on tea in 1770. News of the *Somerset* decision reached the colonies in the summer and fall of 1772.

During those "quiet years," John Adams of Massachusetts and Thomas Jefferson of Virginia had not yet met each other. Even so, they had much in common. They were well-educated, thoughtful, and successful lawyers who had entered the political arenas of their respective colonies.[38] They were both concerned with perceived British intrusions into colonial life and economy.

There were also sharp differences between them, both in appearance and background. Jefferson, the younger of the two, was a tall, thin, soft-spoken aristocrat; a wealthy man by inheritance and marriage, owning about two hundred slaves. He was not a strong public speaker, but the clarity and style of his prose was recognized by all.

Adams was short, stout, and talkative; the product of generations of Massachusetts farmers, his modest wealth was the result of his successful law practice and farming. He frequently spoke at length, seeking to persuade others through reasoning of what he thought was obvious. He was direct rather than diplomatic.

Regardless of these differences in culture and background, Jefferson and Adams were both disappointed that the colonial revolutionary movement had collapsed in 1770.

Jefferson wrote in his autobiography:

> Nothing of particular excitement occurring for a considerable time, our countrymen seemed to fall into a state of insensibility to our situation; the duty on tea not yet repealed, and the Declaratory Act of a right in the British Parliament to bind us by their laws in all cases whatsoever still suspended over us.[39]

At nearly the same time, Adams wrote about the apathy of the people outside of Massachusetts: "Still quiet at the southward; and at New York they laugh at us."[40] By the end of the year, he was also worried about the people of Massachusetts. On December 31, 1772, he wrote to a friend, reporting that his health had returned and he had resumed his law practice.

> The prospect before me, however, is very gloomy. My country is in deep distress and has very little ground of hope that she will soon, if ever, get out of it. The system of a mean and merciless administration, is gaining ground upon our patriots every day.[41]

During the calm, both men went about their personal, political, and professional affairs. In 1770, John Adams was elected a representative to the Massachusetts legislature. Adams moved to Boston from Braintree where he had been born. Riding circuit, he became one of the best lawyers in Massachusetts. In 1772, Abigail had their fifth and last child. The growing Adams family spent long days on the farm.[42] However, John also managed to appear in more than two hundred cases ranging from animals straying into a neighbor's yard to complex commercial matters. He also became more active in political matters. In 1773, when Governor Hutchinson of Massachusetts argued to the colonial legislature that there was no middle ground between parliamentary supremacy and independence, Adams framed an answer that, since Britain never intended the colonials to be slaves, they must be free.[43]

During the calm, Jefferson also lived the full life of a young lawyer. In 1770, his family home Shadwell was accidentally destroyed by fire, burning his books and papers. But he was already at work developing his new house at Monticello, and had begun courting the young widow Martha Shelton, whom he would marry on New Year's Day, 1772.[44] Their first child was born in late September of the same year. He was elected to the House of Burgesses and he handled complex cases, including a divorce case that challenged the supremacy of British divorce law over colonial legislation.

This case crystallized Jefferson's thinking about the relation between Britain and the colonies. Jefferson had been preparing an argument to uphold a colonial legislative divorce. In this effort, he reviewed the basis for the English law concerning divorce.[45] His preparation was aborted by the death of one of the parties. The issue of parliamentary control of divorce matters continued to brew in Pennsylvania, and was finally resolved that same year, against the colonial power.[46]

The research was not lost; Jefferson relied on it in developing his argument for independence published as his "Summary View" in 1774.[47] His argument paralleled that of John Adams in the debate with Governor Hutchinson.[48] It was a difficult argument because Britain had long claimed authority over the actions of the colonies under the original charters of the colonies. The colonial charters that gave each colony the power to adopt legislation contained clauses limiting that power to laws that were not repugnant to the laws of Britain. After the *Somerset* case, there was a prospect that Parliament might tax or abolish the "odious" institution.

The Declaratory Act of 1766 in which Parliament claimed total power over "all cases whatsoever" in the colonies was far more intrusive into colonial authority than the principle that the government could void laws repugnant to British law. This was the state of legal affairs that Jefferson considered a sword of Damocles suspended over the colonies.

Thus the reliance on the "rights of Englishmen" that had emerged during the Stamp Act controversy could not prevail under the Declaratory Act. Furthermore, the southern colonists knew that the senior spokesman for the British colonial administration during the Stamp Act crisis had been none other than Lord Mansfield, who had just declared the basis of their society to be "odious."[49]

Parliament's reaction to the *Somerset* proceedings was not reassuring to the colonists. It had refused to consider legislation protecting slavery in England during Somerset's trial, following Lord Mansfield's advice, and did not take it up after the trial was over. Presumably the people of England did not wish to legalize slavery there.

This treatment of colonial slave owners was in sharp contrast to that in France, where, despite occasional releases of slaves based on the "freedom principle," French colonists had requested, and the government had agreed to, legislation which set conditions that allowed the colonists to bring their slaves to France and retain ownership of them.[50] In the context of increasing colonial distrust of British actions and motives, and the growing belief that the British would not understand their need to be secure in their property, this turn-down by Parliament when compared to the French response on the same issue led many slave owners to make their slaves sign indentures, classifying them as servants, before taking them to England.[51]

Thus both the Court of King's Bench and Parliament rejected the merchant's demands for a decision protecting colonial slavery. To many thoughtful southern colonials, this was the last straw in a decade-long effort by Britain to usurp colonial autonomy. The following year, Adams would argue vigorously and successfully to base the colonists' claims on "natural law" rather than on existing rights of Englishmen under British laws or colonial charters.

Jefferson and Adams both knew that the abstract declaration of the right of Parliament to control the colonies was a weapon that could destroy colonial aspirations to self-government and could shred the economy of each colony. They were not alone among those colonists who worried that Britain would treat the colonies as pawns in the international struggle for power with the French and as sources of revenue for Britain, rather than recognizing that the energies of the colonists could enhance the status of the British empire throughout the world.[52] But now, after *Somerset*, the threat from the government in London was clearer, and if carried out would undermine the rich and powerful southern society dominated by the lawyer-planter-slave-owner political elite.

# Chapter 3

# Virginia Responds to the *Somerset* Decision

The *Somerset* decision, with its slap at the Virginians' way of life, became the subject of serious discussion in drawing rooms during the fall of 1772. With limited mail service and few newspapers, the social exchanges at plantation houses provided the best occasions for people to talk about politics, exchange social gossip, and explore ideas among friends who shared their basic lifestyles.[1] The slave-owner-planter-lawyer political figures met regularly at such affairs. Some visits and parties lasted days.

Slave owners, especially those who owned more than a few slaves, could never be completely at ease. There was an undertone that silently expressed the frustration of most slaves at the futility of their lives. In his book *The Ruling Race: A History of American Slaveholders*, historian James Oakes reviews the manuals developed to help slave owners promote efficiency in production through persuasion, threats, and punishment. He writes:

> Loyal house servants and faithful mammies did not disturb the workings of the slave system; hostile slave laborers did, and there can

be no question that in terms of the master's perceptions, hostility prevailed....For the mass of field hands, daily life was a perpetual grind of hard work characterized by nearly universal hatred of the slave system and punctuated by periodic and often sustained acts of resistance. It was the resistance that made its mark.

Slaveholders complained that their bondsmen were impudent because they *were* impudent; masters complained that their slaves were lazy because they frequently would not work. By deliberate lassitude, by running away, by sabotage, slaves withheld their labor from the master. In effect, they were striking, and to some degree every master succumbed to the slaves' demands. By planning their individual and collective acts of day-to-day resistance as deliberate responses to particular grievances, the slaves were punishing their masters for mistreatment, neglect, overwork.[2]

As a result, the planters and their families were always conscious that their security, both personal and financial, was on shaky grounds. Stories of slave revolts, murders, and lesser violence were extensively discussed and dissected. Virginians knew that South Carolina had an 80 percent slave population. They thought that percentage dangerously high and wished to cut off further importation of African slaves, both to increase their own security and to improve their position as sellers of slaves. These insecurities informed their review of Lord Mansfield's decision that slavery was "so odious" that it could exist only by positive law and was not protected by the common law. That Lord Mansfield would free fifteen thousand slaves in England, leaving the slave owners with no recourse to the courts, and that Parliament showed no interest in the question was appalling to them.[3]

Some historians have questioned the significance of the *Somerset* decision because in later years Mansfield disavowed the intent to abolish slavery and British courts held that if a slave brought to Britain did return to the colonies, his slavery reemerged and attached to him again.[4] However, the decision was in large measure self-executing as slaves walked away from their masters and the masters gave up. Slavery virtually disappeared in England in the early nineteenth century.[5] The importance of *Somerset* in the American colonies was the impression that the decision created in the minds of the colonist planter-lawyer-politicians in late 1772, who could only read the words, not the future.

The attitudes of these men have been examined in depth by historian T. H. Breen. His thesis is that their perceptions of life were influenced by the nature of the planting process: that being known as a successful grower of tobacco was the pinnacle of personal achievement, giving meaning to their lives and assuring what they considered to be their independence.[6]

A far-off and highly placed judge in Britain had labeled slavery, on which the tobacco culture depended, "so odious" that British law would not recognize it. These planters must have taken his criticism as applying to the process of their lives. These proud and independent-minded men were given a double wound: to their honor and to their independence, administered by a stranger who appeared to be ignorant about the fundamentals of life in colonial Virginia.

A deeper issue underlay the uncertainties created by Mansfield's decision. Mansfield's statement pointedly emphasized Parliament's ultimate power over slavery in the colonies under the Declaratory Act of 1766 when he told Stewart that Parliament is the "best and perhaps the only method of settling the point for the future."[7] This statement meant that Parliament's claim of total power over the colonies "in all cases whatsoever" included the institution of slavery. Thus the refusal of Parliament to consider whether to legalize slavery in Britain during Somerset's trial, implying a lack of sympathy toward the slave owners, may have been as upsetting to the southern colonies as the *Somerset* decision itself. If Parliament would allow the abolition of slavery at home, without even hearing the plantation interests, how long would it be before Britain would meddle with or abolish slavery in the colonies?[8]

Lawyers would doubtless think that since Mansfield had declared slavery a disfavored institution, it could be more readily taxed by a regime that was seeking to milk the colonies for the benefit of the homeland. Thus they saw that the attack on slavery involved both colonial control of internal policies and taxation without representation.

In the fall of 1772, the planter-lawyers carried these fears from the drawing rooms to their offices and courthouses where they met. As lawyers pondered the *Somerset* decision published in southern papers, their concern increased. They put together three points of Mansfield's reasoning in the *Somerset* case: (1) slavery was repugnant to the common law, (2) Parliament had the final say concerning the legality of slavery under the Declaratory Act of 1766, and (3) Parliament had claimed the power to tax the colonies in the same Declaratory Act. They realized that slavery was under a double-barreled threat from Britain, under the repugnancy clause and the Declaratory Act. After *Somerset*, slavery and the colonial life it supported existed at the will of an apparently unfriendly Parliament.[9]

Attempts to confine discussions of the *Somerset* decision to drawing rooms and law offices failed. The unobtrusive servants who appeared to be part of the furniture—after all, they were literally property—must have heard the irate slave owners complain about the decision. This incredible news led some slaves to decide to free themselves and go to England.

How did the slave owners and their lawyers react to these threats from the *Somerset* opinion? First, they thought long and hard about the policies, the practicalities, and the legalities of their situation. They could have done nothing and waited to see if their fears were well grounded. But they rejected this course: Lord Mansfield had long been a major political figure in England, as well as a distinguished judge, and his opinion appeared deadly serious.

Second, they could have sought assurances from Britain that it would cease meddling in their internal affairs—to transform their relationship with Britain from that of an inferior jurisdiction to one of a partnership. That would require the British to repeal the Declaratory Act, thereby agreeing to share sovereignty with the colonies. But they knew Britain would not agree to such a partnership.[10] Sovereignty, in the British view, was a unitary concept. A nation either had total control over a territory or none at all. Since the Glorious Revolution of 1688, Parliament had solidified its power over the king, and in 1766 had asserted it over the colonies as well. Lord Mansfield was a firm believer that Parliament was, and had to be, supreme in the British Empire.[11]

Third, the southerners might seek to secede from Britain. There had been much talk during the taxation crisis of 1765–1770 that the British claim of the power to tax the colonies was the equivalent to holding the colonies in slavery.[12] This image could—and did—naturally lead to thoughts of independence. As John Adams wrote later to Jefferson:

> The revolution was in the minds of the people, and this was effected from 1760 to 1775, in the course of fifteen years before a drop of blood was drawn at Lexington.[13]

A revolution would be most hazardous. Britain was the most powerful country in the world, both at sea and on land. Separation by rebellion was conceivable only if all the colonies—already chafing under British rule and worried about perceived threats to their liberty—were willing to unite in a rebellion that would secure the institution of slavery under an American government. The security the South needed was recognition of the complete freedom of each colony to conduct its internal affairs.

Would the northern colonies join in a revolution to protect southern slavery? The southerners were unsure. They
did not know the northerners. Most colonists were provin-
cials, attached to their colony and to Britain more than to
each other. They certainly did not know their neighbors
well enough to believe they would make common cause
with the South to protect slavery. When the colonies had
examined Benjamin Franklin's Albany Plan for a defensive league against the French and Indians in 1754, they
had all rejected it because it interfered with their internal
affairs.[14] The southerners did know that there was already
some antislavery sentiment in the North. Although slavery
was legal in all colonies, it was less prevalent in the North,
particularly north of New York City where slaves provided
much of the labor.

Northern attitudes toward slavery were ambivalent.[15]
Southerners may have heard that James Otis, the leading
antislavery advocate in Massachusetts in the early 1760s,
argued in the Superior Court of Massachusetts against
"writs of assistance," which were general search warrants.
His argument included an attack on slavery as a violation
of natural rights. In 1764, his pamphlet, *The Rights of the
British Colonies Asserted and Proved,* stated, "The
colonists are by the law of nature free born, as indeed all
men are, white or black."[16] Southern papers had reported
that, after the *Somerset* decision, there was dancing in the
streets of Philadelphia.

On the other hand, some northerners had serious interests in slavery that paralleled the southerners. Shipyards
built the cargo ships for the slave trade and other commercial ventures in which New England's bottoms transported

not only slaves, but also the products they produced. Northerners captained and manned these ships and supported their families and local communities with their incomes. They also participated in smuggling that evaded the navigation acts, which required colonial goods to be shipped through British ports.

Astute slave-owner-planter-lawyer-politicians would not jump from the frying pan of the threat from *Somerset* into a fire of northern antislavery attitudes. The South would not join with the North to seek revolution without assurance that southern slavery would be left alone. The generation of brilliant Virginian political figures—perhaps the greatest in our history—would not be so foolish as to leave that question unaddressed. The South would seek liberty from Britain, but only if doing so would protect slavery at home.

One of the most perceptive historians of slavery during the Revolution, Donald L. Robinson, in his *Slavery in the Structure of American Politics, 1765–1820,* identified the tensions between northerners and southerners that existed in the early 1770s. To southerners, slavery was a necessity; to northerners steeped in a philosophy of natural rights, it was inconsistent and hypocritical. Robinson's focus, however, was on the situation of the colonies in 1776, as the question of independence loomed large. But his analysis is equally applicable to the condition of the colonies in early 1773, once the Virginians recognized the need for committees of correspondence to organize the colonies against the British.[17]

In the spring of 1773, Jefferson was still working on his "Summary View of the Rights of British America," a short exposition of his theory of the origin of Virginia which brought him instant fame in the colonies.[18] His basic premise was that Britain never retained power over the internal affairs of the colonies so neither the repugnancy clause nor the Declaratory Act could constitutionally establish British control over the colonies. He shared these views with his closest friends, the younger men in the House of Burgesses, as they considered how to address their fears of loss of slavery and their aspirations for the independence to protect it.

To further both these concerns, they needed to determine how their own leaders, and those in other colonies, felt about slavery, and to measure the strength of these leaders' support for Britain. Both objectives could be achieved by securing a resolution from the House of Burgesses, the lower house of the Virginia legislature, calling on all the colonies to create "committees of correspondence" to communicate with each other concerning British activities unfriendly to colonial interests. Richard Henry Lee, one of the "younger men" who would become prominent in the coming revolutionary period, characterized the measure as "leading to that union, and perfect understanding of each other, on which the political salvation of America so eminently depends."[19]

According to Jefferson's recollection:

> Not thinking our old and leading members up to the point of forwardness and zeal which the times required, Mr. Henry, R. H. Lee, Francis L. Lee, Mr. Carr, and myself agreed to meet in the evening in a private room of the Raleigh to consult on the state of things....We were all sensible that the most

urgent of all measures was that of coming to
an understanding with all the other colonies
to consider the British claims as a common
cause to all, to produce an unity of action:
and for this purpose that a committee of correspondence in each colony would be the best
instrument for intercommunication: and that
their first measure would probably be to propose a meeting of deputies from every colony
at some central place, who should be charged
with the direction of the measures which
should be taken by all.[20]

Some of these younger members were conflicted about
the morality—but not the necessity—of the maintenance of
slavery. Jefferson would later elegantly condemn slavery in
a passage of the Declaration of Independence that was
deleted by Congress.[21] Much later, in his famous letter to
Edward Coles in 1814, Jefferson concluded that public
sentiment indicated "an apathy to every hope" that the
younger generation "would have sympathized with oppression wherever found."[22] Richard Henry Lee's initial speech
to the Burgesses in 1759 had criticized slavery for weakening the energies of white Virginians. The importation of
slaves "has been and will be attended with effects dangerous
both to our political and moral interests." Other colonies
were outmatching Virginia because,

With their whites, they import arts and agriculture, while we, with our blacks, exclude
both...they are deprived, forever deprived,

of all the comfort of life, and to be made the most wretched of the human kind.[23]

Patrick Henry had also bemoaned slavery, while acknowledging its necessity. In Virginia, he wrote,

> When the rights of humanity are defined and understood with precision...we find men, professing a religion the most humane, mild, meek, gentle, and generous, adopting a principle as repugnant to humanity as it is inconsistent with the Bible and destructive to liberty....Would anyone think I am master of slaves of my own purchase!...I am drawn along by the general inconveniences of living without them, I will not, I cannot, justify it.[24]

They all knew that protecting slavery was essential to the political, social, and economic life of Virginia, and to their personal political futures.

They suppressed what negative feelings they may have had about slavery and gave free rein to their desires for independence to protect it. Any impulse to move to end slavery was outweighed by their fears, their guilt, and their need to maintain slavery as well as their desire for independence that had been kindled during the taxation issues of the 1760s and nurtured by British incursions into colonial self-government.

In fact, they were all in a position similar to Jefferson's, as explained by economic historians Stanley Elkins and Eric McKitrick:

[Jefferson] would never, in fact, be anything
but an insider. His rise was swift and smooth
as leaders of the provincial elite quickly recognized his abilities and in effect brought
him into the ruling group while still in his
mid-twenties....The coercions of this insider-
ship were undoubtedly considerable. The
system had given him everything he could
have asked for: wealth, love and a profitable
marriage, social position, the fullest opportunity to engage his talents, and general
recognition. He was thus allowed the luxury
of determining which of these things he valued most, and which least, without having
to give up any of them. Such being the case,
the likelihood of his offering a basic challenge to that system, whatever the defects he
might decide needed remedying, was not
very great. He might suppose himself viewing it with detachment, but he would never
do so from the outside.[25]

Jefferson's sophistry, in his "Summary View" published in
1774, that the slave trade must be eliminated *before* slavery
could be abolished, must be understood as going as far publicly toward restricting slavery as he thought possible without
risking his political influence.[26] But his conclusion was illogical. As historian Duncan MacLeod noted pithily: "It was slavery which supported the slave trade and not the converse."[27]

Once the younger members were satisfied with their
draft, they sounded out some of the senior leaders before

proposing it. Jefferson recalled how the senior members had heckled Richard Bland, one of the most respected of Virginia's elder statesmen, when he proposed a modest easing of the prohibition on manumission of slaves.[28] Jefferson, as pictured by historian Joseph Ellis, did not like personal conflicts or confrontations. His forte was—among other things—in working out wide ranging theories and expressing them brilliantly in his writing. Ellis writes:

> What his critics took to be hypocrisy was not really that at all. In some cases it was the desire to please different constituencies, to avoid conflict with colleagues. In other cases it was an orchestration of his internal voice, to avoid conflict with himself. Both the external and internal diplomacy grew out of his deep distaste for sharp disagreement and his bedrock belief that harmony was nature's way of signaling the arrival of truth. More self-deception than calculated hypocrisy, it was nonetheless a disconcerting form of psychological agility that would make it possible for Jefferson to walk past the slave quarters on Mulberry Row at Monticello thinking about mankind's brilliant prospects without any sense of contradiction.[29]

From their associations with the senior leaders, the younger members had reason to believe that their concerns for the preservation of Virginia's slave system would override the older members' attachment to the empire.

Tobacco cultivation had worn out many acres of Virginia so much that experiments in planting wheat had already been undertaken by George Washington, among others. Wheat required fewer slaves than tobacco. The cultivation of tobacco or wheat was easier than the cultivation of sugar or rice. As a result, in Virginia, slaves multiplied. In the rice fields of South Carolina, slaves died early, and had to be "replenished." West Indian planters also required constant supplies of "new" slaves as the working conditions on the sugar plantations caused slaves to die young, and consequently not reproduce. In Virginia, and most of the South except South Carolina and Georgia, the life of the slave was "less onerous"; slaves did reproduce and increased their population.[30]

Historian Edmund Morgan explains:

> In Virginia not only had the rate of mortality from disease gone down, but the less strenuous work of cultivating tobacco, as opposed to sugar, enabled slaves to retain their health and multiply. To make a profit, sugar planters worked their slaves to death; tobacco planters did not have to.[31]

Some Virginia planters found themselves with surplus slaves to sell to other colonies; others began to "breed" slaves for sale. Cutting off further foreign importation of slaves would enhance the value of the Virginians' slaves. Thus Virginia could oppose the international slave trade while combining conscience and economics. The elimination of the trade would increase the value of the existing slaves and reduce the risk of severe slave over-population, which might threaten slave revolts. In addition, domestic and domesticated slaves were more valuable because they knew the language, work habits, and plantation customs, and were considered more peaceable and better security risks. Economic historian James A. Henretta identified the parallel increase in the price of slaves and the value of land in Virginia between 1750 and 1776.[32]

The leading slave holders had joined in a plea to the king in 1772 to ban foreign traffic in slaves, but had been rebuffed by the British government.[33] The petition read in part:

> The importation of slaves into the colonies from the coast of Africa hath long been considered a trade of great inhumanity, and under its present encouragement we have too much reason to fear will endanger the very existence of Your Majesty's American dominions.[34]

Because Virginia advocated abolition of the international slave trade, it has sometimes been considered an advocate for the abolition of slavery itself. This was George Bancroft's view in his 1854 *History of the United States*. In discussing the Virginia petition to the king to abolish the trade in 1772, he states:

> In this manner Virginia led the host, *who alike condemned slavery and opposed the slave trade.* Thousands in Maryland, and in

New Jersey, were ready to adopt a similar
Petition; so were the legislatures of North
Carolina, of Pennsylvania, of New York.
Massachusetts, in its towns and in its legislature, unceasingly combated the conditions as
well as the sale of slaves. There was no jealousy among one another in the strife against
the crying evil. Virginia harmonized all opinions, and represented the moral sentiment
and policy of them all.[35] (emphasis added)

Bancroft ignored the difference between abolishing
slavery and abolishing the slave trade. He was also wrong
in suggesting that the South was united behind Virginia's
desire to end the importation of slaves.[36] South Carolina
and Georgia imported slaves into the nineteenth century.
The international slave trade was as necessary for them as
for the West Indian planters.

After the younger members had prepared the ground-
work for the resolution for the committees of correspondence, it was presented to the House of Burgesses
controlled by the senior members who dominated Virginia's political landscape. By March 12, 1773, these
men—all of whom had prospered under British rule—
were prepared to take the serious step of uniting the
colonies to oppose British actions that offended their interests. The *Somerset* decision, with its implications for
southern slavery, had been the most recent and profound
event that led them to assert publicly that, since the Stamp
Act of 1765, the British government had demonstrated a
pattern of disregard of colonial interests.

These senior members were listed first among those to serve on the committee of correspondence. The first three men named in the resolution constituting the committee—Peyton Randolph, Robert Carter Nicholas, and Richard Bland—were wealthy planters and staunch supporters of slavery.[37] They had been considered both social and political friends of the governor and no friend of radical talk during the tax crises with Britain of the preceeding years, although they had cautiously supported the boycotts of that time.

The president of the House of Burgesses, Peyton Randolph, was a member (as was Jefferson's mother) of the historic Randolph family, which had enormous interests in Virginia. Robert Carter Nicholas was a member of two of the most important families in Virginia history. He was so sensitive to the need to protect slavery that he led the filibuster against George Mason's draft Bill of Rights for Virginia in 1776, on the grounds that it might incite slave revolts by suggesting that slaves might have rights.[38] Richard Bland was a gentleman-planter-lawyer whose performance in public affairs was said to be "equaled by few and surpassed by no Virginians of the mid-eighteenth century."[39]

The other members in the order named in the resolution were: Richard Henry Lee, Benjamin Harrison, Edmund Pendleton, Patrick Henry, Dudley Digges, Dabney Carr, Archibald Cary, and Thomas Jefferson. All these men were slaveholders and lawyers—the representatives who dominated the Virginia House of Burgesses for at least half a century.[40]

Edmund Pendleton was a well-respected Virginia lawyer and judge who was much more cautious in moving toward independence than others like Patrick Henry, whom Pendleton considered rash. As a judge during the Stamp Act crisis, Pendleton carefully balanced his responsibilities by keeping his court open while using documents that did not require stamps in order to not violate the Act's requirements. In 1775, he successfully discouraged Virginia militia from seeking to recover gunpowder that had been moved to a ship by Lord Dunmore.[41] Pendleton did not believe the Virginia militia was equipped to begin a revolution that he did not yet support. Yet Pendleton's name appeared high on the list of members in a resolution that he knew would draw the wrath of the Board of Trade in London, which later called the resolution "a measure of a most dangerous tendency and effect."[42]

When Patrick Henry, in March of 1775, moved that "this colony be immediately put into a posture of defense" to prepare for a war that was—in his view—already underway (the celebrated "liberty or death" speech), Pendleton opposed the motion.[43] It was adopted, however, and Pendleton was placed on the committee to organize the defense. He was included to assure that all shades of opinion would be represented and because he was one of "the men of business to whom Virginia turned when the decision had been made and trusted leaders were needed to carry it out."[44]

This comment appears to explain Pendleton's and the others' inclusion as members of the committee of correspondence in 1773, long before the antagonism toward Britain had hardened into revolt. Despite his caution and hesitation to cut ties with Britain, Pendleton permitted himself to be included, along with Patrick Henry, on a "dangerous" committee of correspondence, demonstrating his belief that the vital interests of Virginia were at stake. This analysis also applies to Richard Bland, Robert Carter Nicholas, and Benjamin Harrison, whose names appear first in the resolution.

The publication of the resolution upset the British Board of Trade because it prepared the colonies to act in concert. Historian Theodore Draper explains:

> The committees of correspondence transformed the struggle for power from agitation to organization. They were a radical innovation in the colonial struggle, extralegal if not illegal....Governors could and did dismiss or refuse to convene councils and assemblies, but they had no authority over committees of correspondence, which, in effect, existed outside the British imperial system. They again belied the old British assumption that the colonies were not to be feared because they were so diverse that they could not act together. From 1773 on, the colonies were prepared to meet any British threat with organized, collective opposition.[45]

Before the year was out, Samuel Adams and friends in Massachusetts—along with others in New York, Philadelphia, and Charleston—would demonstrate how "collective opposition" worked.

Just as the opinion in the *Somerset* case helped conservative Virginians to make a serious move toward revolution in March of 1773, the same judgment was being made in Massachusetts concerning a totally different issue. Within three weeks of Virginia's resolution to establish intercolonial committees of correspondence, in far-off Boston letters written by Thomas Hutchinson in 1769 when he was lieutenant governor of Massachusetts began to circulate. These letters were written to Thomas Whately, a British friend of Hutchinson. Whately had been secretary to Lord Grenville, who had presided over the adoption of the Stamp Act in 1765.

These letters came into the possession of Benjamin Franklin in 1772 after Whately died. In December, he sent them to Thomas Cushing, Speaker of the House of Representatives in Massachusetts. Franklin was at that time the agent for Massachusetts in Britain. He asked that they not be printed, but shown to important Massachusetts political figures. It was surely too much for Franklin to expect they would not see the light of day.

Franklin said his objective was to demonstrate that the difficulties with Britain were the result of Hutchinson and other individual colonists' despicable policies of secretly seeking to weaken colonial liberties, rather than the fault of the British government.[46] This explanation sounds suspiciously like a Franklin satire, or else a desire to placate both the Massachusetts patriots and the British government at the same time. The letters were incriminating to Massachusetts eyes because they urged a restriction on colonial liberties. Here is a sample:

> This is most certainly a crisis. I really wish
> that there may not have been the least degree

of severity, beyond what was absolutely necessary to maintain, I think I may say this to you, *the dependence* which a colony ought to have upon the parent state, but if no measures shall have been taken to secure this dependence or nothing more than some Declaratory Acts or resolves, *it is all over with us.* The friends of government will be utterly disheartened and the friends of anarchy will be afraid of nothing, be it ever so extravagant.

I never think of the measures necessary for the peace and good order of the colonies without pain. There must be an abridgment of what are called English liberties. I relieve myself by considering that in a remove from the state of nature to the most perfect state of government there must be a great restraint of natural liberty. I doubt whether it is possible to project a system of government in which a colony three thousand miles distant from the parent state shall enjoy all the liberty of the parent state. I am certain I have never yet seen the projection. I wish the good of the colony, when I wish to see some further restraint of liberty rather than the connection with the parent state should be broken for I am sure such a breach must prove the ruin of the colony.[47]

Samuel Adams generated a demand that the papers be published, which they were, in June of 1773. The content of these letters led Adams, and other patriots, perhaps including Franklin, to conclude that there was a conspiracy between Hutchinson and others with the British to restrict the Massachusetts colonials' exercise of their rights as Englishmen. If so, the time to move toward independence was at hand. This is the conclusion of historian John Ferling:

> No one was more touched than John Adams by these occurrences coming one atop another; London's apparent drive to deprive the provincial authority of its independence, the governor's intransigent position on colonial autonomy, and the revelation of a possible plot among imperial officials to destroy the liberties of the colonists, all had a transforming impact on Adams. As if by alchemy, these events changed Adams. The uncertain patriot of the 1760s was at last recast. Never again would he see British policy as merely misguided. When Great Britain next moved against the colonies, John Adams emerged as a committed revolutionary.[48]

By the summer of 1773, the leaders of both Massachusetts and Virginia—approaching the issue from vastly different positions—had made the psychological leap from loyal subjects of the empire seeking their rights as Englishmen to rebels who would soon assert their right to govern themselves. With the initiative of the Virginia House of Burgesses' call for colonial committees of correspondence, the colonists now had a mechanism for communicating with each other that was beyond the control of the colonial governors, but had legitimacy in the public mind because the committees had been created by colonial legislatures.

# Chapter 4

# The Virginia Resolution Unites the Colonies and Leads to the First Continental Congress in 1774

The Virginia Resolution from the House of Burgesses on March 13, 1773, calling for intercolonial committees of correspondence, merits a close analysis. It represented the decision of the leaders of the wealthiest colony that they were ready to defy British policies. This was a step taken seriously by the other colonies. It put Virginia into a leadership role at the Continental Congress in 1774. Decisions taken there, following Virginia's instructions to its delegates, put the colonies on the collision course that led to revolution.

The Virginia Resolution appears here with paragraph numbers and comments added.[1]

> (1) Whereas, the minds of His Majesty's faithful subjects in this colony have been much

disturbed by various rumours and reports of proceedings tending to deprive them of their ancient, legal, and constitutional rights.

This paragraph establishes that the House of Burgesses had a legitimate interest in addressing these "rumours and reports." At the same time, the phrase "ancient, legal, and constitutional rights" is so broad that it encompasses the "original understanding" theories of both Adams and Jefferson that claimed the colonies had always had full control over their internal affairs. The resolution deals with Virginia's interests. This is the foundation for the rest of the document.

As we have seen, both Massachusetts thinkers like Adams and Virginia thinkers like Jefferson had already developed a claim of "ancient legal and constitutional rights" that gave the colonies freedom to conduct their internal affairs without British interference.[2] The assertion of such rights is inconsistent with the repugnancy clauses in colonial charters as well as the declaration of Parliament in 1766 claiming the right to govern the colonies "in all cases whatsoever."

Moreover, while seeming to be specific, the resolution does not identify the "proceedings" that gave rise to the disturbing reports, thus permitting readers to include any British action that offended them. Southerners could understand that Lord Mansfield's decision in Somerset's case was included; northerners would understand that taxation and the quartering of troops were included. All were instances where Britain usurped or threatened to take the colonists' "ancient, legal, and constitutional rights" and their property.

(2) And whereas, the affairs of this colony
are frequently connected with those of Great
Britain as well as of the neighboring colonies,
which renders a communication of sentiments necessary; in order therefore to
remove the uneasiness and to quiet the
minds of the people as well as for the other
good purposes above mentioned.

This paragraph contains the proposition that so upset
the British Board of Trade. It asserts that common interests of the colonies require intercolonial communication of
sentiments. Sentiments may lead to action. This paragraph
incorporates the purposes set out in paragraph one. It also
contravenes Britain's policy of dealing separately with
each colony. No wonder the Board of Trade called it "a
measure of a most dangerous tendency and effect."

(3) Be it resolved, that a standing committee
of correspondence and inquiry be appointed
to consist of eleven persons, to wit, the Hon-
orable Peyton Randolph, Esquire, Robert
Carter Nicholas, Richard Bland, Richard
Henry Lee, Benjamin Harrison, Edmund
Pendleton, Patrick Henry, Dudley Digges,
Dabney Carr, Archibald Cary, and Thomas
Jefferson, esquires, any six of whom to be a
committee, whose business it shall be to
obtain the most early and authentic intelli-
gence of all such acts and resolutions of the
British Parliament or proceedings of

administration as may relate to or affect the British colonies in America, and to keep up and maintain a correspondence and communication with our sister colonies, respecting these important considerations; and the result of such their proceedings, from time to time, to lay before this House.

These three paragraphs are carefully constructed to build upon one another. Paragraph two incorporates paragraph one, by express reference. Paragraph three refers to both paragraphs one and two. Together they make a coherent whole. Paragraph three told both the British and the other colonies that this document expressed the judgment of the political leadership of Virginia, including both the senior and younger members of the House of Burgesses.

They were united in the decision to discuss with the other colonies "acts of Parliament" and "proceedings of administration" which included all British actions which irritated the colonies—including both limiting slavery and imposing taxes. These were to be considered concerns of all the colonies and to be addressed jointly, regardless of Britain's hopes to keep the colonies separate from one another. It also makes clear that the committees would mobilize public opinion. The actions of the committees were not directed only to the political elites in both the colonies and in Britain, but to the citizens of the colonies as well. The resolution provided a model for extralegal committees of correspondence that the other colonies could—and did—follow.[3]

(4) Resolved, that it be an instruction to the said committee that they do, without delay, inform themselves particularly of the principles and authority on which was constituted a court of enquiry, said to have been lately held in Rhode Island, with powers to transmit persons accused of offenses committed in America to places beyond the seas to be tried.

This paragraph refers to an incident that occurred in June, 1772, involving the *Gaspee*, a British antismuggler ship, assigned to Rhode Island in March of 1772. Rhode Island was a notorious home for smugglers engaged in evading British customs regulations. British navy lieutenant William Dudingston had managed to alienate the colonists while stationed in Philadelphia, his previous post, but outdid himself when he arrived in Rhode Island. He routinely stopped ships and helped himself to food and other supplies. His actions generated many complaints from citizens. He ignored Governor Joseph Wanton's demand to present his commission and discuss these complaints.

Finally, he seized the *Fortune*, a ship owned by the family of Thomas Green, a wealthy merchant, and sent it to Boston, instead of nearby Providence, for a trial on smuggling charges. Merchants John and Nicholas Brown and Thomas Green signed a complaint against Dudingston for violating regulations that required such ships to stay within the colony where it was seized and for abusing the citizens.

On June 9, 1772, Dudingston tried to intercept the *Hannah*, a small ship sailing up Narragansett Bay from Newport to Providence. Captain Benjamin Lindsey took evasive action and the *Gaspee* chased him through shallow waters until it ran aground on Namquid Point at mid-afternoon, shortly after low tide. Captain Lindsey knew that Dudingston would be stuck for twelve hours.

Lindsey rushed to Providence and told John Brown what had happened. Brown immediately organized a flotilla of eight longboats and sent Daniel Pearce to march with a drum down Main Street calling out the news, and asking people to come to Sabin's Tavern where an attack on the *Gaspee* was organized by Brown with his captain Abraham Whipple. At ten p.m., sixty-five volunteers rowed on muffled oars from Fenner's Wharf toward the *Gaspee*.

Their surprise was nearly complete. They were under the *Gaspee*'s eight big guns before they were noticed, at about 12:45 a.m. When Dudingston challenged them, someone shot him in the arm; the bullet lodged in his left groin. The Rhode Islanders overwhelmed the crew of twenty-six men and took all of them to shore, returned to the *Gaspee,* and burned her to the waterline.

By the next day, the story was all over Providence, Newport, and Bristol, including the tale of how Justin Jacobs paraded through Providence wearing Dudingston's gold-braided officer's hat. The local government instituted a pro forma investigation that revealed nothing. Amnesia struck all of Rhode Island. The horrified British created a royal commission to identify the culprits and charge them with treason, which could be tried in England. The chief justices of Massachusetts, New York, and New Jersey, along with a judge of the Vice Admiralty Court for New England and Rhode Island's Governor Wanton made up the commission.

The commission decided that they would turn over anyone they captured to Rhode Island authorities, instead of sending them to London. This was done by January 4, 1773, but was not widely publicized. The investigation—scarcely worthy of Sherlock Holmes—failed to identify anyone. It concluded that the attack had been "spontaneous" and not planned in advance as the British thought, and that Dudingston, by his "intemperate, if not a reprehensible, zeal to aid the revenue service" had contributed to the outcome. Dudingston was promoted to rear admiral after the affair was over and the cloud of amnesia over Rhode Island blew away.[4]

Some historians of the twentieth century have brushed off the *Gaspee* incident as an excuse for the Virginia Resolution rather than its cause. Historian Charles Andrews concludes that: "Even the disturbance caused by the burning of the British revenue vessel *Gaspee* in Narragansett Bay near Providence in 1772 did not seriously derange the existing tranquility."[5] The best evidence for this position is that there was no follow-up to the committee of correspondence request for information about the *Gaspee* affair. Apparently, the committee members violated their instructions. They never "informed themselves" of the basis for the creation of a court of inquiry to investigate the *Gaspee* incident. Evidently, once the *Gaspee* had been mentioned as evidence of British misbehavior, the committee of correspondence lost interest. *Gaspee* served its purpose as a propaganda ploy, not a serious concern worth pursuing.

The records of the Virginia committee of correspondence contain no communications concerning the *Gaspee* affair at all. There is no report that the *Gaspee* incident was examined by anyone. There are no reports that the royal commission had decided to turn over any culprits to Rhode Island authorities, rather than transporting them to England. Nor is there a report that no one was caught or transported.

Paragraph four of the Virginia Resolution appears to be an unnecessary afterthought to the Virginia Resolution, because the *Gaspee* incident was one of those "rumours and reports" already identified in paragraph one. But paragraph four did send one important and clear signal to the northern colonists. It demonstrated that the Virginians took northerners problems with the British seriously and were ready to make common cause with them.

While the records of the Virginia committee of correspondence contain nothing about the *Gaspee* affair, they are full of communications congratulating Virginia for its resolution, and planning for a meeting of a Continental Congress. Even though the resolution was condemned by the British government, it received stunning support throughout the colonies. Many more resolutions were adopted by other colonies in praise and support for Virginia's leadership.

> **Massachusetts, May 27, 1773:** "This House have a very grateful sense of the obligations they are under to the House of Burgesses in Virginia for the vigilance, firmness, and wisdom which they have discovered at all times in support of the rights and liberties of the American colonies, and do heartily concur with them in their said judicious and spirited resolves."

**South Carolina, July 9, 1773:** "We are firmly persuaded of the utility of the measure so seasonably proposed by the colony of Virginia and, we hope, universally adopted by the other colonies, and hope thereby to cultivate and strengthen that harmony and union among all the English colonies on the continent."

**Delaware, October 25, 1773:** "This House have a very grateful sense of the obligation they are under to the House of Burgesses in Virginia, for the vigilance, firmness, and wisdom which they have discovered at all times in support of the rights and liberties of the American colonies, and do heartily concur with them in their said judicious and spirited resolves."

**Georgia, September 10, 1773:** "The thanks of this House be transmitted to the...members of the House of Burgesses of Virginia...for communicating their intentions firmly to support the right and privileges of his Majesty's faithful subjects."

**Philadelphia meeting, noted by Charles Thompson, June 13, 1774:** "All America looks up to Virginia to take the lead on the present occasion. Our united efforts are now necessary to ward off the impending blow leveled at our lives, liberty and property.... Some colony must step forth and appoint the time and place. None is so fit as Virginia.

You are ancient. You are respected. You are animated in the cause."

Similar support came from six other colonies and cities including Connecticut, November 4, 1773, New York City, January 20, 1774, New Jersey, February 3, 1774, New York, March 1, 1774, Alexandria, Virginia, May 29, 1774, and North Carolina, June 24, 1774.[6]

The published records of the Virginia committee of correspondence make clear that the resolution was understood by virtually all the colonies as calling for a congress of the colonies for the purpose of countering the offending British actions. This support meant that the leadership in the other colonies was ready, once Virginia acted, to "cross the Rubicon," and risk British displeasure that could ripen into charges of treason, by publicly supporting the Virginians' resolution. Thus the "younger members" of the House of Burgesses learned not only that their senior members were ready to move forward, but that the other colonies were ready to join the march.

After March, 1773, when the House of Burgesses resolution was adopted, British actions that were designed to save the East India Company from bankruptcy encouraged the colonies to unite. In the spring of 1773, Parliament approved a plan to unload seventeen shiploads of East India Company tea in the colonies. The tea scheme was a bail-out for the East India Company that sat with half a million surplus pounds of tea. The plan authorized the Company to make direct sales of cheaper tea to colonists, without the Company paying taxes, thus threatening to disrupt the Colonies' substantial smuggling trade with the Dutch and undercutting the profit of colonial merchants. British favorites among the colonists would be chosen to distribute the cheap tea. This effort was opposed by both merchants and colonists who saw another tax in the making through the creation of a monopoly.[7]

The British plan radicalized the hitherto conservative New York merchants and provided an opportunity for the southern colonies to emphasize their opposition to this parliamentary intrusion into colonial affairs without mentioning slavery. The ports of Boston, New York, Philadelphia, and Charleston repelled the tea shipments in different ways.[8] The colorful actions in Boston in December, 1773, where three shiploads of tea were dumped into the harbor by colonists lightly disguised as Mohawk Indians, became known as the Boston Tea Party.[9] Its fame eclipsed the fact that the colonists refused to allow the tea to be landed anywhere in the colonies.[10] This was the first time that Americans had taken parallel action to deny British commerce physical access to American ports.

The colonists did not need a committee of correspondence to tell them that the tea should be stopped. The existence of the committees, however, with their implied promise of joint action, may have encouraged the boldness that the colonists demonstrated in rejecting the tea. The unity of colonial action disturbed the British as much as the disruption of the tea scheme itself. British colonial policy had sought to retain direct relations with each colony in hopes that the colonies would not become accustomed to acting in concert and would continue to relate to Britain as the source of styles, education, culture, and political guidance.

By the end of 1773, this policy was in shambles and the British understood that there would be further united action by the colonies unless they put a stop to it.[11] This explains the drastic measures taken against Boston, believed by the British to be the center of revolutionary activities. The British demanded that the people of Boston pay for the tea; the demand was refused. The British had learned from the *Gaspee* incident that local law enforcement would not work because local officials were too frightened to enforce London's will. So they acted with a vengeance. They closed the port of Boston, sent troops to occupy it, appointed General Gage as, in effect, a military governor, and adopted other measures later collectively labeled as the "intolerable" or "coercive" acts. Historian Theodore Draper sums up the thrust of these laws:[12]

> The Boston Port Bill effectively closed Boston harbor to commercial traffic. In May, [1774] an Administration of Justice Act sought to protect Crown officials in Massachusetts from standing trial before hostile provincial courts. It revised the judicial system by enabling the governor to appoint and remove inferior judges, sheriffs, and justices of the peace. Next, a Massachusetts Government Bill sought to show that the colony was not going to be governed as before. It partially abrogated the Massachusetts charter of 1691 by giving the London government the power to appoint all members of the council, whose approval of the

governor's actions had previously been required. These Coercive Acts, as they were known, were intended to break Boston's will to resist.

The intolerable acts demonstrated to all the colonists that their rights as Englishmen—the initial basis of their claim to freedom from taxation without representation—was not a fortress, but a sand castle. In fact, just as Parliament had claimed in 1766 in the Declaratory Act, the entire structure of the colonial government could be abrogated and replaced with a military governor, their assemblies could meet only at the will of the British, and the assemblies themselves could be made to consist of London's appointees. Their property—which to southerners included slaves—was now subject to the will of Britain, "without the cause being glossed over by taxation."[13] At this point, concern for protection of property and their systems of self-government merged the interests of northern and southern colonies.

Once again, Virginia formulated the colonial reaction. It sounded out the colonies on the need for a meeting of a general congress of the colonies. Following the British occupation of Boston, the Virginia committee of correspondence, on May 28, 1774, sent letters to the other colonial committees "requesting their sentiments on the appointment of deputies to meet annually in general congress."[14] Then the committee called for observing June 15 as a day of prayer in support of the people of Boston. Massachusetts responded to the May 28 letter from Virginia by calling for a meeting in Philadelphia on September 1.[15] The other colonies agreed. Delegates were

selected informally, except in two colonies where the legislature acted.[16]

The Virginia delegates to the congress were instructed to
insist that colonial legislatures possessed "the sole right of
directing their internal polity," thus directly challenging
both the repugnancy clauses in colonial charters and the
Declaratory Act which claimed such power for Parliament.[17]
The foundation for this claim of independence was provided
by Jefferson's "summary view" that Parliament never had
legislative power over the internal affairs of the colonies.[18]

The instructions explained that the colonies had from
the first acquiesced in British legislation concerning them,
because the legislation was useful and reasonable:

> Wanting the protection of Britain, we have
> long acquiesced in their acts of navigation
> restrictive of our commerce, which we
> consider as an ample recompense for such
> protection; but as those acts derive their effi-
> cacy from that foundation alone, we have
> reason to expect they will be restrained, so as
> to produce the reasonable purposes of
> Britain, without being injurious to us.[19]

This language offered a compromise whereby Britain
could keep its regulation of trade if it gave up its control
over colonial internal affairs and left the judgment of rea-
sonableness to the colonies.

Thus the Virginians arrived in Philadelphia in September
of 1774 with a fixed view that the outcome of the congress
was to include the protection of slavery in each colony as

an aspect of colonial control over "internal policies." They had armed their delegates with the ammunition to assure that this outcome would be reached. The Virginia delegates could effectively veto any alternative proposals by maintaining that they were bound by the instructions and could agree to nothing less.

Because the British pressures in Boston required a collective response from the colonies, and because Virginia was the wealthiest of the colonies, these instructions were the requirements that Virginia demanded as the price of its participation in the Congress. This was the first time the Virginians would set the agenda and the intellectual structure of a national convention. As the next chapter will show, these instructions were the foundation for a decision by the Congress that virtually assured a war for independence between the colonies and Great Britain.

The events which unfolded after the call for colonial committees of correspondence demonstrate the intensity of the southern commitment to both independence and slavery. These developments evolved toward a joining of northern and southern interests around concepts of "liberty and property." Because slavery was subsumed within the concept of property, the South did not need to make a public demand for colonial support of slavery.

Had the colonies based their claims only on the issue of Parliament's power to tax, that issue could, and probably would, have been resolved along the lines of the two previous British efforts at taxation in the 1760s.[20] The South made that impossible by its demand for internal freedom of action. In that sense, American liberty could be defined as the desire to protect black slavery.[21]

# Chapter 5

---

# John Adams Supports the South on Slavery

---

John and Samuel Adams, along with Robert Treat
Paine and Thomas Cushing, were appointed
Massachusetts delegates to the first Continental
Congress in a closed meeting of the General Court. The
doors were locked against the governor so he could not dis-
miss the court. He tried, but was too late.[1] After the
appointment, John Adams moved his family from Boston
back to Braintree for safety.

On Wednesday, August 10, 1774, the Massachusetts delegates rode together in a coach from Boston toward
Philadelphia. Their coach passed British troops who made
no effort to stop them. Along the way, they were escorted by
"anxious" and "expectant" local leaders. This was the first
time either John or Samuel Adams had left Massachusetts
for an extended period, but more importantly, it was proof
of their role as the leading figures in the colony's struggles
with Britain.

While John had become a leading lawyer and
spokesman for colonial rights, Samuel was the consum-
mate agitator for independence, using his writing and ver-
bal skills and taking advantage of every British misstep to
encourage the people of Massachusetts to resent British

interference of their rights. He did all this without crossing the line that would have resulted in a charge of treason or would have gotten too far ahead of public opinion.[2] As long as they claimed their rights as Englishmen, a charge of treason was unlikely. The two Adams had become personal symbols of opposition to the British, especially since the British pressure on Boston during the summer of 1774.

John's diary recorded the receptions, meetings, and a continuous parade as they left their home colony to meet leaders from other colonies. At each stop, they were met by local political figures and members of the committees of correspondence who provided advice, support, news, and gossip. When, on August 20, they arrived within fifteen miles of New York City, John was impressed, as first time visitors often are:

> The streets of this town [Kingsbridge] are vastly more regular and elegant than those in Boston, and the houses are more grand as well as neat. They are almost all painted— brick buildings and all.[3]

On Monday, August 22, he encountered a large number of the New York delegation to Congress, who gave him some advice:

> Mr. McDougal gave a caution to avoid every expression here, which looked like an allusion to the last appeal. He says there is a powerful party here, who are intimidated by fears of a civil war, and they have been

induced to acquiesce by assurances that there was no danger, and that a peaceful cessation of commerce would effect relief.[4]

On Tuesday, August 23, after a day of visiting New York City and meeting many people, John Adams wrote in his diary:

> With all the opulence and splendor of this city, there is very little good breeding to be found. We have been treated with an assiduous respect. But I have not seen one real gentleman, one well-bred man since I came to town. At their entertainments there is no conversation that is agreeable. There is no modesty—no attention to one another. If they ask you a question, before you can utter three words of your answer, they will break out upon you, again, and talk away.[5]

He reached Princeton on Saturday, August 27, examined the library and the planetarium, and drank a glass of wine with the president of the college, John Witherspoon, who would later sign the Declaration of Independence for New Jersey. He told Adams:

> It is necessary that the congress should raise money and employ a number of writers in the newspapers in England, to explain to the public the American plea and remove the prejudices of the Britons.[6]

The eastern colonies through which they traveled were especially supportive. If the British could destroy Boston's commerce and strip her people of their political influence, they could devastate Connecticut, New York, and New Jersey as well. John Adams's mission was to unify the colonies behind Massachusetts in its struggle with the British.

While Virginia had organized the committees of correspondence that created channels of communication between the colonies, Massachusetts had instigated the occasion—the Boston Tea Party—which made the British overreact and brought many people to the view that independence was a plausible solution to British arrogance. Adams and Jefferson, who represented two of the most powerful and politically significant colonies—Virginia and Massachusetts—had reached that same conclusion in the spring of 1773.

As Adams's coach neared Philadelphia, the first hint of difficulties for their mission to Congress came from Dr. Benjamin Rush, who rode out five miles to meet them. Were it not for Benjamin Franklin, he would have been the most distinguished citizen of Philadelphia. A prolific writer and passionately antislavery, Benjamin Rush had studied medicine at Edinburgh. A man ahead of his time, he adopted modern medical techniques and taught that mentally ill people should be treated rather than locked up and that yellow fever was not an inevitable plague. Before it was known that mosquitoes carried malaria, he had recommended that the swamps around Philadelphia be drained, but his advice was not followed.[7]

Joining their coach, Rush explained to Adams that influential delegates in Pennsylvania believed that Adams intended to draw the colonies toward independence. Rush reported that a powerful group of delegates wanted to seek reconciliation with Britain. The group was headed by Joseph Galloway, a former speaker of the Pennsylvania Assembly who had long been associated with Ben Franklin, but broke with him over the issue of independence.[8]

Rush warned Adams that if Massachusetts proposed bold measures that hinted at independence, Adams would be accused of seeking to drag all the colonies into war simply because of Massachusetts's impetuous actions at the "tea party" and its aftermath.[9] Those were the actions that had antagonized the British into taking drastic action against Massachusetts, such as closing the port of Boston, imposing a military governor, and reducing the influence of the elected legislature.

It was a bright, late-August afternoon when they were finally escorted down Broad Street in Philadelphia, "dirty, dusty, and fatigued." Half a dozen delegates from the area took them to the city tavern on Second Street where they met other delegates, had an "elegant supper" and talked until 11 p.m.[10] Philadelphia delighted Adams with its rectangular layout:

> The regularity and elegance of this city are very striking. It is situated upon a neck of land, about two miles wide between the River Delaware and the River Schuilkill. The streets are all exactly straight and parallel to the river. Front Street is near the river, then 2 street, 3d, 4th, 5th, 6th, 7th, 8th, 9th. The cross streets which intersect these are all equally wide, straight, and parallel to

each other, and are named from forest and fruit trees; Pear Street, Apple Street, Walnut Street, Chestnut Street, &c.[11]

And the elegant style of living and eating impressed him as well. On September 22, he wrote:

> Dined with M. Chew, chief justice of the province, with all the gentlemen from Virginia, Dr. Shippen, Mr. Tilghman, and many others. We were shewn into a grand entry and staircase, and into an elegant and most magnificent chamber, until dinner. About four o'clock we were called down to dinner. The furniture was all rich. Turttle, and every other thing—flummery, jellies, sweetmeats of twenty sorts, trifles, whip'd syllabubbs, floating islands...I drank Madeira at a great rate and found no inconvenience in it.[12]

Adams believed that twenty-two of the fifty-six members of the Congress were lawyers, and he enjoyed socializing and theorizing with them. On September 7 he wrote:

> We had a large collection of lawyers, at table. Mr. Andrew Allen, the attorney general; a Mr. Morris, the prothonotory; Mr. Fisher; Mr. McKean; Mr. Rodney—besides these we had Mr. Reed, Govr. Hopkins, and Governor Ward.

> We had much conversation upon the
> practice of law, in our different provinces,
> but at last we got swallowed up, in politicks,
> and the great question of parliamentary
> jurisdiction. Mr. Allen asks me, from
> whence do you derive our laws? How do you
> intitle yourselves to English priviledges? Is
> not Lord Mansfield on the side of power? [13]

At first he was also impressed with the intellect and wisdom of the delegates from the other colonies. But after some weeks, Adams grew restless at the seemingly endless arguments while Boston remained under occupation.

Adams worried as he arrived in the city after the warning from Rush and others. How would he be received by the delegates? Was he up to the task of representing Massachusetts, both intellectually and with good judgment? When he was appointed, he wrote to Abigail:

> This will be an assembly of the wisest men
> upon the continent, who are Americans in prin-
> ciple, i.e., against the taxation of Americans by
> authority of Parliament....I feel myself
> unequal to the business. A more extensive
> knowledge of the realm, the colonies, and of
> commerce, as well as of law and policy, is nec-
> essary, than I am a master of. [14]

As he considered Rush's advice, Adams realized that his skills at legal reasoning and argument would have to be supplemented by caution and indirection.

After all, Rush's warning was apt—John Adams was spokesman for the colony that had aggravated the British by the contest over taxes in the 1760s, the Boston Tea Party, and the struggle with Governor Hutchinson. If Massachusetts took the lead in organizing the challenge to Britain by seeking independence, other colonies might resent being asked to bail out Massachusetts from a mess of its own making.

Britain blamed Massachusetts, particularly the people of Boston, and especially the Adams cousins, for the disturbances in all the colonies. Adams was concerned that in Philadelphia, Massachusetts would appear to be pleading primarily for help in its own struggle against the mother country.

The delegates knew that Adams had bested Governor Hutchinson after he had lectured the Massachusetts assembly on the nature of the British Empire. Hutchinson had argued that there could be no intermediate position "between the supreme authority of Parliament and the total independence of the colonies." This belief that sovereignty was an "all or nothing" concept was central to the way Britain ruled the colonies—not by force, but by fostering the belief of the colonists that they were part of the empire.

The Massachusetts assembly, with John Adams's advice, drew a different conclusion from Hutchinson's premise. Since there was no original intention by the British to "reduce us to a state of vassalage, the conclusion is that it was their [original] sense that we were thus independent [of Parliament]."[15] This jousting between a disliked governor and a restive House of Representatives was not far from an assertion of independence.

After only four days in Philadelphia, days filled with dinners and excursions as the delegates became familiar with one another, Adams identified a group of men who reminded him of Massachusetts governors Francis Bernard and Thomas Hutchinson, who had publicly "professed to be Friends of Liberty" until Hutchinson's letters to British officials urging a reduction in colonial rights were discovered.[16] Among them were Joseph Galloway of Pennsylvania and James Duane of New York. They would pose the greatest challenge to the delegates who sought serious action against the British.

Adams sensed these difficulties when he began to mingle with the delegates. He wrote to his friend William Tudor in mid-September:

> We have had numberless prejudices to remove here. We have been obliged to act with great delicacy and caution. We have been obliged to keep ourselves out of sight, and to feel pulses, and sound the depths—to insinuate our sentiments, designs, and desires by means of other persons, sometimes of one province and sometimes of another.[17]

Adams was not alone in his uncertainties about his new colleagues. All of them were "skitterish" during their first weeks together.[18] For example, Joseph Galloway made a private report to New Jersey governor William Franklin, Benjamin Franklin's son, of a conversation he had with John Rutledge, leader of the South Carolina delegation.

The report showed that Galloway and Rutledge withheld information from each other. Galloway did not think that Rutledge was among the supporters of the "Boston Commissioners" who wished for a non-importation agreement and a refusal to pay tea taxes. He explained that in his meeting with:

> the elder Rutledge of South Carolina, whose sentiments and mine differ in no one particular so far as I explained myself—and I was reserved in no point save that of a representation in Parliament. He is a gentleman of an amiable character—has look'd into the arguments on both sides more fully than any I have met with, and seems to be aware of all the consequences which may attend rash and imprudent measures.[19]

Galloway did not tell Rutledge of his plan for a joint British-American Parliament and Rutledge concealed from Galloway that he was a staunch supporter of both slavery and independence.

In Philadelphia, each group took the measure of the men with whom they would share power if independence should ever come. They did this during the socializing that occupied most of their dinners taken after morning sessions, often elaborate affairs as Philadelphia hostesses showed the city's cultivation. John Dickinson invited the delegates to his country estate. He was one of the richest Philadelphians, and was known for his "Letters from a Farmer in Pennsylvania," favoring the "no taxation without representation" principle. He had now joined in efforts to find a compromise with Britain.

In those early days, many delegates hesitated to express their views candidly. The Virginians may have brought the basis for revolution with them in their demand for independence from Parliament, but they, too, had to be cautious in how to present it. The threat that someone might make a charge of treason for seeking independence was never far from their minds.

After some days of sounding out each other, John Adams and the Virginians forged a friendship. Adams wrote: "These gentlemen from Virginia appeared to be the most spirited and consistent of any."[20] Richard Henry Lee reciprocated his admiration, and thus was formed the "Adams-Lee junto," an alliance between Virginia and Massachusetts that would be important for years to come.[21] The initiation of that friendship had come a year earlier when Lee wrote to John Adams to introduce himself. When Adams first met Lee face to face, he wrote: "He is a masterly man."[22] Lee's friendship with and admiration for the spartan qualities of the New Englanders would grow in the years ahead.[23]

The southerners knew that Massachusetts had led the opposition to British taxes of the 1760s with great success. But this movement had dissipated as soon as the taxes were repealed. Some southern delegates may have noted that, under Massachusetts leadership, the northerners appeared to be more concerned with avoiding taxes than with freedom from Britain.

Slavery, although legal, was much less prevalent in the northern colonies and northern attitudes toward slavery were uncertain.[24] The southerners needed to understand the

Massachusetts view of slavery. Southerners would have heard that radical lawyer James Otis's argument before the Superior Court of Massachusetts in 1760 against "writs of assistance" included an attack on slavery as a violation of natural rights.[25] In 1764 he wrote: "The colonists are by the law of nature free born, as indeed all men are, white or black."[26]

Southern leaders would not join with the North to seek revolution without assurance that slavery would be left alone by the newly constituted free country. The southerners were concerned with problems that went far beyond the issues that were to be decided at the First Congress. Their need to protect slavery would continue as events unfolded after the Congress had finished its work.

In this atmosphere, the southerners, faced with the assault of the *Somerset* case, would seek separation from Britain only with the explicit understanding that slavery would be recognized and protected by the other colonies.

This was the view of Virginia historian Hugh Blair Grigsby, writing in 1855 describing the dominant view of the moderates in the Virginia Constitutional Convention of 1776. With reference to slavery, he considered that these men, "however prompt in resisting aggression from without, were cautious in remodeling the domestic policy of the state when a civil war was raging in the land."[27]

The southerners also tested the views of the delegates. Among the most dogmatic on the necessity for independence was Christopher Gadsden, a major plantation and slave owner in South Carolina. A constant replenishment of slaves was needed there because slaves died young in the

malaria-ridden swamps, which they cleared for rice production.[28] Adams reports that Gadsden was:

> violent against allowing to Parliament any
> power of regulating trade, or allowing that
> they have any thing to do with us. Power of
> regulating trade, he says, is power of ruining
> us—as bad as acknowledging them a
> supreme legislative in all cases whatsoever.
> A right of regulating trade is a right of legis-
> lation, and a right of legislation in one case,
> is a right in all.[29]

Adams wrote that he disagreed with Gadsden's conclusion, but spent considerable time with him, and with
Thomas Lynch, also of South Carolina.

After studying John Adams, the southerners decided
they had found the man they could trust. Adams was no
abolitionist. Long after Adams heard James Otis's declaration that "all men, white or black" are free born, he wrote:

> Not a Quaker in Philadelphia, or Mr. Jefferson
> of Virginia ever asserted the rights of
> Negroes in stronger terms. Young as I was,
> and ignorant as I was, I shuddered at the
> doctrine he taught; and I have all my life-
> time shuddered, and still shudder, at the
> consequences that may be drawn from such
> premises. Shall we say that the rights of
> masters and servants clash, and can be
> decided only by force? I adore the idea of

gradual abolition! But who shall decide how fast or how slowly these abolition shall be made?[30]

In his later life, Adams sounded exactly like his "southern friends" of 1774 when he described his attitude toward slavery:

> The turpitude, the inhumanity, the cruelty, and the infamy of the African commerce in slaves has been impressively represented to the public by the highest powers of eloquence, that nothing that I can say would increase the just odium in which it is and ought to be held. Every measure of prudence, therefore, ought to be assumed for the eventual total extirpation of slavery from the United States. If, however, humanity dictates the duty of adopting the most prudent measures for accomplishing so excellent a purpose, the same humanity requires that we should not inflict severer calamities on the objects of our commiseration than those which they at present endure by reducing them to despair, or the necessity of robbery, plunder, assassination, and massacre, to preserve their lives, some provision for furnishing them employment, or some means of supplying them with the necessary comforts of life. The same humanity requires that we should not by any rash or

violent measures expose the lives and property of those of our fellow-citizens who are so
unfortunate as to be surrounded with these
fellow-creatures, by hereditary descent, or by
any other means without their own fault.[31]

This is essentially the position taken in the 1770s by
Jefferson, Patrick Henry, and the other Virginians as we
saw in Chapter Three.

By agreeing to protect slavery in the new nation Adams
would live up to his promise to bring help to Massachusetts.
In cementing his relations to Virginia, he supported Peyton
Randolph of Virginia for president of the Continental Congress in 1774 and nominated Virginian George Washington
to command the Continental Army in 1775.

During the Revolutionary War, Adams effectively
buried a letter to Congress relating to a bill to free Negroes
in Massachusetts. When the Massachusetts legislature
tabled the bill to abolish slavery in the state, Adams was
pleased. "We have causes enough of jealousy, discord, and
division, and this bill [to free Negroes] will certainly add to
the number." In August, 1776, a New Jersey official proposed a black unit to serve as a home guard, but Adams
objected. "Your Negro battalion will never do. S. Carolina
would run out of their wits at the least hint of such a measure."[32] Historian Henry Wiencek has concluded, "Adams
was always concerned over the potential southern response
to the use of black troops or emancipation proposals."[33]

Adams shared the view that Congress should not be
asked to pay salaries to boys, old men, Negroes, and others
"unsuitable for service."[34] Early during the war, at the end

of 1775, a congressional delegation from South Carolina and Virginia, along with Ben Franklin, met with civilians from Massachusetts, Connecticut, and Rhode Island and concluded that Negroes, slave or free, should be "rejected altogether" from military service.

Historian Donald Robinson says the primary factor in the decision to reject new black recruits was "the effect such a policy would have in other colonies...not an animus against Negroes, out of a desire for a strong national union in the effort against England."[35] The petition of blacks who had served at Bunker Hill and the demands of war caused a change in this policy later in the Revolution, but the policy itself was a reflection of northern acceptance of the southern view concerning blacks.

Adams made clear in later life that he had deferred to the southerners on the issue of slavery: "I constantly said in former times to the southern gentlemen, I cannot comprehend this object. I must leave it to you. I will vote for forcing no measure against your judgments."

This statement makes clear that the southerners had questioned Adams on his view of the slavery question. John Adams knew, when he gave his answer, that the "southern gentlemen" intended to protect the foundation of their society—slavery. Their resolve was spelled out in the instructions from Virginia to secure full control of their internal affairs so that, among other things, they could maintain slavery.[36] Adams's statement to Jefferson is evidence that the most influential colonies—Massachusetts, Virginia, and the slave colonies—agreed to protect colonial slavery when they first met in 1774. Protecting slavery was such an important issue that it was resolved in favor of the South early in the first session of the Continental Congress. As a result, there was never a discussion of it on the floor of Congress. Such a discussion did not take place until many years later when John Adams and Thomas Jefferson were both retired.

Adams's "confession" that he had accepted the South's position on slavery was part of his late-in-life correspondence with Jefferson, who had been his political enemy in earlier years. Jefferson had defeated Adams for the presidency in 1800, and Adams had been bitter. Benjamin Rush arranged a reconciliation between the two, taking three years to accomplish it, between 1809 and 1812.[37]

From that time forward they exchanged elegantly composed correspondence drawing on their current interests, their recollections of their exciting past, and their problems of aging, wondering if their prodigious efforts had been worthwhile. Their correspondence about slavery began in 1819, the first year of the conflict over admitting Missouri as a slave state. The issue of whether a state should be "free" or "slave" had up to that time been avoided by admitting states in pairs—one free for one slave state. This meant that state equality in the Senate had been maintained. Northerners attempted to block Missouri's admission as a slave state, and southerners held the admission of Maine hostage to block that effort. The issue was resolved by admitting Missouri as a slave state, Maine as a free state, and extending, to the west, the line between slave and free territory that had been drawn in the Northwest Ordinance of 1787.[38] But before the compromise was reached on March 3, 1820, Jefferson and Adams began an exchange of letters that included the following:

Adams wrote to Jefferson, November 23, 1819, listing a series of issues facing the new Congress, including "the Missouri Slavery," writing, "Clouds look black and thick...threatening thunder and lightning."[39]

Jefferson to Adams, Dec. 10, 1819: Jefferson dismisses the other issues:

> They are occurrences which like waves in a storm will pass under the ship. But the Missouri question is a breaker on which we may lose the Missouri country by revolt, and what more, God only knows. From the battle of Bunker's Hill to the treaty of Paris, we never had so ominous a question.[40]

Adams to Jefferson, Dec. 21, 1819:

> The Missouri question I hope will follow the other waves under the ship and do no harm. I know it is high treason to express a doubt of the perpetual duration of our vast American Empire and our free institutions...but I am sometimes Cassandra enough to dream that another Hamilton, another Burr might rend this mighty fabric in twain.[41]

Jefferson to Adams, Jan. 22, 1821, after the adoption of the Missouri Compromise:

What does the Holy Alliance, in and out of Congress, mean to do with us on the Missouri question....The real question, as seen in the states afflicted with this unfortunate population is, Are our slaves to be presented with freedom and a dagger? For if Congress has the power to regulate the conditions of the inhabitants of the states, within the states, it will be but another exercise of that power to declare that all shall be free. Are we then to see again Athenian and Lacedemonian confederacies? To wage another Peloponnesian war to settle the ascendancy between them? Or is this the tocsin of merely a servile war? That remains to be seen, but not I hope, by you or me. Surely they will parley a while, and give us time to get out of the way.[42]

Adams to Jefferson, Feb. 3, 1821:

Slavery in this country I have seen hanging over it like a black cloud for half a century. [He then alludes to a vision of] armies of Negroes marching and counter-marching in the air, shining in armour. I have been so terrified with this phenomenon that I constantly said in former times to the southern gentlemen, I cannot comprehend this object. I must leave it to you. I will vote for forcing no measure against your judgments.[43]

This statement, made in 1821, explains his actions supporting the South on slavery issues at the First Continental Congress in 1774, and continuing in the following years.[44] Older histories emphasized the unity of the colonies, not their differences. Twentieth century histories continue to minimize the influence of slavery on the Revolution.[45]

Modern historians Joseph Ellis, Richard Brookhiser, and David McCullough have minimized Adams's "confession." Ellis assumed that there had been an "unspoken promise" to Adams that the South would engage in gradual emancipation. An unspoken promise, if there can be such a thing, sounds at most like wistful thinking by an Adams who needed the South to join the move against Britain. The Virginians' position that slavery was an evil that would be addressed some time in the future was certainly no promise. South Carolina would never have made such a promise. The idea that the southerners would have left the issue of slavery in the South an open question to be resolved through "unspoken promises" ignores both the intensity of southern interest in the issue, and the high quality of southern lawyers, who would have insisted on clarity on this issue.[46]

Brookhiser believed that John Adams had "absolutely clean hands" on the slavery issue. He even quotes Adams's statement to the southern gentlemen that he would "leave it to you. I will vote for forcing no measure against your judgments" in support of his proposition. Brookhiser's explanation is that Adams engaged in wistful thinking about letting slavery die a "natural death."[47] David McCullough, in his *John Adams,* also quotes the statement, but contends that Adams had no solution to the slavery issue.[48] Obviously,

Adams did have a solution—he supported "the southern gen-tlemen," thus assuring that Massachusetts would have the support of the wealthiest and most important of the colonies.

Edward Cody Burnett, a compiler of letters of members of the Continental Congress, did note the potential issue of counting slaves for purposes of state contributions to the federal treasury.

> Should the criterion for contributions be population or wealth? If wealth, should it be land values or some broader measure of property values? If population, what about slaves? Should they be counted as part of the population or as property? Though the determination of the latter question may not have seemed so vital a consequence as that of voting, nevertheless, here, at the very begin-nings of the nation was sounded an alarum bell that may well have roused the deepest slumber. It would ring out again and more insistently when the Federal Convention should assemble, and yet once more a few years later, even "as a fire bell in the night."[49]

The phrase "fire bell in the night" comes from Jefferson's letter to Congressman John Holmes relating to the Missouri Compromise in 1820 that extended the slave-free area of the country, established in the Northwest Ordinance of 1787, beyond the Mississippi to the west. To Jefferson it was "like a fire bell in the night, awakened and filled me with terror. I consider it at once as the knell of the Union."[50] By quoting his "fire bell" letter, Burnett made clear that, to him, the slavery issue raised its head in 1774.

Most modern historians who write about the First Continental Congress in 1774 mention slavery only with respect to the issue that Burnett addressed, and some quote or summarize Thomas Lynch's statement in July, 1776, that if it were to be debated if slaves were property, the confederation would be at an end.[51] Others speak only about the various and usually failed antislavery activities in the North, and include the banning of the international slave trade long proposed by Virginia for its own interests.[52] Jack Rakove, in his highly influential *Beginnings of National Politics*, does not mention slavery at all in connection with the First Congress. He treats Virginia during that period as a subordinate player on a field dominated by northern and middle colonies.[53]

Some historians have challenged the "majority view" that slavery was not an important issue in the period from 1774–1787. Staughton Lynd, in "Class Conflict, Slavery and the United States Constitution," and Gary Nash, in *Race and Revolution,* emphasized the choices that were made at the Constitutional Convention regarding slavery-related issues. Other authors who have addressed the slavery issue directly include Donald Robinson (1971), Duncan MacLeod (1974), and Donald Fehrenbacher (2001). Fehrenbacher develops the experiences in the First and Second Continental Congress to a greater depth than the others, but the bulk of his concern is with events occurring after the Constitutional Convention.

It appears that the limited number of written materials concerning the decisions made in the early 1770s has led historians, critical of the decisions concerning slavery at the Constitutional Convention, to accept without serious challenge the older analysis that slavery was essentially irrelevant to the earlier period of the Revolution.

John Adams was afraid that something like this would happen.

He wrote to Benjamin Rush in 1806:

> The secret of affairs is never known to the public until after the event, and often not then....And very often, the real springs, motives, and causes remain secrets in the breasts of a few, and perhaps one, and perish with their keepers.[54]

In 1815, he raised the same question in his correspondence with Thomas Jefferson.

> Who shall write the history of the American Revolution? Who can write it? Who will ever be able to write it? The most essential documents, the debates and deliberations in Congress, from 1774 to 1783, were all in secret, and are now lost forever.[55]

Jefferson replied,

> Nobody, except merely its external facts. All its councils, designs, and discussions having been conducted by Congress with closed doors, and no member, as far as I know,

having even made notes of them, these, which are the life and soul of history must be forever unknown.[56]

Was Adams, in his letter of 1821, telling Jefferson about his early relations with the southern gentlemen, revealing one of those secrets "in the breasts of a few" that might otherwise have perished "with their keeper"?

By 1819 and 1821, when the correspondence between them quoted above took place, their views on slavery had diverged. Jefferson was for states' rights, and the "diffusion" theory of slavery—let it expand to the west, where it will be spread out so thin that it will fade away. Adams was opposed to this theory, and did not want to see slavery in Missouri.

Adams knew that publishers would be interested in his correspondence with Jefferson, and that these letters would reach the public in the future.[57] Knowing this, Adams may have wanted to disclose his agreement to protect slavery at the beginning of the revolutionary struggle in order to distinguish it from his view in 1821. This would not be surprising, given his concern about the writing of history and his well-known propensity for telling the blunt truth.

In 1774, with Boston occupied by the British, the bargaining power of the South as compared to the North was overwhelming. Had Adams, or any northerner, raised the issue of the legitimacy of slavery, the South could simply have walked away from Philadelphia and allowed Massachusetts to sink under the weight of the British forces then in possession. What real choice did John Adams have at that time? When he was old, and opposed to the expansion of slavery, he may have had a wish to, while he was still alive, explain his 1774 actions.

The Marquis de Lafayette, the French nobleman who served as Washington's aide during the Revolution and who led a charge at Yorktown, certainly felt that way:

> I would never have drawn my sword in the cause of America, if I could have conceived that thereby I was founding a land of slavery.[58]

# Chapter 6

# The Colonies Claim Independence from Parliament

T he issue of slavery was presumably resolved to the satisfaction of the slave-holding colonies at the First Continental Congress in the first few days of September, 1774. At that point the Congress began to discuss how to stop British incursions into colonial affairs. As historian Jack Rakove has observed, the authority of the delegates arose from the ways that they had been selected and then instructed on what to do or say at the Congress. Many of the colonies instructed their delegates to support whatever policies the Congress chose to adopt, thus conferring on a majority of the colonies present the power to bind the other colonies.[1]

Virginia did not so casually surrender its freedom of action to a majority vote in the Congress. Rather, it instructed its delegates specifically with a date when a boycott of British goods and an embargo on sales to Britain should begin. Beyond that, the delegates were urged to "cordially cooperate with our sister colonies in general congress in such other just and proper methods as they, or the majority, shall deem necessary for the accomplishment of the valuable ends."[2] This allowed the delegates to pass judgment on whether the proposals were "just and proper" methods to the valuable end. This drew a critical comment from Jefferson, who noted that it "totally destroys that union of conduct in the several colonies which was the very purpose of calling a congress."[3] From another perspective, it gave the Virginia delegates broad discretion to choose among possible conflicting proposals, and to help shape those that would serve Virginia's interest. Virginia, having been very specific that the assemblies of each colony possessed "the sole right of directing their internal polity," would not surrender that authority to a group whose direction, at that point, was unknown.

The provisions discussed and adopted by the Congress included a petition to the king to redress grievances, the endorsement of the Suffolk Resolves calling for preparations for war, the boycott of British goods, the forming of an association to enforce the boycott, a ban on the foreign slave trade, and plans for a future meeting if the grievances were not resolved.[4] These techniques were all familiar. They had been used successfully during the earlier taxation crises. As a consequence, they caused but limited controversy.[5]

A declaration of rights was another matter. The relations between the colonies and Great Britain had worsened greatly since the Coercive Acts of the Spring of 1774, when Britain closed the port of Boston, sent troops to occupy it, appointed a military governor, and reduced the power of the legislature. Until those acts, the colonists had largely based their grievances on their rights as Englishmen. But the Coercive Acts demonstrated that Parliament would exercise the power it had claimed in the Declaratory Act of 1766 to govern the colonies "in all cases whatsoever." In the Coercive Acts, it demonstrated that it could and did redefine their rights as Englishmen. Parliament's view was that the colonies had only such rights as it chose to grant—or take away. Some of the colonists were now ready to deny Parliament such extensive control over their destiny.

John Adams was at the center of this controversy. He believed that the union of the colonies depended on its outcome.[6]

Adams described that these were the questions before them:

> What authority we should concede to Parliament: whether we should deny the authority of Parliament in all cases; whether we should allow any authority to it in our internal affairs; or whether we should allow it to regulate the trade of the empire, with or without any restrictions.[7]

There were sharply differing views on these issues. Christopher Gadsden of South Carolina favored total separation from Parliament. The Virginia instructions, while seeking independence in matters of internal policy, favored continuing the navigation acts by which Britain controlled colonial commerce by requiring that raw materials be exported to Britain, and excluded foreign ships from carrying goods to or from the colonies. Men from the middle colonies, such as Joseph Galloway from Pennsylvania and James Duane from New York, sought to retain the existing relation with Britain, but to guarantee that Britain could not regulate without colonial consent.

The language that challenged parliamentary supremacy over the colonies included Virginia's August, 1774, instructions to its delegates that claimed for the colonies "the sole right to direct their internal polity," and gave them discretion to accept or reject proposals by the Congress.[8]

John Rutledge of South Carolina, a careful proponent of slavery, drafted a more comprehensive resolution for the Congress in early September. His resolution combined the southern concern for internal liberty with the northern emphasis on freedom from taxation by England:

> They [the colonists in the several colonies] are also entitled to the [immunities] and privileges which have been from time to time granted to them respectively by royal charters; and to a free and inclusive power of legislation in *all cases of taxation and internal policy....* They cannot be altered or abridged by any authority but our respective legislatures. (emphasis added)[9]

This resolution combined the northern preoccupation with unfair taxation with the southern desire for freedom for each colony concerning internal affairs—including slavery. Rutledge's contribution consisted of linking these two issues at the Congress.[10] This linkage forged the common cause that generated a sense of the "united states."[11] The connection was expressed three times in extensive proposals drafted by Rutledge.[12]

The language combining taxation and internal affairs would become Article IV of the Declaration of the Rights of the Colonies.[13] It was drafted in early September, 1774, during the first week of the Congress, in a subcommittee of the Committee on Rights and Grievances.[14] This subcommittee agreed on a recommendation to Congress except for one provision that concerned the authority that should be conceded to Parliament. Following a long debate, Rutledge asked John Adams to prepare a draft that might resolve the issue. Adams described what happened:

> Mr. John Rutledge of South Carolina, one of the committee, addressing himself to me was pleased to say, "Adams we must agree upon something; you appear to be as familiar with the subject as any of us, and I like your expressions *the necessity of the case* and *excluding all ideas of taxation external and internal*. I have a great opinion of that same idea of the necessity of the case and I am determined against all taxation for revenue. Come take the pen and see if you can produce something that will unite us." Some others of the committee seconding Mr. Rutledge, I took a sheet of paper and drew up an article. When it was read I believe not one of the committee were fully satisfied with it, but they all soon acknowledged that there was no hope of hitting on any thing in which we could all agree with more satisfaction. All therefore agreed to this, and upon

this depended the union of the colonies.

The subcommittee reported their draught to the grand committee, and another long debate ensued....The articles were then reported to congress.[15]... The difficult article was again attacked and defended.[16] Congress rejected all amendments to it, and the general sense of the members was that the article demanded as little as could be demanded, and conceded as much as could be conceded with safety, and certainly as little as would be accepted by Great Britain; and that the country must take its fate, in consequence of it. When Congress had gone through the articles, I was appointed to put them into form and report a fair draught for their final acceptance.

This experience was another demonstration of the working relations between Adams and the southern gentlemen. Here is the language of Article IV that resolved the "great issues" identified by Adams. The boldface language challenges the authority of Parliament over the colonies, while allowing a circumscribed power to the king. The language in italics provisionally consents to Parliament's authority over external trade.[17]

**The foundation of English liberty, and of all free government, is a right in the people to participate in their legislative council: and as the English colonists are not represented,**

**and from their local and other circumstances, cannot properly be represented in the British Parliament, they are entitled to a free and exclusive power of legislation in their several provincial legislatures, where their right of representation can alone be preserved, in all cases of taxation and internal polity, subject only to the negative of their sovereign, in such manner as has been heretofore used and accustomed.**

*But, from the necessity of the case, and a regard to the mutual interests of both countries, we cheerfully consent to the operation of such acts of the British Parliament, as are bona fide restrained to the regulation of our external commerce, for the purpose of securing the commercial advantages of the whole empire to the mother country, and the commercial benefits of its respective members excluding every idea of taxation, internal or external, for raising a revenue of the subjects in America without their consent.*[18]

Political leaders on both sides of the Atlantic understood the import of the boldface language. Thomas Jefferson had challenged the Declaratory Act of 1766 where Parliament claimed to control the colonies "in all cases whatsoever" in his "Summary View."[19] John Adams had raised the same issue in the debate with Governor Hutchinson of Massachusetts.[20] Both Rutledge and Adams were aware that the assertion of colonial rights in Article IV contained the seeds of a possible treason charge, because it constituted a direct challenge to Parliament.[21] This may explain the paucity of written records concerning this issue at the time.

Lord Mansfield, in England, analyzed the colonial declaration of 1774 in exactly the same way. In November of that year, he wrote:

> The Congress sum up the whole of their grievances in that passage of the Declaratory Act which asserts the right of Great Britain to make laws which bind them in all cases whatsoever. They positively deny the right, not the mode of executing it. They would allow the king of Great Britain a nominal sovereignty over them, but nothing else.[22]

George III himself recognized that the declaration created a "serious crisis" in relations with the colonies in a long memorandum sent to Lord North. The king declared:

> There is no denying the serious crisis to which the disputes between the mother country and its North American colonies are growing, and that the greatest temper and firmness are necessary to bring matters to a good issue....Had the Americans in prosecuting their ill-grounded claims put on an appearance of mildness it might have been very difficult to chalk out the right path to be pursued; but they have boldly thrown off the mask and avowed that nothing

less than a total independence of the British legislature will satisfy them.

This indeed decides the proper plan to be followed, which is to stop the trade of all those colonies who obey the mandate of the Congress for non-importation, non-exportation, and non-consumption, to assist them no further with presents to the Indians, and give every kind of assistance to those who conduct themselves other ways; which will make them quarrel among themselves. Their separate interests must soon effect this, and experience will then show them that the interference of the mother country is essentially necessary to prevent their becoming rivals.[23]

Thus, on both sides of the Atlantic, two years before the Declaration of Independence and a year before hostilities broke out, American and British leaders agreed that the issue of parliamentary control raised in Article IV of the declaration was the crucial issue separating the mother country and the colonies.

Article IV is the origin of the states' rights doctrine that would protect southern slavery for 86 years and racial superiority for 104 more. The assertion that legislative power rested in the individual colonies laid the foundation for a weak national government. It asserted that sovereignty over internal affairs would lie with each colony. Under these circumstances, southerners would be free to maintain slavery, even as they agonized over the difficulties of ending it.[24]

The boldface language follows the Virginia instructions, Jefferson's "Summary View,"[25] and reflects Rutledge's draft of early September, 1774. It declares independence in all cases of taxation and internal polity from British Parliament, and locates all such power in the "several provincial legislatures."

Thus it embodied the deal to preserve slavery as the price of revolution. The agreement was hardly incidental, but was a response to the demand for internal freedom for the colonies that came specifically from the South.[26]

As noted earlier, the British actions against Boston in 1774 that had already occurred by the time the First Continental Congress met in September aroused such colonial anger that the southerners did not have to publicly assert their desire to preserve slavery. The South cloaked that desire within the general demand for colonial liberty and the protection of property—concepts which were broad enough to encompass both the commercial interests of the North and the slavery interests of the South.

Northerners and southerners could both seek independence in their internal affairs, with the northerners viewing liberty as the right to engage in commercial activity and to be taxed only by their own representatives, while the southerners insisted upon liberty primarily to maintain slavery. Both of these ideas fit under the common banner of independence for the colonies in their internal affairs.

By breaking from Parliament, the colonies also broke from their traditional assertion of "rights as Englishmen." Parliament had amply demonstrated how easily it could destroy those rights by the Coercive Acts and the occupation of Boston. What then was the foundation for the colonial claims? Adams said that Galloway and Duane would only look to the British Constitution and the American charters and grants, while he urged that the colonies look to natural law "as a resource to which we might be driven by Parliament much sooner than we were aware."[27] Events after the Continental Congress proved him right.

Some historians minimize the significance of the Declaration of Rights and Grievances of 1774, and conclude that other actions taken by the Congress were more serious, particularly the boycott and the local associations formed to enforce it. All these actions were ambiguous. They were negotiating tactics similar to those that had succeeded in securing repeal of the Stamp Act and the Townshend taxes on imported glass, paint, lead, and tea. The Townshend taxes of 1768 had been withdrawn in 1770 under pressure of a boycott. All of these tactics held the prospect of terminating as soon as particular colonial demands were met.

But Article IV was different. For the first time, the colonists struck at the heart of British rule. This was not a temporary negotiating position. It called for abolition of the existing relations with Britain. All British relations with the colonies would in some way relate to internal activities of the colonies. The claim in Article IV was—and was seen as—a major step toward total independence.

Historian Merrill Jensen made this point clear: "By 1774, the American and British positions on the power of Parliament were irreconcilable."[28] English historian Lawrence Henry Gipson wrote, "Here was the **real** American revolution."[29] Historian Theodore Draper concluded, "the Declaratory Act was the true causus belli of the American Revolution."[30]

The Declaratory Act of 1766, claiming parliamentary power over "all cases whatsoever" in the colonies, in conjunction with the *Somerset* decision, was an assertion of parliamentary power to destroy the southern economy and the social conditions built upon slavery. The southerners had to insist that Parliament have no control over internal affairs and policies. This challenge to the jurisdiction of Parliament, according to legal historian John Phillip Reid, made war inevitable, because:

> If the Americans had acknowledged an abstract supremacy, Parliament could then have devised a constitutional mechanism to check any threat from the crown should the colonies provide the king with revenue. But the Americans could not acknowledge [that supremacy] without risking their constitutional security to the whims and changing politics of some future parliament.[31] The controversy, therefore, became too legal not in an abstract sense, but because the procedures or mechanics of constitutional advocacy provided no opportunity for a political solution unless either the British or the Americans surrendered a constitutional principle they thought essential for their constitutional liberty. ...American liberty—the right to be free of arbitrary power—could not be secured under parliamentary supremacy. British liberty— the representative legislature over the

crown—could not be secured without parliamentary supremacy.[32]

Thus, states rights, slavery, and liberty were inextricably linked in the 1774 Declaration of Rights and Grievances.

The Continental Congress was presented with a serious and powerful alternative to the Adams-Rutledge provision by Joseph Galloway of Pennsylvania supported by James Duane of New York. This presentation came on September 28, while the Adams-Rutledge declaration was being debated by the Congress. Galloway's alternative was to create an American colonial parliament, which, with the British parliament, could legislate on matters affecting the colonies.[33]

The "American Parliament" was to be an "inferior and distinct" branch of Parliament. A president-general, appointed by the king, with the advice and consent of the "Grand Council" chosen by representatives of colonial legislatures, would:

> hold and exercise all the legislative rights, powers, and authorities necessary for regulating and administering all the general police and affairs of the colonies, in which Great Britain and the colonies, or any of them, the colonies in general, or more than one colony, are in any manner concerned, as well civil and criminal as commercial.[34]

The approval of both the American and British Parliaments would be necessary for the adoption of "all such general acts and statutes," under Galloway's plan. Thus the plan fully addressed all expressed northern concerns: the grievance concerning taxation without representation, the quartering and support of British troops without consent, as well as the closing of the port of Boston and the other Coercive Acts. These things could not take place without the agreement of the colonies acting within the "British-American Parliament."

It gave the American Parliament a veto over such legislation and made clear that Britain could not rule the colonies without their consent. It effectively answered all issues concerning taxation or anything else that might be done "without representation" by the colonies. It was carefully crafted to meet the issue of representation by reducing Britain's ability to control the colonies. It would repeal the Declaratory Act of 1766 that so upset many colonists.

At the same time it retained the basic structure of the empire. It permitted joint British-American parliamentary legislation concerning a wide range of matters. Under the plan the "joint" parliament could exercise legislative power asserted in the Declaratory Act over "all cases whatsoever." The joint parliament could adopt "positive law" as well as the British Parliament. The institution of slavery fell squarely within the jurisdictional grant proposed by Galloway because it fit the definition of:

> affairs of the colonies, in which Great Britain and the colonies, or any of them, the colonies in general, or more than one colony, are in any manner concerned, as well civil and criminal as commercial.

The Preamble to Galloway's plan stated that "within and under [the British-American] government each colony shall retain its *present* constitution and powers of regulating and governing its own internal police in all cases whatsoever." (emphasis added)[35] Galloway's plan accepted the British claim to Parliament's overriding power but expanded the Parliament to include representatives of the American colonies, thus meeting the demand for colonial representation.

While the issue of "taxation without representation" was fully addressed, the risks to slavery were not. The South could not assume that the colonial representatives to the Parliament would always vote to protect slavery. Antislavery views of the northern and middle states might prevail among the "American" delegation to the Parliament.[36] The South had little reason to trust Massachusetts, Rhode Island, or Pennsylvania more than the British Parliament, on the slavery question.[37]

Virginia delegates Richard Henry Lee and Patrick Henry raised this issue sharply in the debate on September 28 when Galloway's plan was introduced. Lee exercised the veto power that Virginia had built into the instructions to its delegates. He told Congress that Galloway's plan, "would make such changes in the legislatures of the colonies that I could not agree to it without consulting my constituents." His constituents had already spoken in the Virginia instructions to the delegates demanding for each colony the "sole right of directing their internal polity."[38]

John Jay of New York defended the plan, maintaining that it did not interfere with any liberty or right of the colonists:

It is objected that this plan will alter our constitutions and thereafter cannot be adopted without consulting constituents.

Does this plan give up any one liberty— or interfere with any one right?

But the argument that the plan did not "give up" any liberties or rights could not succeed against those who sought liberty from any superior parliament as the Virginians did.

Patrick Henry made this clear in his pithy rebuttal. Under the plan, he said:

We shall liberate our constituents from a corrupt House of Commons, but throw them into the arms of an American legislature that may be bribed by that nation which avows in the face of the world that bribery is a part of her system of government....*We are not to consent by the representatives of representatives.* (emphasis added)[39]

This last sentence made clear that Henry—and through him Virginia—would not admit of supervision of the colonies by any government, even one that included other American colonies.[40] The Galloway plan, on its surface, preserved the supremacy of an expanded parliament, including its jurisdiction over slavery.[41] The Virginia instructions prohibited any governmental body, British, American, or joint, from obtaining jurisdiction over the internal affairs of Virginia. Lee and Henry succeeded in burying the Galloway plan.[42]

As previously shown, the Galloway plan was a powerful counter to the Adams-Rutledge language of Article IV because it fully satisfied the "taxation without representation" issue. The colonists could well assume that their fellow colonies would be alert to ward off any British taxation scheme that offended them. But, as Patrick Henry suggested, the southern colonists would not assume that the same thing would be true when the British raised questions about slavery. The northern and middle colonies might conclude that their self-interest lay in limiting or eliminating slavery. The clearest evidence that the South insisted on independence in its internal affairs from any "superior" legislative body lies in the rejection of the Galloway plan.[43]

Six colonies voted to give further consideration to the Galloway plan at the end of the sharp debate on September 28, but no such direct consideration ever took place. Adams had dinner that day with a large company at Richard Penn's house, considered the single best house in the city. He spent the evening at home with Richard Henry Lee, Dr. Shippen, and George Washington.

This was the first known intimate contact between Adams and Washington.[44] The meeting took place following a debate in which Galloway's supporters suggested his opponents favored separation from Britain. It was crucial for the future relations between the Massachusetts and Virginia delegations. Washington, not yet committed to revolution, needed to believe that Adams and his delegation were not seeking separation from Britain. Adams gave Washington that assurance, and Washington believed him. The success of that meeting was reflected in Washington's correspondence with Lieutenant Robert

McKenzie, who had served under him since 1755 and was then stationed in Boston with General Gage's forces. McKenzie described Massachusetts as:

> this unhappy province,...their tyrannical oppression over one another,...their fixed aim at total independence, of the weakness and temper of the main springs that set the whole in motion, and how necessary it is that abler heads and better hearts should draw a line for their guidance: even when this is done 'tis much to be feared they will follow it no further than where it coincides with their present sentiments....
>
> The rebellious and numerous meetings of men in arms, their scandalous and ungenerous attacks upon the best characters in the province, obliging them to save their lives by flight, and their repeated but feeble threats to dispossess the troops, have furnished sufficient reasons to General Gage to put the town in a formidable state of defense, about which we are now fully employed.

Washington responded on October 9, from Philadelphia. He expressed "pleasure" receiving McKenzie's letter, and invited him to visit Mount Vernon. He then, "with the freedom of a friend," wrote:

> I view things in a very different point of light to the one in which you seem to

consider them, and though you are led to believe by venal men...that the people of Massachusetts are rebellious, setting up for independency, and what not,...you are abused—grossly abused; and this I advance with a degree of confidence...having better opportunities of knowing the real sentiments of the people you are among, from the leaders of them, in opposition to the present measures of administration, than you...I can announce it as a fact, that it is not the wish, or the interest of the government, or any other upon this continent, separately, or collectively, to set up for independence; but...none of them will ever submit to the loss of those valuable rights and privileges which are essential to the happiness of every free state, and without which life, liberty, and property are rendered totally insecure.[45]

Washington may have reached this judgment through his discussions with John Adams. Adams was clearly accepted by Washington as a patriot seeking redress within the empire, not as a revolutionary. Rush's advice on Adams's arrival that he should be discrete had proved to be correct.

From October 12 to 14, Congress debated the Declaration of Rights and Grievances, including Article IV, as drafted by Adams. As of October 13, Congress was evenly divided on the question of parliamentary power to regulate trade. Adams reported that five colonies were for allowing

Parliament's participation, five were against, and two divided among themselves, i.e. Massachusetts and Rhode Island.[46] But on October 14, Congress resolved the issue against the principles of the Galloway plan by adopting the declaration that denied any parliamentary power over the colonies.[47] This decision effectively killed Galloway's proposal. His plan was not further considered. He complained bitterly for years from England that it had not appeared in the public record because his opponents had not wanted it discussed.[48]

In retrospect, it is clear that the fundamental difference between Galloway and Adams lay in the fact that Galloway insisted on basing his analysis on British law, while Adams had moved to the principles of "natural law." The concept of natural law developed by John Locke in his *Second Treatise on Government* was premised on an assumed equality of all members of a society who then consented to form a government to protect their individual interests.[49] Locke presented a challenge to arguments for the divine right of kings. The Virginians, already suffering the sting of the *Somerset* decision under English law, were also prepared to abandon English law as the basis for separation from Britain. Once the colonists took the step that both Adams and Jefferson adopted—moving to a natural law principle to support the Revolution—it was easier to emphasize the principle of equality than it would have been under the British monarchial system.

Had the delicate balance in Philadelphia tipped the other way—had the Galloway plan or something like it been adopted—the Revolution might have been avoided. The magical images in Jefferson's Declaration might never

have been written, and authority in the people might not
have become the foundation of America.

# Chapter 7

# The Immortal Ambiguity: "All Men Are Created Equal"

T he year 1775 saw the beginnings of war as the British responded to the 1774 Continental Congress declaration of independence from Parliament. British forces sought out caches of colonial gunpowder in Lexington and Concord, nearly capturing John Adams and John Hancock, a wealthy merchant who had been active in Revolutionary affairs and who would be president of the Continental Congress. The British fired on local militia, but were forced to retreat to Boston. During the retreat, they were severely mauled by armed farmers.

At about the same time, the Virginia governor, Lord Dunmore, had his royal marines remove gunpowder from the powder magazine in Williamsburg to the schooner *Magdalen*. Militia men under the direction of Patrick Henry demanded that he return the gunpowder to an arsenal on land so that the colonists could get at it. Dunmore refused, but to avoid a march on Williamsburg, gave his note for £330 to cover the cost of the gunpowder.[1]

The Second Continental Congress meeting in Philadelphia in 1775 began to conduct war against the British in Boston. British governance of the colonies was in shambles. In the fall of 1775, Lord Dunmore, unable to cow the Virginians who had established their own militia, promised to free all slaves who would join him in his struggle to maintain control of the colony:

> I do require every person capable of bearing arms, to resort to His Majesty's standard, or be looked upon as traitors to His Majesty's crown and government, and thereby become liable to the penalty the law inflicts upon such offenses; such as forfeiture of life, confiscation of lands....And I do hereby further declare all indented servants, Negroes, or others (appertaining to rebels) free that are able and willing to bear arms, they joining His Majesty's troops as soon as may be, for the more speedily reducing this colony to a proper sense of their duty to His Majesty's crown and dignity.[2]

Historian John C. Miller wrote, "To Virginians this was nothing less than a call for race war."[3] Dunmore's approach was supported by Samuel Johnson in Britain, who wrote that it would be cheaper and easier to subdue the colonies by encouraging slave uprisings than to send a large military force.[4] Many slaves took up the offer of freedom and joined Dunmore's forces. Landon Carter, probably the richest slave holder in Virginia, was frustrated by

the rebellion of eight of his slaves, but bragged that in
their leaving, they had not touched anything belonging to
his person.[5] Dunmore's action confirmed colonial fears
that the British would use the colonies for their own purposes, even to the extent of prompting slaves to murder
their masters.

Virginia responded by offering amnesty to those slaves
who returned, and death to those who fought against it:

> Whereas, by an act of the general assembly
> now in force in this colony, it is enacted that
> all Negro or other slaves, conspiring to rebel
> or make insurrection, shall suffer death and
> be excluded all benefit of clergy. We think it
> proper to declare that all slaves who have
> been, or shall be seduced by his lordship's
> proclamation, or other arts, to desert their
> masters' service, and take up arms against
> the inhabitants of this colony, shall be liable
> to such punishment as shall hereafter be
> directed by the general convention. And to
> that end all such who have taken this unlaw-
> ful and wicked step may return in safety to
> their duty and escape the punishment due to
> their crimes, we hereby promise pardon to
> them, they surrendering themselves to Col.
> William Woodford, or any other commander
> of our troops, and not appearing in arms
> after the publication hereof. And we do far-
> ther earnestly recommend it to all humane
> and benevolent persons in this colony to

explain and make known this our offer of
mercy to those unfortunate people.[6]

In late 1775, the Continental Congress urged the
colonies to adopt their own constitutions to fill a vacuum
left by the absence of government.[7] Starting in the autumn
of 1774, Massachusetts became ungovernable; the courts
could not operate, juries would not serve, and the milita
was training. Other states began arming themselves and
ignoring the existing governments.[8] On May 15, 1776, a
Virginian convention, called to shape a new government
for the state, instructed its delegates to the Second Continental Congress in Philadelphia to propose that Congress
declare independence from Great Britain.[9]

On June 7, Richard Henry Lee made the motion. A vote
was delayed while the delegates from several colonies
sought permission to approve it. In the interim, a committee
of five members was formed to draft a declaration of independence. Members of the committee were John Adams,
Benjamin Franklin, Thomas Jefferson, Robert Livingston
of New York, and Roger Sherman of Connecticut. The
committee outlined the structure for the declaration, and
assigned the initial drafting to Jefferson. He worked in
haste and under serious time pressures while worrying
about the health of his wife Martha back at Monticello.[10]

Jefferson modestly said that he had not attempted any
original statement, but was only reflecting views current in
the society. He did not consider his draft to be of value in
the "originality of principles or sentiments, nor yet copied
from any particular and previous writing. It was intended
to be an expression of the American mind....All its

authority rests on the harmonizing sentiments of the day."[11] This modesty was without foundation, as we shall see.

Jefferson closely followed the events that transpired at the Virginia Convention while he was preparing his draft of the Declaration of Independence. He viewed himself as a Virginian, and always remained attuned to his political base among the slave owning planter-lawyers of the Virginia elite.[12] In this instance, he was wise to pay such close attention.

The Virginia Convention, after proposing that America declare independence, asked George Mason, a well-loved older planter, to draft a declaration of rights and principles of government for Virginia. Mason was forty-eight years old and had long taken an interest in patriot causes, but had not previously engaged openly in politics because he despised most aspects of it. Mason was not a lawyer, but had studied deeply the principles that lay at the base of colonial differences with Britain.[13] His draft was reviewed and approved by a small committee, probably because it was a pure statement of the natural law principles made popular by John Locke.[14] It was then circulated among the delegates in preparation for a discussion that began on May 29, 1776. It was made public and circulated so widely through the colonies that it became the model for several state constitutions.[15] But it was not popular with the Virginia Convention.

The first paragraph of Mason's declaration read:

All men are born equally free and independent and have certain inherent natural rights
of which they cannot, by any compact,

deprive or divest their posterity; among
which are the enjoyment of life and liberty,
with the means of acquiring and possessing
property, and pursuing and obtaining happiness and safety.[16]

This was a "pure" statement of the natural rights theory
developed by Locke and others, which the colonists
adopted late in their struggle with the British. Mason had
faithfully restated the principles of natural law that were
the foundation of colonial claims that Britain was attempting to enslave them.

The convention included members who had shouted
down Richard Bland in 1769 when he had proposed a modest extension of slave owners rights to manumit their slaves.
There were men who knew of the *Somerset* decision and that
Virginia had thereafter called for committees of correspondence that led to the First Continental Congress, where the
deal to protect slavery had been made with John Adams.

Some members of the Virginia Convention were aghast
that, in their view, George Mason was encouraging slaves
to rebel. The leading slaveholders at the Virginia Convention could not believe the language he had used. As the
debate began on May 29, "all were struck with the force of
the objection" made by Robert Carter Nicholas and others
that the first article was "inconsistent with the state of slavery then existing in Virginia" to proclaim the equality of
men in a "fundamental act," for doing so would "have the
effect of abolishing that institution."[17]

One of their own appeared to be a traitor to their class.
They filibustered against Mason's draft for at least two

days. The proposal clearly and unequivocally denied the basic principle of slavery, that children born of slave women "belonged" to their master. It also prohibited anyone from contracting into slavery "to deprive their posterity" of the named rights. Black slavery was hereditary through the mother. There was no ambiguity—no way around the plain meaning of these words. "They saw in the sweeping phraseology of the declaration that its adoption into the fundamental law would immediately emancipate the slaves."[18] And they would have none of it.

Richard Henry Lee was attending the Continental Congress in Philadelphia during the Virginia Convention. His brother, Thomas Ludwell Lee, wrote to him that:

> A certain set of aristocrats—for we have such monsters here—finding that their execrable system cannot be reared on such foundations, have to this time kept us at bay on the first line, which declares all men to be born equally free and independent. A number of absurd or unmeaning alteration have been proposed, yet by a thousand masterly fetches and stratagems the business has been so delayed that the first clause stands yet unassented to by the Convention.[19]

Did Mason think that the slave owners who ruled Virginia would consent to this statement? We do not know. Mason, like Jefferson, Richard Henry Lee, Patrick Henry, and other colonial leaders, had pointed out the evils of slavery, but when faced with the reality of its importance, became impotent to take action against it. Why then present such a stark challenge to the Convention?

The answer lies in the issue that Mason was addressing—the colonial claims against England, which had begun as the claims of Englishmen but had become converted to claims under natural law that the British were out to "enslave" them. In that context, the words were a clear justification for separation from a Britain that sought to consume the riches from the colonies while ignoring their liberties.

But the slave holders at the Convention had their eyes clearly fixed on protecting slavery no matter what general principles of the revolution were involved. The intensity of their conviction in protecting slavery is ignored by some historians who focus on the contributions of Mason's original draft to Jefferson's proposed national declaration of independence, without addressing the hostile reaction to that draft in the Virginia Convention.[20]

During the first week in June, the Virginia delegates sought "to vary the language, as to not involve the necessity of emancipating the slaves."[21] There were those, such as Robert Carter Nicholas, who would have deleted Mason's first principle altogether, as Thomas Ludwell Lee had suggested to his brother, Richard Henry. But wiser heads prevailed. The draft was already known to the public.[22] To adopt it without the first paragraph would tell the world that Virginia intended to protect slavery at all costs. But it could not be adopted without change because slave holders feared correctly that it could be used to abolish slavery or encourage slave revolt.

We do not know how Mason argued the matter, if he did. He may have responded, as some did later, that slaves were excluded from the statement because they had no right to contract and therefore no rights under the clause —or that they were property and similarly excluded— arguments that were vague at best in light of the specificity in the language Mason had drafted.

Judge Edward Pendleton came to the rescue of the Convention. He was the shrewd Virginia judge who had balanced his distaste for the Stamp Act against his duty as a justice by trying to keep his court open in 1765. He also joined in the call for committees of correspondence in 1773.

During the debate, in late May and early June, the word "born" was deleted in deference to the hereditary nature of slavery, but the Convention was still unsure how to make clear that the declaration did not apply to slaves. Pendleton finally proposed at least one amendment which achieved this objective. He suggested inserting the phrase, "when they enter a state of society," as a condition to the exercise of any of the rights that Mason had described. As a result, *all* men continued to be "equally free and independent"— the word "born" being already deleted. Their "natural rights" were no longer "natural" but were "inherent." But these rights did not arise by birth, but came into being only "when men enter a state of society."

This amendment answered the slave holders' complaints, "slaves being no part of the society to which the declaration applied and the masters having control over when those outside should enter."[23] Until they had "entered" such a state, they had none of the rights that Mason had outlined. And finally, the door on the expansion of these "inherent rights" was slammed by striking the phrase "among which are" and replacing it with the phrase "namely," making clear that no other rights could be considered inherent under the Virginia Declaration of Rights. Thus, Pendleton persuaded the slave owners that slavery would remain fully protected under the new constitution. With some other modifications —none of them touching the first paragraph—the Mason draft was adopted on June 12.[24]

Here is the Mason draft, with changes indicated. Deletions are italicized and in parenthesis, additions are in boldface.

> All men are *(born)* equally free and independent and have certain inherent *(natural)* rights, of which, **when they enter a state of society,** they cannot, by any compact, deprive or divest their posterity; *(among which are)* **namely** the enjoyment of life and liberty, with the means of acquiring and possessing property, and pursuing and obtaining happiness and safety.[25]

Modern scholars are satisfied that Jefferson had access to Mason's draft, somewhere between June 6 and 12. Historian Joseph Ellis explained:

> Throughout late May and early June couriers moved back and forth between Williamsburg carrying Jefferson's drafts for a new constitution to the Convention and reports on the debates there to the Continental

> Congress.... Since we know that Jefferson regarded the unfolding of events in Virginia as more significant than what was occurring in Philadelphia and that he was being kept abreast by courier, it also strains credibility to deny the influence of Mason's language on his own.[26]

Jefferson was appointed to a committee of five to draft the declaration on June 11. The committee met and outlined the contours of the declaration before Jefferson was singled out to prepare the draft.[27] His appointment to the committee in early June would have focused the busy Jefferson's mind on the events that were taking place at the Virginia Convention in Williamsburg. Since Virginia politics was his lifeblood, he would have paid close attention to the mutilation of Mason's first paragraph. He and Mason were engaged in the same enterprise at about the same time, and he had "volunteered" his ideas about the shape of Virginia's government to the Virginia Convention.

Jefferson's appointment by the subcommittee to draft the declaration probably took place on June 23, nine days after the Virginia convention had modified Mason's draft.[28] There were eleven days between June 12, when the final version was adopted by Virginians in Williamsburg, and June 23, when Jefferson was appointed to draft the national declaration of independence. When Washington, Henry, and Pendleton had ridden to Philadelphia for the first Continental Congress in 1774, the trip, with some delays, took five days.[29] There was more than enough time for news of the final adoption of the Virginia Declaration of Rights to reach Jefferson as he began work on the national declaration. Jefferson prepared his draft and had it reviewed by Franklin and Adams between the 23 and the 28 of June.

Probably the most important information Jefferson obtained before he prepared his declaration of independence was the reaction of the Virginia Convention to Mason's draft. The uproar by the slave owners and the ensuing modifications of Mason's declaration sent Jefferson a warning. If he followed the Mason draft he could expect that southerners in the Congress would react exactly as they had at the Virginia Convention. They would demand that it be changed to protect slavery in unequivocal language. The slave-holding colonies could explode and show the world how disunited the colonies were. Such a reaction might destroy the nation before it was born.

When Jefferson studied the draft as modified by the Virginia Convention, he realized that he could not use it either. Mason had written that "all men are born equally free and independent." This language—particularly the word "born"—had infuriated the Virginia Convention because it was a direct contradiction of slavery. There was no way to save the word "born" because it was so specific. But the words that remained, "all men are equally free and independent," as a statement of fact was absurd. Some were well born, others were not, even if slaves were not considered. It would not do to start the declaration with an assertion that no one would believe.

Furthermore, the modification to Mason's draft adopted by the Virginia Convention was seriously offensive to Jefferson. Pendleton's modification—"when they enter a state of society"—blew a huge hole in the "natural rights" theory on which the revolution from Britain now depended. Rights did not flow from nature, rather they arose after some white men made a judgment about when other men "entered a state of society." The phrase could not be explained as meaning that slaves were not in "society" at all because the purpose of the document was to establish principles for society that included slaves.

While John Locke relied on an analysis that began with hypothetical men in a state of nature, and from that, built a rationale for government to be based on the consent of the governed, the colonists turned the hypothetical state of nature into a present-day reality. The words "all men are created equal" or "born free," are not introductions to a cause in political theory. They are an assertation of a present day reality or human aspiration. To carve out an unlimited exception from this assertion is to undercut the primary rationale for the Declaration of Independence.[30]

Jefferson's assignment was to provide a consensus document, showing that America was united in its determination to be free. He had to be sure that his declaration did not meet the same fate as Mason's.

The exclusion of slaves from the domain of natural rights, as was done in the Virginia Declaration, would be obvious to both the northern colonies and to Britain. The British would certainly accuse the Americans of seeking freedom to enslave blacks. Furthermore, the right of "obtaining and possessing property" would confirm the accusation, because it was well known that, to southerners, slaves were property.

This concept that slaves were property was dramatically expressed in the very Congress that proclaimed independence. In late July, 1776, Congress debated whether it should vote by colony or by some other measure. This led to a discussion of how state contributions to the federal treasury should be determined. One proposal was that the colonies contribute according to the number of "inhabitants of every age, sex, and quality, except indians." Jefferson's notes go on:

> Mr. Chase [MD] moved that the quotas should be fixed, not by the number of inhabitants of every conditions, but by that of white inhabitants....He observed that Negroes are property, and as such cannot be distinguished from the lands or personalities held in those states where there are few slaves....There is no more reason therefore for taxing the southern states on the farmers head, and on his slaves head, than the northern ones on the farmers heads and the heads of their cattle.[31]

Rep. Thomas Lynch of South Carolina—one of the southern gentlemen with whom John Adams had associated at the First Continental Congress—added:

> *If it is debated whether their slaves are their property, there is an end to the confederation.* Our slaves being our property, why should they be taxed more than the

land, sheep, cattle, horses, etc.[32] (emphasis added)

The inclusion of "property" in the declaration would have enabled the slave owners to base their claims to own slaves on the declaration itself. They could maintain that the Revolution was fought to protect their property in slaves.[33] In fact, one petition *against* manumission of slaves in 1785 in Virginia did just that. It claimed that slavery was protected by the Virginia Declaration of Rights:

> When the British Parliament usurped a right to dispose of our property, it was not the matter but the manner adopted for that purpose that alarmed us, as it tended to establish a principle which might one day prove fatal to our rights of property. In order therefore to fix a tenure in our property on a basis of security not to be shaken in future, we dissolved our union with our parent country, and by a self-erected power bravely and wisely established a constitution and form of government, **grounded on a full and clear declaration of such rights as naturally pertain to men born free** and determined to be respectfully and absolutely so as human institutions can make them.[34] (emphasis added)

The slave owners' arguments for the maintenance of slavery would have been even more powerful if they had been rooted in an unalienable property right in a national declaration of independence. Jefferson knew that if he included the term "property," he would protect the institution of slavery as it then existed.

This was not his position. In 1769, he had encouraged Richard Bland to move an amendment to Virginia's law to permit the manumission of slaves. Jefferson seconded the motion. Jefferson recalled that Bland was "denounced as an enemy of his country and treated with the grossest indecorum."[35] In his "Summary View" in 1774, Jefferson presupposed that domestic slavery might be abolished in the future. Thus Jefferson was prevented by his own known position on slavery from copying the draft as adopted by the Virginia Convention. Jefferson knew he was drafting a document for public consideration abroad as well as at home. Had he included the term "property," those opposed to the Revolution in both Britain and America would have immediately accused the colonies of seeking their liberty in order to oppress slaves. This criticism was in fact made concerning the remnant of Jefferson's attack on the king for encouraging slave rebellion.

> It is their boast that they have taken up arms in support of these their own self-evident truths—that all men are created equal, that all men are endowed with the unalienable rights of life, liberty, and the pursuit of happiness. Is it for them to complain of the offer of freedom held out to those wretched beings; of the offer of reinstating them in

that equality which, in this very paper, is
declared to be the gift of God to all; in those
unalienable rights with which, in this very
paper, God is declared to have endowed all
mankind?[36]

Whatever one thinks of Jefferson's views or actions concerning slavery over his lifetime, in 1776 he opposed the
existing concept of slave property. In addition, he had proposed an end to existing property rights of primogeniture
(real property held at death descended to the oldest son) and
entail (real property held at death could not be divided),
both of which contributed to the maintenance of the great
slave plantations. He would not consciously write into a
declaration language that would be used against the very
reforms he had proposed.

The alterations made by Virginia to Mason's original
draft suggested to Jefferson that its primary difficulty lay
in its specificity. Jefferson solved this problem by using
language that was more general, and therefore more
ambiguous and less likely to appear objectionable.

For the word "born," which had caused the first out-
burst at the Virginia Convention, he substituted the word
"created" which did not specify the process of birth by a
woman. This enabled Jefferson to return to his beloved
natural law principles, and attributed the conclusion of
equality to god or nature—"all men are 'created' equal."
What happened to them after they were created is not discussed. Thus he reasserted the creator—god or nature—as
the source of the rights. Having elevated the source of the
rights to god or nature, he could insist that this source had

not necessarily exhausted itself in the creation of the specified rights. They were only "among these rights," leaving open the possibility of recognition of other rights in the future. This was a fateful change: it empowered the nation, as it grew, to create new rights, mainly by legislation, which became as fundamental as those recognized in the declaration. Since then, America has created many important rights by statute, as well as expanding constitutional rights as we did in 1865 and 1920.

Finally, Jefferson solved the problem attached to the word "property." He erased it, subsuming property in the generality of "pursuit of happiness."[37] By using the more abstract term "pursuit of happiness," he did not embed slavery in the document expressing our national *raison d'être*. Balancing his views on human worth against the slave owners' interests, he declined to enshrine slave property in the Declaration. The result was the language that still resonates around the world.

> We hold these truths to be self-evident, that all men are created equal, that they are endowed by their Creator with certain unalienable Rights, that among these are Life, Liberty and the Pursuit of Happiness—That to secure these rights, Governments are instituted among Men, deriving their just powers from the consent of the governed—That whenever any Form of Government becomes destructive of these ends, it is the Right of the People to alter or to abolish it, and to institute new Government, laying its foundation on such

principles, and organizing its powers in such form, as to them shall seem most likely to effect their Safety and Happiness.

The statement that emerged was of such profound quality that it has captured the hearts and minds of men and women ever since. Historian Pauline Maier believes that it was Jefferson, the literary genius, who produced these words. Referring to his use of the phrase "pursuit of happiness," she writes that Jefferson "meant to say more economically and movingly what Mason said with some awkwardness and at considerably greater length."[38] But it was Jefferson the lawyer—who knew how to make use of ambiguity when it would better serve his objective—who was equally its author. Underpinning his literary and lawyer skills was the ability to synthesize all that he had studied of past political theory. That profound learning has, over the centuries since, generated brilliant discussions of the concepts embedded in those words.[39]

The Congress did not approve of all of Jefferson's language. It made numerous changes in the later parts of the document. But only one minor change was made in the crucial second paragraph, which is remembered long after the specific grievances outlined against King George have been buried in the dust of history.[40] It is ironic that but for the desire of Virginians to retain and perpetuate slavery, the clarion call to liberty that is the Declaration might never have been heard.

Jefferson's direct criticism of slavery in his draft of the declaration did not fare as well. He composed a complicated provision blaming the king for enslaving blacks and then inciting them to revolt and murder their masters by offering them freedom.[41]

> He has waged cruel war against human nature itself, violating its most sacred rights of life and liberty in the persons of a distant people who never offended him, captivating and carrying them into slavery in another hemisphere, or to incur miserable death in their transportation thither. This piratical warfare, the opprobrium of infidel *powers, is the warfare of the Christian king of Great Britain. Determined to keep open a market where men should be bought and sold, he has prostituted his negative for suppressing every legislative attempt to prohibit or to restrain this execrable commerce; and that this assemblage of horrors might want no fact of distinguished die, he is now exciting those very people to rise in arms among us, and to purchase that liberty of which he has deprived them, and murdering the people upon whom he also obtruded them; thus paying off former crimes committed against the* **liberties** *of one people, with crimes which he urges them to commit against the* **lives** *of another.*

The Congress rejected that provision, which contained an internal contradiction. King George was condemned for forcing Africans into slavery and bringing them to the colonies. But this same criticism inferentially condemns the colonists for maintaining slavery.[42] This is a strange point to make in support of a struggle for equality. Why then include it?

The first part of Jefferson's attack was on the slave trade itself. That was in the Virginia tradition. Virginia had publicly opposed the foreign slave trade since 1772, partly for fear of an overly large population of slaves who might be difficult to control, and partly because Virginia, with a surplus of slaves, was prepared to sell them to others.

The second part of his criticism capitalized on the fear of black uprisings, made imminent by Lord Dunmore's call in 1775 for slaves to join in upholding the empire. The Virginians believed that Dunmore's action would encourage slave revolts that would inevitably lead to rape, pillage, and murder. Jefferson's clause emphasized this threat to the lives of the white colonists. He may have believed that the fear of black revolts would lead the slave interests to permit the antislavery comment and ignore the implicit condemnation of their activities. If so, he was disappointed.

Jefferson explained the deletion of the clause, while emphasizing its antislavery character and ignoring its criticism of the encouragement of slave revolts:

> The clause...reprobating the enslaving the inhabitants of Africa, was struck out in complaisance to South Carolina and Georgia, who had never attempted to restrain the importation of slaves, and who on the contrary still wished to continue it. Our

northern brethren also I believe felt a little tender under those censures; for tho' their people have very few slaves themselves, yet they have been pretty considerable carriers of them to others.[43]

The clause did criticize the king for enslaving Africans, but it also criticized him for offering to free them if they turned against the colonists. To characterize the clause as one "reprobating slavery" is to tell but half the story.[44]

Jefferson's list of colonial grievances that make up the body of the Declaration is haunted by the *Somerset* decision in which Lord Mansfield stated that Parliament had the final authority over slavery in the colonies. The king is accused of conspiring with Parliament to enact "pretended legislation" and "declaring themselves invested with power to legislate for us in all cases whatsoever." This is a clear reference to the Declaratory Act, and its threat, after *Somerset*, to the institution of slavery.

The penultimate paragraph repeats this grievance, this time against "our British brethren." "We have warned them from time to time of attempts by their legislature to extend an unwarrantable jurisdiction over us."

The "unwarrantable jurisdiction" included the *Somerset* case, the Declaratory Act of 1766, and the repugnancy clause in the colonial charters—all of which converged to create a hazard to the institution of slavery.

The agreement to preserve slavery in the colonies, negotiated at the First Continental Congress in 1774 with John Adams, was kept in the Declaration of Independence. Judge A. Leon Higginbotham, reviewing the history of slavery in Virginia and several other states, concluded: "From the perspective of the black masses, the Revolution merely assured the plantation owners of their right to continue the legal tyranny of slavery."[45]

The white delegates who voted for the Declaration of Independence would have agreed with these "black masses." The same Congress that voted for the Declaration of Independence in 1776 promptly made clear that slaves were the property of their masters and that the principle of the *Somerset* decision had no place in the government established by the Articles of Confederation.

# Chapter 1. Leading Figures in the *Somerset* Case

RUN away on the 16th inſtant *(June)* from the ſubſcriber in *Auguſta*, a negro man named B A C C H U S, a thick, ſtrong, well made fellow, about 5 feet 6 or 7 inches high, 30 years of age; took with him two white ruſſia drill coats, one turned up with blue, the other is quite new. plain made, with white figured metal bottons; alſo a pair of blue pluſh breeches, a fine cloth pompadour waiſtcoat, two or three thin or ſummer jackets, ſundry pair of white thread ſtockings, 5 or 6 white ſhirts, two of them pretty fine, neat ſhoes, ſilver buckles, a fine hat, cut and cocked in the macaroni figure, a double milled drab great coat, and ſundry other wearing apparel. He formerly belonged to Doctor *George Pitt,* in *Williamſburg,* and I imagine is gone there, under pretence of my ſending him upon buſineſs, as I have frequently heretofore done. He is cunning, artful, and ſenſible, and very capable of forging a tale to impoſe on the unwary, is well acquainted with the lower parts of the country, having conſtantly rode with me for ſome years paſt, and has been uſed to waiting from his infancy. He was ſeen a few days before he went off with a purſe of dollars, and had juſt changed a 5l. bill; moſt or all of which, I ſuppoſe, he muſt have robbed me of, which he might eaſily have done, as I truſted him much, and placed too great a confidence in his fidelity. It is probable he may endeavour to paſs as a free man, by the name of *John Chriſtian,* and endeavour to get on board ſome veſſel bound for *Great Britain,* from a knowledge he has of the late determination of *Somerſet*'s caſe. Whoever takes up the ſaid ſlave, and delivers him to me, ſhall receive FIVE POUNDS.

GABRIEL JONES.

While slave owners may not have wanted their slaves to hear about the *Somerset* decision, it was impossible for them to keep it secret. Slaves learning of it may have sought to take ships to freedom in England, or their masters might have thought that this is what they would do. In either case, the masters blamed Britain for encouraging slaves to escape as a result of the *Somerset* decision. Slave owner Gabriel Jones thought that Bacchus, who ran away, had been motivated by the *Somerset* decision, as the bottom of his ad makes clear.

William Murray, Lord Mansfield, Chief Judge of the Court of King's Bench. A reluctant emancipator who, in the *Somerset* case of 1772, decided that slavery was "so odious" that it could not exist, except by the positive law of Parliament and there was no such law. Therefore, the owner of a slave who had freed himself and was later recaptured could not ship the slave from England to the Caribbean to be sold. Lord Mansfield freed the slave, James Somerset. By freeing a slave, he threatened the economic and social foundation of the southern colonies.

Granville Sharp, practically a one-man antislavery society in London, who challenged slavery in his writings and in Mansfield's court by developing his theory that slavery was contrary to the common law of England.

# Chapter 2. The Tinderbox

Courtesy of the National Archives (69-N-4877)

The Boston Massacre in 1770 involved a crowd who John Adams later called "saucy boys, Negroes and mulattos, Irish teagues, and outlandish jack-tars," that surrounded some British troops who opened fire. They killed five in the crowd, including Crispus Attucks. Adams successfully defended the troops and their captain. The event did not disturb the calm that had descended in the colonies after the British repealed the Townshend taxes.

# Chapters 3 and 4. Leading Figures in Virginia's 1773 Call to the Colonies to Create Committees of Correspondence

Edmund Pendleton was a conservative judge who nevertheless joined the Virginia committee of correspondence knowing that Britain would condemn his action. Later he proposed to modify the Virginia Declaration of Rights by limiting it to persons who had "entered a state of society," thus excluding slaves.

Courtesy Library of Congress

Patrick Henry was a spellbinding orator, and an early advocate of preparing for a war of independence against Britain.

Courtesy U.S. Senate

Richard Henry Lee, a leading member of the Lee family of Virginia, who would make the motion for independence at the Continental Congress, and eventually become president of the Continental Congress. He contributed to resolving the deadlock in the Constitutional Convention of 1787 by supporting the antislavery provision of the Northwest Ordinance.

Courtesy Library of Congress

The *Gaspee,* a British anti-smuggling ship whose captain had antagonized the people of Rhode Island, was burned to the waterline in 1772 by the colonists. In retaliation, Britain threatened to transport the culprits to England for trial. But this threat was blunted by a commission of judges, and no one was ever convicted of any crime. Nevertheless, this was one of the specific events that was singled out in Virginia's call to the colonies to create committees of correspondence.

Courtesy Library of Congress

# Chapters 5 and 6. Events and Leading Figures at the First Continental Congress in 1774 that Declared Independence from Parliament

Courtesy National Archives (148-GW-439)

The Boston Tea Party, in December 1773, involved Bostonians, thinly disguised as Mohawks, dumping huge amounts of tea into the harbor in protest over a British plan to create a tea monopoly for the East India Company. The British reacted by closing the port of Boston, imposing a military governor, and reducing colonial rights of self-government. This harsh reaction led to the First Continental Congress in Philadelphia in the fall of 1774.

John Adams was a leading spokesman for an already-occupied Massachusetts, who agreed with the "southern gentlemen," at the Congress and later, to protect slavery in the new nation.

John Rutledge, a leading slave owner from South Carolina, who urged John Adams to draft the language declaring independence from Parliament.

Samuel Adams, John's cousin, masterminded the Boston Tea Party and maneuvered at the First Continental Congress to derail a plan by Joseph Galloway that would have rejected independence and established a British-American Parliament.

George Washington was one of the few colonists with leadership experience in the military. He sought to assure himself that the northerners wished to remain connected to the British Empire, if the Empire would recognize colonial rights.

Courtesy U.S. Senate

Dr. Benjamin Rush, the second-best-known professional man in Philadelphia, rode out to meet the Adams cousins before they entered the city in order to warn them not to appear to support a revolution because influential members of Congress would be in serious opposition. John Adams followed this advice, allowing the "southern gentlemen" to appear to be radicals, while reassuring Washington that the northerners were not.

Courtesy National Archives (148-CP-200)

# Chapter 7. The Preparation of the Declaration of Independence, 1776

Thomas Jefferson, chosen to draft the Declaration of Independence because of his prior writings, knew he had to avoid the mistake that George Mason had made in Virginia by writing that all men were "born free." Instead, Jefferson wrote "all men are created equal."

Courtesy Library of Congress

Jefferson, Adams, Franklin, Robert Livingston, and Roger Sherman: the committee appointed to develop the Declaration of Independence reviewed Jefferson's draft.

Courtesy Library of Congress

Excerpt from the draft Declaration of Independence, beginning with the second paragraph, "We hold these truths..."

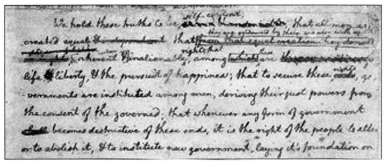

Courtesy Library of Congress

# Chapter 8. Writing the Articles of Confederation, 1776–77

John Dickinson, author of the famous "Letters from a Farmer in Pennsylvania," was asked to prepare a draft for Articles of Confederation of the colonies. His draft proposed a powerful central government, with states required to follow federal policies. His proposal ran into stiff opposition and was rejected in favor of a much more limited federal authority.

Courtesy Dickinson College

Thomas Burke opposed Dickinson's proposed strong central government. Burke prevailed; the Articles created a weak government with no taxing power and no chief executive.

Courtesy Library of Congress

Henry Laurens, a leading South Carolina slave holder, stated in 1776 that "I abhor slavery." He was president of the Continental Congress in 1777, which ensured that slaves could not gain their freedom by being taken into a "free" state, as had Somerset. As a commissioner at the Paris Peace Treaty ending the Revolutionary War, Laurens insisted that Britain return the slaves who had joined the British forces.

Courtesy Library of Congress

# Chapter 9. Development of the Land Ordinances of 1784, 1785

James Monroe surveyed the northwest territory in 1786 and, thinking it unsuitable for farming, urged the reduction of the ten states proposed by Jefferson to no more than five. His recommendation was accepted in the Northwest Ordinance and agreed to by Virginia.

Courtesy Library of Congress

Courtesy Library of Congress

Jefferson had proposed a prospective antislavery clause in 1784 that was not adopted. Rufus King prepared a similar bill in 1785, but did not put his proposal before Congress because he knew it would fail.

# Chapter 10. Leading Figures in the Beginning of the Constitutional Convention of 1787 and in the Deadlock that Occurred in July

James Madison masterminded Virginia's approach at the Constitutional Convention. Virginia sought a strong central government with one house elected by the people and votes distributed among the states so slaves would count as three-fifths of a person in determining representation in Congress.

Courtesy Library of Congress

Oliver Ellsworth of Connecticut threatened that the North would leave the Union over Virginia's proposal to count slaves as three-fifths of a person for representation purposes.

Courtesy Library of Congress

Abraham Baldwin of Georgia, a transplanted Connecticut Yankee, split the Convention equally so that a committee was appointed to avoid the breakup of the Union.

Courtesy Library of Congress

Benjamin Franklin may have saved the Union by conceiving the idea of dividing the territory of the United States along the Ohio River, and prohibiting slavery north of that line.

Courtesy Library of Congress

# Chapter 11. Nathan Dane, Draftsman of the Prohibition on Slavery in the Northwest Ordinance of 1787

Courtesy Library of Congress

Nathan Dane of Massachusetts placed the prohibition against slavery in the northwest territory at the end of his draft, because he thought it would not pass. When the rest of his draft was accepted, he heard favorable comments from delegates who represented four slave states and four free states. These circumstances suggest that the prohibition on slavery had been arranged at the Convention in Philadelphia and implemented at the Congress in New York without consulting Dane in advance.

# Chapter 13. The Aftermath of the Constitution and Northwest Ordinance

Courtesy Library of Congress

Edward Coles, well-born slave owner from Virginia, Madison's secretary, and friend of Jefferson, urged Jefferson (after he had served as president) to make public his opposition to slavery. Jefferson refused. Coles took his slaves to Illinois and liberated them, providing them with support while they became farmers and agriculture workers. In 1822, Coles was elected governor of Illinois. He defeated an effort to repeal the antislavery clause in the Illinois Constitution by a vote of 6,822 to 4,950.

Abraham Lincoln, the Civil War president from Illinois (formerly part of the northwest territory), who emancipated the slaves in Confederate territory, leading to the Thirteenth Amendment ending slavery.

Courtesy U.S. Senate

Courtesy Library of Congress

Ulysses S. Grant was the general Lincoln sought to bring an end to the Civil War. Grant was born in Ohio, the first state to be carved out of the northwest territory. His victory at Vicksburg, along with the victory at Gettysburg, assured that the North would ultimately prevail.

General John Buford saved Cemetery Ridge for the Union Army the first day at Gettysburg, with troops from the former northwest territory.

Courtesy Library of Congress

Courtesy Library of Congress

George Armstrong Custer frustrated a Confederate cavalry charge on the third day at Gettysburg, with cavalry from the former northwest territory.

Benjamin Franklin, in 1789, became the great-great-godfather of affirmative action by proposing programs to assist newly freed slaves in becoming full participants in the economy of Philadelphia in connection with housing, employment, and business opportunities.

Courtesy Library of Congress

President Lyndon B. Johnson signing the Civil Rights Act of 1964, a law encouraged by Republicans William McCullough of Ohio and Everett Dirksen of Illinois,
both from the former northwest territory. In his Howard University speech a year
later, Johnson echoed Benjamin Franklin's concern that it was important to provide assistance and support to those who had recently gained their full freedom.

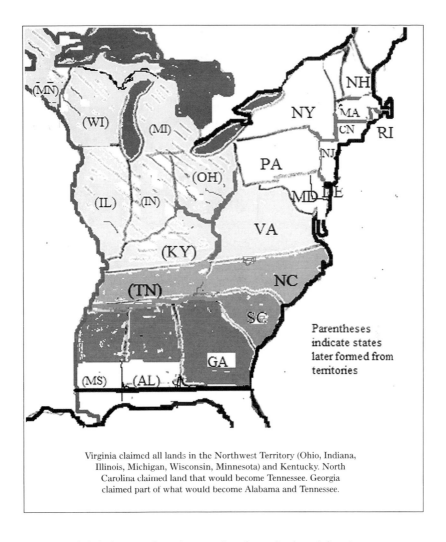

Virginia claimed all lands in the Northwest Territory (Ohio, Indiana, Illinois, Michigan, Wisconsin, Minnesota) and Kentucky. North Carolina claimed land that would become Tennessee. Georgia claimed part of what would become Alabama and Tennessee.

The British left the new American nation the task of straightening out a complicated set of overlapping land claims, and a fear by those without land claims that they would be overpowered by states with such claims. They insisted that these claims be ceded to the federal government before they would sign the Articles of Confederation. Cession was completed sufficiently and the Articles went into effect in 1781. The land claims were formalized after Britain ceded its claims in the Treaty of Paris, finalized in 1784. The Northwest Ordinance of 1787 created a slave-free area, shown with slanted lines, north of the Ohio River. Slavery continued to be lawful south of that river, as new states were created.

**State Claims to Western Lands, 1791**

Thirteen states (shaded dark) were created from the former colonies in 1776. Their western borders were settled as they ceded western lands at the demand of the "landless" states. This map shows their conflicting claims in detail. The territory that was declared slave-free in the Northwest Ordinance of 1787 is in the upper left (lighter portion) of the map. The southern border of the northwest territory follows the Ohio River from the Mississippi to Pennsylvania. The claims of Virginia north of the Ohio became the slave-free states of Ohio, Indiana, Illinois, Michigan, Wisconsin, and part of Minnesota The claims of the southern states, that bordered the Atlantic, including Virginia, became the states of Kentucky, Tennessee, Mississippi, and Alabama.

# Chapter 8

---

# The Articles of Confederation Reject *Somerset* and Protect Slavery

---

R ichard Henry Lee's motion for independence on
June 7, 1776, required the Congress to establish a
national government to replace British rule.[1] Congress promptly asked John Dickinson of Pennsylvania to
prepare a draft of Articles of Confederation among the former colonies that now called themselves states. Dickinson
was a slave-holding lawyer and the richest man in
Philadelphia. He was already famous as the author of "Letters from a Farmer in Pennsylvania," which in 1767 and
1768 challenged the authority of Parliament to levy any
taxes on the colonies.[2] Dickinson, while still unsure of the
wisdom of separation from Britain, prepared his draft
promptly. The Congress began to debate this draft on July
12, 1776, only a week after the Declaration was adopted.

Dickinson proposed a central government with general
powers in the legislature while it was in session, and in a
"Council of State" when it was recessed.[3] With respect to

the relation between the central government and the colonies, his draft stated:

> Article XVIII. The United States assembled shall have authority for the defense and welfare of the united colonies and every of them.[4]
>
> Article III. Each colony shall retain and enjoy as much of its present laws, rights, and customs as it may think fit, and reserves to itself the sole and exclusive regulation and government of its internal police, **in all matters that shall not interfere with the articles of this confederation.**[5] (emphasis added)

> Article XVIII. The United States assembled shall have the sole and exclusive right and power of appointing a council of state and such committees and civil officers as may be necessary for managing the general affairs of the United States, under their direction while assembled, and in their recess, of the council of state.[6]

These provisions relating to the authority of Congress over the states sounded similar to the Galloway plan that had been buried by the First Congress in 1774.[7] The national government had authority for defense and welfare of each colony. State control of internal affairs was subject to the power of the central government to manage these "general affairs"—just as the British Declaratory Act of

1766 gave Parliament control of the colonies in "all cases whatsoever." [8] The Galloway plan had centralized control of such matters in the American-British Parliament.[9] As in both of these earlier situations, these "general affairs" included slavery.

This possibility appalled John Rutledge of South Carolina when he saw the Dickinson draft in late June. He wrote to John Jay of New York on June 29, 1776, asking him to come to Philadelphia to review Dickinson's plan:

> If the plan now proposed should be adopted nothing less than ruin to some colonies will be the consequence of it. The idea of destroying all provincial distinctions and making every thing of the most minute kind bend to what they call the good of the whole, is in other terms to say these colonies must be subject to the government of the eastern provinces....I dread their low cunning, and those levelling principles which men without character and without fortune in general possess, which are so captivating to the lower class of mankind, and which will occasion such a fluctuating of property as to introduce the greater disorder. I am resolved to vest the Congress with no more power than what is absolutely necessary, and to use a familiar expression to keep the staff in our own hands, for I am confident if surrendered into the hands of others a most pernicious use will be made of it.[10]

This candid comment captures the concerns that the new government, influenced by northerners, would destabilize the political and economic order. Rutledge feared that the poorer but more numerous would take or tax the property (slaves) of the rich.

The southern leaders of the time saw risks to slavery at every turn; from Richard Bland's proposal for manumission in 1769, the *Somerset* decision in 1772, and their need for John Adams's support for slavery in 1774, to their mutilation of George Mason's declaration of rights in Virginia in 1776 and South Carolina's Thomas Lynch's threat to walk out of the Congress in July of 1776 if slaves were not recognized as "property."

Thomas Burke of North Carolina shared Rutledge's perception that the Dickinson draft would permit the general government virtually as much power as the British government had claimed over the colonies before the Revolution:[11]

> I thought [Article III] left it in the power of the future Congress or general council to explain away every right belonging to the states, and to make their own power as unlimited as they please. I proposed, therefore, an amendment, which held up the principle that all sovereign power was in the states separately, and that particular acts of it, which should be expressly enumerated, would be exercised in conjunction and not otherwise; but that in all things else each state would exercise all the rights and powers of sovereignty, uncontrolled.[12]

Burke and Rutledge won their battle. The Articles of Confederation were adopted in November 1777, while Henry Laurens, a South Carolina planter and former slave trader, was president of the Congress.[13] They provided:

> Each state retains its sovereignty, freedom, and independence, and every power, jurisdiction, and right which is not by this confederation expressly delegated to the United States, in Congress assembled.[14]

The shift is stark, from a draft which granted general powers to the federal government to a states' rights provision which limited the powers of government so that there would not be "fluctuating of property"—feared by Rutledge and Burke because it jeopardized slavery.[15] Slavery within a colony could not be regulated by the Congress under the Articles.[16] Thus the South preserved that freedom from external regulation of slavery that it had sought in moving toward independence from Britain.

This freedom was made more secure by other provisions in the Articles which required unanimity in order to amend an article, nine states to agree on many important matters, and a majority of seven states to act on other matters.[17]

There was, as yet, no concept of American national citizenship. If there was to be a union of states, each state would have to be obligated to respect the rights of people from other states to reside, work, and engage in commercial activities. In July, 1774, Rhode Island adopted a statute that had an anti-slavery tone. Its preamble stated, "Those who are desirous of enjoying all the advantages of liberty should be willing to extend personal liberty to others."[18] This high sounding phrase was followed by major restrictive qualifications.[19]

Dickinson devoted two articles in his draft to the privileges of "inhabitants" of one colony while in another.[20] Article VI prevented a state from reducing the existing rights of inhabitants of another state. Article VII assured that the inhabitants of one state would have the same rights in another state with respect to commercial activities and movement as that state's own citizens. Dickinson's draft did not address the issue of a slave entering a state that prohibited slavery.[21] This issue was only faced in November, 1777.

Between the time of the Declaration of Independence and the autumn of 1777, Congress was preoccupied with conducting the war and avoiding capture as the British occupied New York and New Jersey and overran Philadelphia. When Congress moved to York, Pennsylvania, in late September, 1777, it made a sustained effort to finish work on the Articles.[22]

On November 1, Henry Laurens of South Carolina became president of the Congress. Laurens was a planter and former slave trader, which was said to have made him the richest man in the colony. He had been in London at the time Lord Mansfield decided the *Somerset* case and had written to a friend and associate that the lawyer for Somerset's owner had been a failure, but—as a cautious man—would put nothing further in writing.[23] He had abandoned the slave trade in the early 1760s for reasons that appeared more practical than moral, enabling him to concentrate on planting and his childrens' education. But he continued to advise and provide financial assistance to younger men going into the trade as late as 1774.[24]

Henry Laurens had spent 1770–1773 in Europe supervising his son's education. His son John was intensely antislavery, and futilely sought to raise black regiments during the latter part of the war. John was killed in one of the last skirmishes of the war, on August 27, 1782, nearly a year after the British defeat at Yorktown.[25]

When Henry Laurens returned to South Carolina in 1773, he was elected to the first Continental Congress, where he attracted favorable attention from John Adams. In August, 1776, a month after the Declaration of Independence, he wrote, "I abhor slavery." He also said that he planned to free a large number of his own slaves.[26] His awareness of the *Somerset* decision, discussed in Chapter Two, established a link between that decision and the actions of the Congress after he became president on November 1, 1777.[27]

The work on the Articles of Confederation was thought to be completed by Friday, November 7. Nevertheless, on Monday, November 10, a group of additional propositions were referred to a committee consisting of Richard Henry Lee of Virginia, Richard Law of Connecticut, and James Duane of New York.[28] One of the new propositions addressed the rights of slave owners to take their slaves into other states. This amendment made clear that the privileges and immunities of a person in state A who was a resident of state B applied only to the "citizens," not the "inhabitants" of state B. The amendment allowed the people in each state free movement to and from other states for their "persons and property."[29] This change should have been enough to calm fears that the *Somerset* decision might apply under the Articles, because slaves were not "citizens"—but it did not, possibly because slaves could still have been considered "people." Two days later the proposal was sharpened to make clear that *only* "free inhabitants" and "free citizens" were entitled to this freedom of movement between the states.[30]

This change should have settled the question of whether slaves had freedom of movement but, again, it did not. What was to happen if a state chose to adopt the rule of the *Somerset* case, that a slave brought into its jurisdiction became free? That possibility lurked only because many southerners, including President Laurens, knew about the ruling in *Somerset*. They could readily imagine that a northern state opposed to slavery, such as Rhode Island, might apply the common law as announced in *Somerset*, and free the slaves that entered its jurisdiction.[31]

This risk was addressed directly. On November 14, the clause was amended again to state explicitly that the free people of each state shall have free access to and from any other state, and enjoy :

> The privileges of trade and commerce, subject to the same duties, impositions, and restrictions as the inhabitants thereof respectively, **provided that such restrictions shall not extend so far as to prevent the removal of property imported into any state to any other state of which the owner is an inhabitant.**[32] (emphasis added)

Reading this clause with an understanding that slaves were property, it is a direct repudiation of the decision in

Somerset's case. Legal historian Charles Warren observed, "though phrased in general terms [this section] was intended to apply to slave property."[33] Under this clause, a slave could not become free by entering or escaping into a "free" state, regardless of the laws of that state.[34]

The slave owners' rights regarding his slave property were guaranteed in all states where he had taken his slaves, even if the law of that state would have set them free. Legal historian William Wiecek states that "the clause might have been construed to restrain the states from interfering with a sojourning or in-transit master's rights in his slave."[35]

This "restraint" is inconsistent with the principle of state autonomy that had been so important to Rutledge and Burke, when they were insisting that each state have full control over its internal policies. States' rights were recognized to protect slavery from outside interference and slave owners' rights were recognized to protect slavery in states that sought to reject it.[36] Every state was required to recognize "property in slaves" created by the laws of the other states.[37] Thus the articles prevented northern whites from excluding slavery from their states. In this sense, the clause was the precursor of the fugitive slave clause in the United States Constitution, the Northwest Ordinance, and in subsequent federal laws.[38] The issue of states' rights to deny slavery would become a cause celebre in nineteenth-century events leading to the Civil War when supporters of slavery sought to impose their will on whites, both North and South, who opposed slavery.[39] Laurens's apparent antipathy toward slavery in 1776 did not prevent him from presiding over its protection in 1777.

The agreement to protect slavery that was reached at the First Congress in 1774 and maintained in the Declaration of Independence in 1776, was kept in the Articles of Confederation in 1777. Slaves remained property, regardless of the law of the state where a slave might be found. Five years after Lord Mansfield had declared slavery so odious that it could be justified only by positive law, and one year after the colonies seceded from Britain under a banner reading "all men are created equal," the Continental Congress adopted positive law that made sure that the rule in the *Somerset* case did not apply in the colonies.

The Articles were sent to the states for the unanimous ratification required for adoption. Ratification was delayed for four years as a result of conflicts concerning the lands west of the colonies, between Virginia and New York, who had major claims, and the "landless states," including Maryland, that had none. These states feared that the states with land claims would become more important and influential over time. Maryland would not ratify the Articles until both New York and Virginia agreed to surrender their claims to the Continental Congress.[40]

With the war going badly, particularly in the South where the British made a major invasion in 1778, these states agreed to cede their land claims to Congress, creating a territory that was not part of any state. When Virginia ceded a huge land area that included all the territory north of the Ohio River, the agreement provided that "certain settlers...who have professed themselves citizens of Virginia, shall have their possessions and titles confirmed to them, and be protected in the enjoyment of their rights and liberties."[41] Presumably this included protecting their property in slaves, even though they would no longer be Virginians.

Maryland was the last state to ratify the Articles of Confederation. They became effective on March 1, 1781. Slavery was then safe from Somerset's ghost as long as the Articles of Confederation were the basis for the union of the states. The surrender of British troops at Yorktown occurred on October 19, 1781. It was a victory for the Revolutionary Army that effectively ended the war. With the Treaty of Paris in 1783, the United States acquired a huge territory, all of which was subject to the government under the Articles of Confederation.

# Chapter 9

# The Lure of the West: Slavery Protected in the Territories

I n the early 1780s, two streams of events merged to create a huge national territory on the American mainland that was not a part of any state. The original thirteen states had three hundred twenty-five thousand square miles. By 1790, the territory had increased to 864,746 square miles as a result of the Treaty of Paris which ended the Revolution. The American-French victory over the British at Yorktown on October 19, 1781, assured that the Revolution would succeed. The Treaty of Paris in 1783, negotiated by John Adams, Benjamin Franklin, and John Jay confirmed that the United States would "own" 539,746 square miles to the west of the colonies as far as the Mississippi River, except for parts of Florida, southern Louisiana, and Canada.[1]

By 1781, the states with western land claims had agreed to cede them to the Continental Congress in order to secure adoption of the Articles of Confederation. The major cession agreements came from Virginia and New York. The Virginia cession agreement conveyed to the Continental

Congress "all right, title, and claim, as well of soil as jurisdiction, which this Commonwealth hath to the territory."[2]

Thus a huge national territory was created, more than double the size of the thirteen colonies combined. The lure of the West was felt by northerners and southerners alike. They saw great opportunities this territory created for expansion of agriculture, for settling the nation's war debts to both citizen soldiers and foreign countries, and for land speculation that could generate great riches. From the beginning, northerners and southerners had different perspectives on one crucial matter in the new territory—slavery.[3]

Southerners producing tobacco needed new land because tobacco ruined the soil after a few years. Northerners, especially former military personnel, wanted new space in the Ohio country—space that was free of slavery. Most of the work of settling new lands was hard labor, and the presence of slavery would have reduced the value of white labor by half.

Land speculators from the 1760s on had seen the great fortunes to be made by selling shares in the expanded west, once British restraints on settlement were removed. Political figures both North and South believed that the West, when settled, would weigh heavily in the political future of the nation.

The Treaty of Paris was ratified by the Congress under the Articles of Confederation, with the requisite nine states present.[4] The Articles of Confederation gave the Congress "the sole and exclusive right and power of...entering into treaties and alliances...[if]...the delegates of nine colonies freely assent to the same."[5] But it did not expressly state that Congress had any power to govern territories that were outside of any state. The Articles had been written while the nation's survival was hanging by a thread. Congress was fleeing for its life from the British forces, not thinking about the vast expansion of their then unstable union.

Once the Treaty of Paris had been ratified by Congress and by Britain in 1784, the cession agreements enabled the United States to take control of the ceded territory. This power was asserted in early 1784, a month after Virginia ceded her claims to Congress. Much of the territory, both north and south of the Ohio River, had been claimed by Virginia and other southern states where slavery was established and protected by law. The law of Virginia included its Declaration of Rights in 1776 that had been carefully written to assure that slaves would have no constitutional rights.[6] These laws were not affected by the treaty or by the cession agreements to the United States.[7] As a result, slavery was lawful in all the territory acquired by the United States under treaty and cession agreements until the law of that territory was changed. By 1784, Pennsylvania had enacted a gradual abolition program. Massachusetts had already abolished slavery by judicial decision in 1783.

The issue of slavery in the territories was raised in 1783, the year before the Treaty of Paris was fully ratified. The man who raised it was Timothy Pickering from Massachusetts, the highly regarded quartermaster general in the Revolutionary Army and a puritanical opponent of slavery all his life.[8] He petitioned Congress to purchase land that had been ceded to it in order to create a new state in the Ohio country to be settled by veterans who had been paid in script that was "not worth a continental."[9] His petition included an express prohibition on slavery.[10]

Congress never acted on that petition, but the importance to the northern states of a territory free of slavery,
suggested by a respected leader of the now disbanded Revolutionary Army, demonstrated the thinking of many veterans. Living and laboring in the highly populated
northeast held little future for them. Their attention, as
Pickering's proposal demonstrated, focused on unsettled
lands to the west. Settling uncleared lands was hard farm
labor; clearing, planting, and defending the emerging farm-
land. Because of the increasing recognition that slavery
was wrong, arising from religious and revolutionary rheto-
ric, more white workers were now opposed to slavery on
principle. They also knew that they would have great difficulty competing with slave labor that was "free" to the
plantation owner and that they would have lessened influence in any state dominated by the plantation owners. The
perception and reality that the presence of black labor
reduced the value of white labor was probably a significant factor in the hardening of a negative perception of
blacks on the part of white laboring class workers.[11]

The restlessness of these unpaid veterans in post-war
economic conditions was demonstrated most vividly by
Shays's Rebellion in Massachusetts in 1786. This rebellion
of veterans turned into debtor-farmers who closed some
courts, was put down by a force paid for by the eastern
merchants.[12] Similar resistance by debtors to court enforcement of their obligations—which included imprisonment
for debt—flared that year along the eastern seaboard.[13]

In 1784, after the treaty with Britain was formalized,
Jefferson prepared a plan for the temporary government of
present and future territories.[14] It divided the territory into

fourteen future states, ten of them north of the Ohio, and authorized the settlers to establish a temporary government adopting "the constitution and laws of any one of the original states." Each new territory could thus choose to be a free or slave territory.

Jefferson addressed the issue of slavery as follows:

> After the year 1800 of the Christian era, there shall be neither slavery nor involuntary servitude in any of the said states, otherwise than in punishment of crimes, whereof the party shall have been convicted to have been personally guilty.

This position was a far cry from the Jefferson of 1776. In the same month that he drafted the Declaration of Independence, he submitted to influential friends in Virginia a draft constitution for Virginia. It included this language under the heading "Slaves:" "No person hereafter coming into this county [?] shall be held within the same in slavery under any pretext."[15]

This provision was consistent with the Virginia opposition to the importation of slaves, but it was not Jefferson's position in 1784 when drafting a plan for the territories. There, he permitted slavery to continue with respect to all slaves, imported or otherwise, for another sixteen years. However, even this position fell one state short of adoption. Massachusetts, Connecticut, Rhode Island, New Hampshire, New York, and Pennsylvania supported it; Maryland, South Carolina, and Virginia voted against it. North Carolina was divided. Jefferson later blamed John

Beatty of New Jersey who had a cold and stayed home.[16] Had John Beatty voted for the measure, it would have passed. Jefferson wrote to a French historian:

> The voice of a single individual would have prevented this abominable crime from spreading itself over the new country. Thus we see the fate of millions unborn hanging on the tongue of one man, and Heaven was silent in that awful moment![17]

Did Jefferson mean to blame God or Beatty? Either way, his analysis was wrong. Beatty was not the only delegate who could have changed the result. If Monroe of Virginia, a follower of Jefferson and Madison, had been present and voted to support the provision and either Hardy or Mercer been absent, it would have passed.[18] In any event, southern votes defeated Jefferson's modest proposal.[19] The rest of the ordinance was adopted ten to one, South Carolina dissenting.[20]

Jefferson's proposal for delayed emancipation has been criticized as giving sixteen years for slavery to become established in the territories.[21] Surely the prospective operation was calculated to reduce southern opposition. Jefferson's proposal also required that the new states created in the territory be bound by the Articles of Confederation. Those Articles, as we have seen, permitted slave owners to take their property into other states without losing them.[22] Thus the states would have been prohibited from fully abolishing slavery even within their own borders. If adopted, his proposal would have created a conflict in the year 1800 with the

Articles of Confederation permitting free movement of property. Jefferson's antislavery amendment applied to all present and future territory.[23] Its defeat meant that slavery continued to be lawful in the entire territory.

Jefferson and his colleagues believed that a law was necessary to prevent "this abominable crime from spreading itself over the new country."[24] Otherwise, why propose a statute at all? When his proposal was defeated, as his above quoted letter indicates, he believed that slavery remained lawful. He was not alone in this view. In fact, there was no other view. His conclusion was shared by all who addressed the slavery question. Those who opposed slavery in the territory believed that it was necessary to pass a law to prohibit it. No one argued that slavery had been abolished by the cession of the land to the Continental Congress. They agreed that the defeat of Jefferson's proposal meant that slavery was permitted in all the territory. The historians who concluded that Congress in 1787 had tacitly approved of southern slavery when it prohibited slavery north of the Ohio River ignored the fact that "everyone knew" that slavery was already lawful in the South.[25]

The defeat of Jefferson's 1784 proposal did not discourage the persistent Timothy Pickering from continuing to seek slave-free land for former soldiers. In early 1785, he urged Rufus King, then a member of the Continental Congress, to forbid slavery in the territories before they were settled:

> It will be infinitely easier to prevent the evil
> at first than to eradicate it or check it at any

future time....To suffer the continuance of slaves until they can gradually be emancipated in states already overrun with them may be pardonable, because unavoidable without hazarding greater evils; but to introduce them into countries where none now exist, countries which have been talked of—which we have boasted of—as an asylum to the oppressed of the earth—can never be forgiven. For God's sake, then, let one more effort be made to prevent so terrible a calamity.[26]

Pickering's letter does not suggest that slavery might be illegal without the passage of new legislation, although his abhorrence of slavery drove him to consider a northern separation from the union in the early nineteenth century.[27]

The rejection of Jefferson's proposal was a vote by Congress that slavery continued to be lawful in the territory. There was no realistic third possibility.[28] This form of legal reasoning—the rejection of one proposition meant the approval of its opposite—was commonly used by lawyers of that era.[29] Chief Justice John Marshall used it in one of the most important decisions of the Supreme Court in its early years. In *McCulloch v. Maryland,* he held that Congress had the power to create a national bank, even though this power was not expressed in the Constitution. He reasoned that the word "expressly" had appeared in the Articles of Confederation in order to restrict Congress to powers which were named in the Articles.[30] However, the word "expressly" did not appear in the Constitution or in the Tenth Amendment. This omission demonstrated the intent of the framers to permit "implied powers" in addition to those expressly granted.[31] Under this form of reasoning, the congressional decision not to prohibit slavery in the territories, like the decision not to limit Congress to expressed powers, was equivalent to a decision that slavery was permitted.[32]

At the root of these legal forms lay the concept that slaves were property, and that the owner of female slaves "owned" her children and prospective children. Slavery had been lawful in all states at the time they ceded their jurisdiction to the Congress. The cession agreements did not alter or abridge any existing rights to property. Thus slavery would remain lawful in the territory until the Congress acted to change its status. These principles were so elementary that they were imbedded in the actions of both pro-slavery and antislavery forces.[33]

In response to Pickering's urgings in 1785, on March 16 King moved a resolution prohibiting territorial slavery, as an amendment to the land ordinance then under consideration.[34] It would have had immediate effect. By a vote of eight states to four, the resolution was committed to a committee he chaired. The vote reflected a straight North-South split.[35] The northern states were prepared to discuss the slavery issue—the southern states were not. Both sides assumed that such legislation was necessary if slavery was to be prohibited.

The committee reported a resolution that reinstated Jefferson's prospective abolition principle of the previous year, and added a fugitive slave clause to sweeten the proposal for slave owners:[36]

That after the year 1800 of the Christian era that there shall be neither slavery nor involuntary servitude in any of the states, described in the resolve of Congress of the 23 April, 1784, [the 1784 land ordinance] otherwise than in punishment of crimes, whereof the party shall have been personally guilty: And that this regulation shall be an article of compact, and remain a fundamental principle of the constitutions between the thirteen original states, and each of the states described in the said resolve of the 23 April, 1784, **any implication or construction of the said resolve to the contrary notwithstanding**—provided always, that upon the escape of any person into any of the states described in the said resolve of Congress of the 23d day of April 1784, from whom labor or service is lawfully claimed in any one of the original states, such fugitive may be lawfully reclaimed, and carried back to the person claiming his labor or service as aforesaid.[37] (emphasis added)

King's motion, as amended by the committee, would have allowed slavery in all the territory for fifteen years, after which it would have been prohibited in all of the territory. It also provided for the return of fugitive slaves who had escaped from the original states. Thus the principle of containment of slavery to the original states was included in his resolution. This appears to follow Pickering's suggestion to limit slavery to the states where it already existed, although the fifteen year permission for slavery to grow would not have pleased him.

These sweeteners were not enough to accommodate the South. The southern opposition to the freedom principle was as strong in 1785 as it had been in 1776. King did not submit this amended proposal to a vote. He must have concluded that he would suffer the same defeat as had Jefferson in 1784.[38] King's failure to press his motion to a vote strengthened the inference that slavery was permitted in all U.S. territory.

The boldface clause is evidence that the defeat of Jefferson's 1784 antislavery proposal was viewed by lawyers as authorizing slavery in all the territories. The only purpose of the clause is to rebut that inference once the year 1800 arrived. This is strong evidence that the lawyers understood that language in the 1784 ordinance meant that slavery was permitted in the entire territory.[39] In an era where there was no federal supremacy clause and no full federal court system, the lawyers' understanding was law.

The next major step in developing a program to govern the territory was a report by James Monroe who had visited the northwest territory. He concluded that Jefferson's proposed division of the area in the 1784 legislation would produce states that were so small that they would be unlikely to obtain a population entitled to statehood. Monroe had a low opinion of the area:

> A great part of the territory is miserably poor, especially that near Lakes Michigan and Erie; and that upon the Mississippi and

Illinois consists of extensive plains which
have not had from appearances and will not
have a single bush on them for ages.[40]

Monroe recommended asking the states which had
ceded lands conditioned on the creation of nine to ten states
provided in the 1784 ordinance to amend their cession
agreements to permit fewer states north of the Ohio River.[41]
In July 1786, Congress asked Virginia to modify its act of
cession to permit the establishment of three to five states in
that area.[42] The ten states that Jefferson had proposed—if
settled by northerners—would have given the North
a more decided advantage over the South in any future
government which, it was thought, might give an equal
votes to each state. On the other hand, an increase in four
states to the north would be balanced by an equal number
of slave states east of the Mississippi. Was Monroe not
much of a farmer, or was he a far-sighted politician who did
not want to give the North such a voting advantage?[43]

On September 19, 1786, another bill concerning the
governance of the territories was proposed to Congress.[44] It
recommended a more formal governmental structure than
had the 1784 ordinance and adopted most of the proposals
in the report Congress had considered.[45] This bill reflected
both a distrust of what the settlers might do if left to themselves and a desire for greater congressional supervision of
the territorial government than Jefferson had planned.
The bill passed its second reading on May 9, 1787.[46]

The same day, Congress received a petition from the
Ohio Company seeking land at a convenient place for officers and soldiers. This was the same group of veterans that

Timothy Pickering had been working with since 1783, seeking a slave-free area.

Congress then lost its quorum and was unable to do business, because some of its members were also delegates to the Constitutional Convention that convened in late May in Philadelphia. The Congress could not reconvene until enough delegates returned to create a quorum. Around July 6, five delegates from Virginia, North Carolina, and Georgia reached New York and created a quorum so that Congress could do business. To understand the extraordinary events that occurred after their arrival in New York, we must examine what happened at the Constitutional Convention in Philadelphia during the last week in June and the first two weeks in July. As Historian H. J. Henderson wrote:

> Only by perceiving the Northwest Ordinance in the context of the proceedings of the Constitutional Convention can one properly understand its passage, and only by viewing the debates of the Convention as an extension of Congressional factionalism can we understand why the Convention had such a vital influence on the ordinance.[47]

# Chapter 10

# Deadlock over Slavery in the Constitutional Convention

The alliance of states that had fought the Revolution was weakened once the war ended. The Continental Congress had deliberately created a frail central government in the Articles of Confederation.[1] There was no executive branch. Each state had one vote, and could veto any changes to the Articles. The Congress had no taxing power, and could raise money only by begging the states for it. It had no power to prevent the states from taxing goods exported to other states. Thus New Jersey, whose goods were taxed at port cities of both New York and Philadelphia, was "like a cask tapped at both ends; and North Carolina, between Virginia and South Carolina...a patient bleeding at both arms."[2]

After disbanding the army, the Congress had no federal military force. In Massachusetts during the recession of 1786, war veteran Daniel Shays led a crowd of disgruntled former soldiers in a "rebellion." They had been paid with paper that was growing worthless, causing the loss of their farms to foreclosures and leaving them facing imprisonment for debt. They closed the courts in several towns and headed toward the arsenal in Springfield. Local militia dispersed them. The discontent was not limited to Massachusetts, however. Up and down the eastern seaboard, courts with the power to imprison debtors were closed by mob violence.[3] To the political and economic leadership, the impotence of the federal government was proving a disaster. The state governments looked no better, printing paper money that rapidly became worthless, thus contributing to the general collapse of the economy. Finally, twelve states agreed to a call by Virginia for a convention in Philadelphia in May 1787, to consider amending the Articles of Confederation to strengthen the powers of the federal government.

The Virginia delegation came to Philadelphia prepared to dominate the convention. The distinguished group was headed by George Washington, and included Governor Edmund Randolph, James Madison, George Mason (who had drafted the Virginia Constitution of 1776), and George Wythe (a judge, a mentor of Jefferson's, and the first law professor in an American college).[4] They planned to create a strong national government that would be controlled by the larger states, based on population—Virginia, Massachusetts, and Pennsylvania were the most populous at the time. They spent nearly two weeks preparing their proposal—known as the Virginia or Randolph plan. It was designed to create a strong federal government by giving the central government the power to tax, and weakening the states' ability to prevent, delay, or interfere with federal government programs.

Virginia's governor, Edmund Randolph, presented the plan on May 29.[5] It featured a two-part national legislature that was based on the single principle of representation. The number of representatives that each state would have in Congress was to be based on "the quotas of contribution," meaning each state's share of contributions to the federal budget. This proportion had been set in a political compromise by Congress in 1783 as counting each slave as three-fifths of a person for purposes of setting each state's contribution to the federal government.[6] An alternative proposal was to measure representation by the "number of free inhabitants" but Madison quickly moved to strike this alternative because he said, "it might occasion debates which would divert the Committee from the general question whether the principle of representation should be changed."[7]

Only one body, the House of Representatives, would be elected by the people of each state.[8] The second and smaller body, the Senate, would be elected by the House of Representatives from among persons nominated by the state legislatures.[9]

On June 11, James Wilson of Pennsylvania and Charles Pinckney of South Carolina proposed that the three-fifths formula be applied to determine membership in the House of Representatives.[10] This would give the slave-holding states a greater representation in the House than they would have if only whites were counted. The proposal passed in the committee, nine to two,[11] but only after Elbridge Gerry of Massachusetts asked, "Why should the blacks, who were property in the South, be in their rule of representation more than the cattle and horses of the North?"[12]

Nevertheless, Massachusetts supported the motion because the state would benefit. The result of this vote was that the states that contributed more to the federal budget would effectively dominate the House and the Senate because both were based on the same principle of representation. The large states and a few supporting states would control the Congress. The smaller states, foreseeing a loss of influence, immediately fought back.

Roger Sherman and Oliver Ellsworth of Connecticut proposed that states have equal votes in the Senate. If not, "The smaller states would never agree to the plan." Madison was adamant that giving the states equal voting power in any form would merely replicate the weakness of the Articles of Confederation. The Sherman-Ellsworth motion was defeated six to five. The larger free states plus the slave states ganged up on the smaller states.[13] The small states obtained a day's adjournment to consider what to do.

On June 15, Patterson presented the New Jersey Plan on behalf of New York, New Jersey, Delaware, and Luther Martin of Maryland.[14] It insisted on an equal vote for each state in a single legislative body, as was the case under the Articles of Confederation.

This issue was debated until June 19, when the committee of the whole rejected the Patterson plan by seven votes—Massachusetts, Connecticut, Pennsylvania, Virginia, the Carolinas, and Georgia—to three—New York, New Jersey, and Delaware, those states that had originally proposed it.[15] The committee recommended that the Virginia plan be adopted. For ten more days, the convention debated inconclusively. Tempers and temperatures rose as the debate grew more heated inside the hall, as did the weather outside.

On June 28, Hugh Williamson of North Carolina added a new dimension to the debate. He:

> begged that the expected addition of new states from the westward might be kept in view. They would be small states, they would be poor states, they would be unable to pay in proportion to their numbers; their distance from market rendering the produce of their labor less valuable; they would consequently be tempted to combine for the purpose of laying burdens on commerce and consumption which would fall with greatest weight on the old states.[16]

On the same day, Benjamin Franklin, whose experience and judgment, according to historian Walter Isaacson, "exemplified qualities of enlightenment, tolerance and pragmatic compromise," expressed the frustration of the convention:[17]

> The small progress we have made after four or five weeks close attendance and continual reasonings with each other—our different sentiments on almost every question, several of the last producing as many noes as ayes, is methinks a melancholy proof of the imperfection of the human understanding....
>
> In this situation of this assembly, groping as it were in the dark to find political truth, and scarce able to distinguish it when

presented to us, how has it happened, Sir, that we have not hitherto once thought of humbly applying to the father of lights to illuminate our understandings?

Franklin recommended prayer. When delegate Hugh Williamson of North Carolina pointed out that the Convention had no funds to pay a minister, the proposal was dropped.[18]

On Friday, June 29, the debate continued, culminating in a six to four vote rejecting the equality of states principle of the Articles of Confederation in the House and proposing that it be "according to some equitable ratio."[19] The six states voting against equal representation were Massachusetts, Pennsylvania, Virginia, the two Carolinas, and Georgia; the three largest states by population and the four slave states. The Convention was precisely at the same point it had been on June 14, before the Patterson plan for equal votes in the state legislature had been proposed. The Patterson plan was dead and at that point, small state representatives fought back to save equal representation for states in the Senate with their strongest weapon.

On Friday, June 29, Oliver Ellsworth of Connecticut moved to save some influence for the states. This time he moved that each state should have an equal vote in the Senate, and accepted a two house legislature as in the Virginia plan. Madison reported Ellsworth's speech:

The proportional representation in the first branch was conformable to the federal principle and was necessary to secure the large states against the small. An equality of voices was conformable to the federal principle and was necessary to secure the small states against the large. He trusted that on this middle ground a compromise would take place. He did not see that it could on any other. And if no compromise should take place, our meting would not only be in vain but worse than in vain. To the eastward, he was sure that Massachusetts was the only state that would listen to a proposition for excluding the states as equal political societies, from an equal voice in both branches. The others would risk every consequence rather than part with so dear a right. An attempt to deprive them of it was at once cutting the body (of America) in two, and, as he supposed would be the case, somewhere about this part of it.[20]

Ellsworth may have used much more colorful language. Rufus King of Massachusetts reported that he had said, "the political body must be cut asunder at the Delaware."[21] Abraham Yates of New York reported that he said, "If the great states refuse this plan, we will be forever separated."[22]

This was the strongest threat to split the country made by a northerner at the Convention. Ellsworth demanded an equal vote in both House and Senate for the states, but if the larger states insisted on proportional representation in both houses, he was willing to compromise on equality in one and proportionality in the other.

Suddenly, the entire convention was facing an abyss. They had come together to strengthen the union; now they were coming perilously close to dissolving it. They were all men of business, law, and politics. Division of the union threatened the economic and social stability of the states they represented, and of their own generally prosperous lifestyles.[23]

Southerners—who frequently used the threat themselves —had to take this threat seriously.[24] They could ill afford to be cut loose from the northern states. They had not recovered from the brutal warfare in the later years of the war or the loss of a quarter of their slaves who had been liberated by the British. The South was economically and militarily weaker than it had been in 1774, compared to the North. It had been devastated by the later years of the war. It had no navy and it was exposed to hostile Native Americans, possible British meddling to the west, and the Spanish to the south. A division of the nation would have left it prey to external forces as well as to the risk of slave uprisings and poor white protests over debts as in Shays's Rebellion.[25]

The next day, June 30, Madison responded to Ellsworth's threat to split the union. His speech was the analytical and thoughtful Madison at his best. He had reached a new understanding of the real issue before the Convention. Since the beginning of the Convention, the dispute had appeared to be between small and large states. But it was really about slavery.

> The States were divided into different interests not by their difference of size, but by

other circumstances; the most material of
which resulted partly from climate, but principally from (the effects of) their having
or not having slaves. These two causes
concurred in forming the great division of
interests in the U. States. It did not lie
between the large and small states; it lay
between the northern and southern. And if
any defensive powers were necessary, it
ought to be mutually given to these two
interests.[26]

This powerful analysis from the most respected thinker
at the Convention constituted the first public acknowledgment of the central role of slavery at the Convention. Even
if it was overstated, it sank into the collective consciousness of the Convention. By July 14, Madison could report
that his analysis had been accepted.

It seems now to be pretty well understood
that the real difference of interests lay, not
between the n(orthern) and southern states.
The institution of slavery and its consequences formed the line of discrimination.
There were five states in the South, eight on
the northern side of this line.[27]

Madison may have exaggerated the slavery issue by
suggesting it was the only difference between the states.
But he made his point that it was the important issue
before the Convention. The Convention had heard little

concerning slavery prior to this time. Gerry's statement of June 11—that if slaves were property, they should have no more votes than cattle and horses—is the only direct critical statement concerning slavery made between May 28 and June 30.[28] Either Madison and the other note takers did not report such statements, or, more likely, they were made off the floor in social contacts between the delegates.[29]

We assume that most of the comments which were made on the record—everyone knew that Madison was taking copious notes—had first been discussed off the floor. We know that the delegates had a busy social life but we know little of the content of the conversations and discussions that took place because the delegates were sworn to secrecy. Particularly since some of the delegates did not know each other well it was likely that comments made on the record had been carefully thought out beforehand.[30]

Those informal antislavery comments must have been sufficiently strong that the southerners had to mount a major defense of their states' rights position. These southern responses began on May 30, shortly after the convention convened.[31] If the discussions about large versus small states scattered throughout the record really described differences between slave and free states, then there was extensive deliberation on the issue. Ellsworth's threat to "cut the political body asunder" on June 29, along with Madison's the next day that slavery was the central issue between the North and the South, forced the Convention to face the reality that the union of the colonies was likely to break up at the Convention.

Madison's comment was a result of careful reflection, not a spontaneous expression. As the concluding lines of his statement indicated, he was searching for a balanced approach to the issue of slavery: "If any defensive powers were necessary, it ought to be mutually given to these two interests."

Madison continued, in his notes:

> He [Madison] was so strongly impressed with this important truth that he had been casting about in his mind for some expedient that would answer the purpose. The one which had occurred was that instead of proportioning the votes of the states in both branches to their respective numbers of inhabitants computing the slaves in the ration of five to three, they should be represented in one branch according to the number of free inhabitants only; and in the other according to the whole n[umber] counting the slaves as (if) free. By this arrangement the southern scale would have the advantage in one House, and the northern in the other. He had restrained from proposing this expedient by two considerations; one was his unwillingness to urge any diversity of interests on an occasion when it is but too apt to arise itself—the other was the inequality of powers that must be vested in the two branches, and which would destroy the equilibrium of interests.[32]

The thrust of Madison's proposal—that the two houses of Congress could be based on different principles of representation—was a striking departure from the original Virginia plan that relied on a single principle of representation in both houses.[33] But there was a problem: in one house he would count slaves as free men, upping the ante from three-fifths to counting all slaves the same as free people. Nevertheless, Madison's analysis that the basic difference between the states was over slavery gave rise to the possibility of different ways to achieve a balance between these interests.

Ben Franklin pounced immediately on the possibilities of a new framework based on the Ellsworth and Madison statements:

> The diversity of opinions turns on two points. If a proportional representation takes place, the small states contend their liberties will be in danger. If an equality of votes is to be put in place, the large states say their money will be in danger. When a broad table is to be made, and the edges (of the planks do not fit) the artist takes a little from both and makes a good joint. In like manner here both sides must part with some of their demands, in order that they may join in some accommodating proposition.[34]

He proposed equal numbers of delegates from each state to the Senate and that states have "equal suffrage" on three issues, all of which related directly to the ever-present concern of the South to protect slavery: (1) those issues involving individual state sovereignty; (2) where state authority over their own citizens might be diminished or augmented; and (3) where appointments to federal offices were subject to Senate confirmation.

Franklin may have urged prayer on Wednesday, but once Madison's analysis had created the opportunity he was quick to seek a practical compromise on Saturday. His proposal was only partially followed up.[35] Nevertheless, Madison's and Franklin's proposals initiated a search for a compromise that took account of how slavery in the territory would affect the future growth of the nation.

The question of how the western lands would evolve into states was already an issue before both the Convention and the Continental Congress. The North had been seeking a slave-free area where its citizens could expand since Pickering's proposal in 1783, but had been rebuffed by the South at every turn. The South wanted to develop the western territory by using slaves to do the heavy work of clearing and planting.

The western territory was an enormous reservoir for future growth. Discussion at the Convention made clear that the West would inevitably gain increased political influence as the territory was settled and achieved statehood under the "equal footing" doctrine.[36] This meant that the West would affect the political balance concerning slavery as well as many other issues.[37]

The assumption of many at the Convention was that expansion of the country would be to the southwest and therefore pro-slavery. This assumption was in part based on Monroe's negative report on the soil in the northwest.[38] Southerners using slave labor could clear land more cheaply than northerners using either paid labor or the "sweat equity" of new settlers. Moreover, southerners—despite being discouraged by both the British and American governments from settling west of Appalachians—were already on the move.[39] Historian Lance Banning writes:

> In 1786, the West was everywhere perceived as an extension of the South. Western settlement was still almost exclusively on lands south of the Ohio, and as population moved increasingly into the old Southwest, it was becoming ever more apparent that admission to the union of new southwestern states would fundamentally affect the federal balance.[40]

The Massachusetts men—particularly Timothy Pickering—had been urging the development of a slave-free northwest territory for years.[41] It was understood that the northern territory would be developed by people from New England who would bring their antislavery politics with them. They expected prompt settlement activity as soon as land became available in the northwest, without competition from plantation owners using slave labor.

Land developers, particularly the energetic Manasseh Cutler and the persistent Samuel Parsons from Massachusetts, were pressing hard for a national settlement policy that would unleash this pent-up demand and make great fortunes for the developers. The rapid population increase in the colonies was creating these pressures for more land up and down the east coast.[42] Speculators believed that the system of government might be changed, and wanted to seal their arrangements before that happened.

On Monday, July 2, the Convention voted on Ellsworth's motion to allow each state one vote in the Senate. It split the convention, 5-5-1.[43] In support were Connecticut, New York, New Jersey, Delaware, and Maryland. Opposed were Massachusetts, Pennsylvania, Virginia, and the Carolinas. Georgia, which would have voted against the motion along with the other southern states, was divided and therefore its vote did not count. The delegate who created this situation in Georgia was Abraham Baldwin, a transplant from Connecticut. Well-educated, he had been a chaplain in the Revolutionary Army. After the war he moved to Georgia, became a lawyer, and a two-term congressman. He created the dead-lock by supporting the motion for equal representation because he thought the North would split the union rather than lose its equality in the Senate.[44] Baldwin's switch was critical because it meant that Georgia's vote—which would have been against equal votes in the Senate—did not count. Convention rules prohibited counting a state's vote unless a majority of its delegates supported it. Baldwin thought that a deadlock was preferable to a six to four vote against the equality of states in the Senate and a walk out by the smaller states.

The deadlock shocked delegates from every quarter. Madison noted that Charles Pinckney from South Carolina immediately saw its seriousness. He was:

> extremely anxious that something should be done, considering this as the last appeal to a regular experiment. Congresses have failed in almost every effort for an amendment of the

federal system. Nothing has prevented a dissolution of it, but the appointment of this Convention; and he could not express his alarms for the consequences of such an event.[45]

He added, "Some compromise seemed to be necessary; the states being exactly divided on the question of an equality of votes in the second branch." He proposed a committee of one from each state to recommend a way out of the impass.[46]

Roger Sherman of Connecticut: "We are now at a full stop, and nobody...meant that we should break up without doing something."[47] He supported the committee concept.

Edmund Randolph of Virginia: "favored the commitment [to a committee] though he did not expect much benefit from the expedient."[48]

Hugh Williamson of North Carolina: "If we do not concede on both sides, our business must soon be at an end."[49]

Elbridge Gerry of Massachusetts:

Something must be done, or we shall disappoint not only America but the whole world. He suggested a consideration of the state we should be thrown into by the failure of the union. We should be without an umpire to decide controversies and must be at the mercy of events. What too is to become of our treaties—what of our foreign debts, what of our domestic? We must make concessions on both sides. Without these the constitutions of the several states would never have been formed.[50]

The enormity of a failure of the Convention and its impact on the lives and futures of the delegates, their families, their prosperity, and indeed the independence for which many of them had fought, was sinking into the delegates' consciousness. They were all men who had prospered under the admittedly creaky and ineffective Articles of Confederation; many had helped create them. Even if they thought the group of like-minded states could go it alone, they must surely have feared being torn apart from internal dissension and outside forces.

Shays's Rebellion of 1786 and similar evidences of discontent up and down the continent showed that white colonists could disturb a domestic government as well as a British one. In addition, slave revolts were always on the minds of the southerners. Britain, Spain, and Native American tribes surrounded them on all sides. As Gerry said, amidst a growing sense of anarchy and unbridled self-interest among the people, they had come to strengthen the national government to increase security and stability. The results of their deliberations, however, were heading toward the dissolution of the union.

The issue was sharply drawn. It was about slavery.[51] The South wanted slaves to count in their representation in order to preserve slavery; the North would not stand for a government where whites, with the advantage of votes assigned because they had slaves, would create a slave nation.

The committee recommended by General Pinckney was established by a vote of nine states to two.[52] The committee met and voted on Tuesday, July 3.[53] It recommended that the House have one representative for each forty thousand inhabitants, counting slaves as three-fifths; and that each state should have equal votes in the Senate.[54] This recommendation was the death knell for the Virginia plan that had sought a single principle of representation, but it assured southern power in the House by counting of three-fifths of the slaves to determine representation.[55] By July 3, it appeared that each state would have equal votes in the Senate and that slaves would count in the South's representation in the House.

The North would not accept the results of the vote even though they had won equal votes in the Senate. Delegates realized that with growth to the west, southern votes in the house would increase more rapidly than northern votes; inevitably the South would dominate the Congress and slavery would become a nation-wide phenomenon, with a northern enclave of free labor. The deadlock seemed impenetrable. Neither Madison's proposal nor Franklin's were acceptable because neither addressed the North's basic concerns. Although Madison had made the first breakthrough in publicly recognizing that the issue of slavery was important, he was so strongly against the "equal votes" principle that he was unlikely to envision a solution that accepted it.[56]

The cluster of ideas circulating at the Convention included (1) Madison's idea that the slavery difference had to be resolved, (2) Ellsworth's threat to split the union at the Delaware, (3) Monroe's recommendations to reduce the maximum number of northern states possible in the territory from ten to five, and his view that much of the land there was useless, (4) the North's demand for slave-free territory and equal state votes in the Senate, (5) the Ohio Company's pressure for a land sale, (6) the recognition that slavery in the future would be determined by the position of those states that would be formed in the West, and (7) the South's demand for "security in their slaves."

Who among the delegates in Philadelphia could make the creative link that would absorb these often conflicting ideas and conceive a solution that would satisfy both northern and southern interests in the slavery issue, and then manage its adoption?[57]

Our hypothesis, and that is all it can be, is that there were two men at the Philadelphia Convention who played roles in the solution. Benjamin Franklin had the breadth of experience, temperament, history, and perspective to perceive that creating a slave-free area north of the Ohio would address the real and immediate concerns of the northern states. Historian Walter Isaacson's penetrating portrait of Benjamin Franklin at the Convention, suggests a man, even in old age, still able to sense the perhaps unexpressed but nonetheless real needs of parties in conflict, and able to nudge them toward a solution.[58] He had already proposed ideas that the committee had incorporated into its report.[59]

Over the years, Franklin had become more and more hostile toward slavery.[60] This led him to accept the presidency of the Pennsylvania Society for the Abolition of Slavery in 1787, while still governor of Pennsylvania. The society wanted him to present a petition against slavery to the convention, but he declined.[61] He was able to think his way through the web of ideas that had led up to the deadlock of July 2 and by being silent about slavery at the

Convention, maintain his credibility with all parties. In 1789 and 1790, he would make proposals with respect to slavery that made him the founding godfather of modern day affirmative action.[62]

Whether it was Franklin or someone else who thought through the haze of ideas to the solution to the deadlock at the convention, the result was elegant, simple, and Solomon-like. It involved cutting the new territory of the United States in half. That part north of the Ohio River would be without slavery; that part south of the Ohio River would continue to maintain slavery. This would satisfy the northern wish to expand into lands to their west, confident that they would not have to compete with slave labor or live in a slave state. The states north of the Ohio would be free, and give the North a balance with the South in the Senate.

In addition, the solution would prevent the operation of the three-fifths rule in the northwest. At the same time, it would also satisfy the southern wish to expand slavery further into the western lands where they had already moved, whereas slavery had only gained a limited foothold on the north bank of the Ohio. It was, in short, a way of "cutting the nation asunder" as Ellsworth had threatened on June 29, but doing so without destroying it.

But the Convention alone could not achieve that result. Not only did it lack authority to solve this particular problem, but if it tried to do so, it would foster a huge public debate about slavery which would not have assisted in the continuance of the union, and might have hastened its demise—as the secret debate nearly did at the Convention. On the other hand, the Continental Congress waiting in

New York because it lacked a quorum could address the issue. It had asserted its authority to regulate the territory in 1784, as we have seen in Chapter Nine. Once this idea had been formulated, the question became how could it be brought to fruition in time to save the Convention and perhaps the union itself? We can only speculate about the details, but the consequences tell the story.

First, would the southern representatives to the Convention and the Congress go along with the idea of a no-slave zone? It ran counter to their fiercely held position during the last thirteen years. They would have to be made to understand that this concession was necessary to save the union. Who could persuade them?

Second, would the northerners accept the promise of southerners at the Convention to try to accomplish this task as a reason to drop their threat of separation? Probably not. After all these years of protecting slavery, why should the northerners believe a promise of a southern change of heart? But if the southerners could actually foreclose slavery in the northwest, what would the North do? Would it still walk out and guarantee a separation, or would it settle for the solution to its constituents' immediate problems, and let the future take care of itself? Did Franklin discuss these questions in his comfortable house near the Convention with some of his Virginia friends, or northern friends, or both? Or did he decide to act without consulting the North, presenting it with a *fait accompli*? We do not know, but we do know the outcome.

Franklin was eighty-one and infirm. Although he lived nearby, it was difficult for him to attend all the convention meetings because of his health. He wrote out some of his comments, rather than delivering them himself. He could not have converted this idea into legislative action. He had to find other delegates who had the physical energy, the talent at persuading legislators, the breadth of vision, and the respect of the legislators at the Convention and at the Congress in New York to make the concept work. Franklin's home was only a few doors away from the hall where the Convention met, and it would require little energy to discuss the prospect with men like Richard Henry Lee. It is likely that it was Richard Henry Lee who carried out Franklin's plan because of his standing among the southerners in both Philadelphia and in New York. Richard Henry Lee was a member of Congress, but not the Convention. He had appeared in Philadelphia at the end of June en route to the Congress in New York just as the Convention appeared to be deadlocked.[63] It is possible that Lee never knew it was Franklin's plan. While appearing all innocence, Franklin was wise in devious ways of proceeding.[64]

One difficulty with this analysis is that Lee and Franklin were not friends. Both Walter Isaacson and Gordon Wood, who have recently published books about Franklin, trace the strained relationship back to Arthur Lee, Richard Henry's brother, who invoked family support in pursuit of his dislike of Franklin.[65] Historian J. Kent McGaughy attributes the hostility to the fact that Franklin had sided with Pennsylvanians in a conflict with Virginians over expansion into western lands.[66] Isaacson does say that "on rare occasions, Lee and Franklin put aside their animosity as they discussed their common cause."[67] Saving the union from dissolution at the Convention could have qualified as one of those "rare occasions."

Now we leave the realm of speculation for facts. Shortly after the Grand Committee had voted for equal representation in the Senate and population plus three-fifths of slaves in the House, five members of the Continental Congress rode north from Philadelphia and joined the proceedings of the Continental Congress in New York. On July 3 or 4, William Blount and Benjamin Hawkins of North Carolina and William Pierce and William Few of Georgia left for New York City. These four were members of both the Convention and the Congress.

Richard Henry Lee probably left Philadelphia on July 5, arriving in New York on July 7, and taking his seat in Congress on July 9.[68] Thus he would have had a day in Philadelphia before he left and a day in New York before he took his seat in Congress to discuss the proposal to prohibit slavery north of the Ohio River with delegates in both places.

Although the meetings of the Constitutional Convention were secret, Lee was not an outsider. McGaughy writes, "In spite of the Convention delegates' efforts to maintain security, Richard Henry Lee obviously found a line into the inner workings of the gathering."[69]

He was privy to the thinking of the leaders from both the South and North with whom he had worked during the Revolution and at the Continental Congress. In the previous year, he had served as president of the Congress. Lee took this role seriously, living and entertaining lavishly after Congress decided to pay the expenses of its president.[70] He had declined membership in the Constitutional Convention because he viewed it as a body that would report to Congress; and that Congress would make the "real" decisions. He thought it inappropriate to be a member of this "subordinate" body.[71]

Lee enjoyed his role in the pantheon of the American Revolution. His eloquence and reasoning as a speaker, and his unceasing activity in the name of colonial freedom, coupled with a desire for recognition on a national scale, made him a public figure recognized by both North and South.[72] Historian Jack Greene describes Richard Henry Lee thusly:

> Unlike John Wilkes or Patrick Henry, he seems to have lacked the inclination or the necessary breadth of appeal to secure a broad following among the public at large and become a demagogue. His proper forum was the legislative chamber; his audience, his fellow legislators....He was not an ideologue who would take his case to the country, but a "parliamentary politician" who preferred to operate inside the legislative halls and within the small circles of the politically powerful.[73]

Lee had often been the public voice of Virginia in legislative halls. He had vetoed the Galloway plan at the First Congress in 1774 by threatening to walk out and had been selected to make the motion for independence in 1776. That year he also circulated a draft constitution for Virginia developed in consultation with John Adams. The draft, according to historian Robert Sutton, was, "pivotal in persuading the delegates [to the Virginia Convention] that there was a better government than royal authority."[74] He had been treated as a senior statesman for a decade, having served as president of the Continental Congress during passage of the Land Ordinance of 1785. That year, he had presided over—and helped defeat—Rufus King's effort to revive Jefferson's antislavery clause.[75] As a result, he knew firsthand the problems of the territory; the interest of the North in a slave-free area as well as the concerns of the South. By 1787, the increasing pressures of the Ohio Company to purchase land free of slavery also would have focused Lee's attention on the northern territory.

The capacity to translate political sentiments into legislative action was a major hallmark of his career. It makes him the preeminent candidate as the promoter of the antislavery clause in the Northwest Ordinance at both the Constitutional Convention and the Continental Congress in New York.

Lee's own attitude toward slavery and the North had distinctive characteristics. His initial speech in the House of Burgesses in 1759 blamed slavery for Virginia's cultural backwardness.[76] Lee, in his youth, saw that the evils of slavery adversely affected whites as well as blacks who were "equally entitled to liberty and freedom by the great law of nature."[77] Beyond that, Lee had cultivated friendships with New Englanders, beginning in 1773, with a letter to Samuel Adams and followed up with long-term relations with John Adams, that sometimes got him into trouble with fellow Virginians.[78] Lee was more friendly toward the New Englanders than to some of his Virginia colleagues, whose "hasty, unpersevering, aristocratic genius of the South suits not my disposition and is inconsistent with my ideas of what must constitute social happiness and security."[79]

According to historian Pauline Maier, he was not only among the Jeffersonians in his opposition to slavery while living on its proceeds, but was an admirer of the spartan culture of New England. Maier captured the complex forces animating his distinguished Revolutionary career in her essay on Lee.[80] It concludes:

> Men like Lee were hardly conservative revolutionaries, dedicated only to preserving Virginia's past. Their Virginia was by nature too impermanent to afford men like Lee the "social happiness and security" they sought. The task they faced was to wrest from instability a more satisfying world. If Lee abandoned the prospect of personal migration [to Massachusetts], he could still hope to resolve his own dilemmas and those of his family not by independence alone but through a larger moral redefinition that for him and others was integral to the Revolution of 1776—by refashioning all America after his image of a sober, diligent, meritocratic northeast. Thus it was that the ways of New England, which for Richard Henry Lee as for Samuel Adams came to represent the hope and meaning of a new American republic, had great appeal to a Virginian of good family, but poor prospects.

This portrait of Lee's character enhances the likelihood that he supported the expansion of northern culture both because he thought it would limit slavery and because he saw virtues in a slave-free society. Although the date he left for New York is uncertain, he arrived there in time to take his seat on July 9. While the five delegates made their way to New York and the Continental Congress, the Convention in Philadelphia spent the week arguing about a number of issues that always seemed to return to the question of slavery. The level of depression rose as the risks of failure discussed on Monday, July 2, continued to mount. On July 10, the New York delegation pulled out of the Convention altogether. George Washington wrote to Alexander Hamilton asking him to return, but painting a woeful picture of what he would find if he did:

> The state of our councils which prevailed at the period you left this city…are now, if possible, in a worse train than ever; you will find but little ground on which the hope of a good establishment can be formed. In a word, I almost despair at seeing a favorable issue to the proceedings of the convention, and do therefore repent having had any agency in the business.[81]

Historian Richard Brookhiser emphasized the importance that Washington placed on his reputation, and how he considered the risks to that reputation of each new venture that presented itself as an opportunity. But the risks to his reputation in attending the Convention were simultaneously risks to the principle of self-government that he valued so highly.[82] Washington's unhappiness in his letter to Hamilton reflected the condition of the convention on July 10. It worsened the next day. Some examples of comments concerning slavery made between July 11 and 14 come from Madison's notes, taken to record the proceedings.[83]

On July 11, Gouverneur Morris of Pennsylvania told the Convention he was:

> Reduced to the dilemma of doing injustice to the southern states or to human nature, and he must therefore do it to the former. For he could never agree to give such encouragement to the slave trade as would be given by allowing them a representation for their Negroes, and he did not believe those states would ever confederate on terms that would deprive them of that trade.

The next day, July 12, William Richardson Davie of North Carolina became impatient. He said it was

> high time now to speak out. He saw that it was meant by some gentlemen to deprive the southern states of any share of representation for their blacks. He was sure that North Carolina would never confederate on any terms that did not rate them as at least three-fifths. If the eastern states meant therefore to exclude them altogether the business was at an end.

Gouverneur Morris responded that

> He came here to form a compact for the good of America. He was ready to do so with

all the states. He hoped and believed that all
would enter into such a compact. If they
would not he was ready to join with any
state that would. But as the compact was to
be voluntary, it is in vain for the eastern
states to insist on what the southern states
would never agree to. It was equally vain for
the latter to require what the other states can
never admit; and he verily believed the people of Pennsylvania will never agree to a
representation of Negroes.

Gouverneur Morris continued the next day, July 13,
when he saw that:

The southern gentlemen will not be satisfied
unless they see the way open to their gaining
a majority in the public councils....Either
this distinction [between northern and
southern states] is fictitious or real. If fictitious let it be dismissed and let us proceed
with due confidence. If it be real, instead of
attempting to blend incompatible things, let
us at once take friendly leave of each other.
There can be no end of demands for security
if every particular interest is to be entitled to
it. The eastern states may claim it for their
fishery, and for other objects, as the southern
states claim it for their peculiar objects.

In response, Pierce Butler of South Carolina explained:

The security the southern states want is that their Negroes may not be taken from them which some gentlemen within or without doors, have a very good mind to do.

On Saturday, July 14, Luther Martin of Maryland took on the larger states:

They are...the weakest in the union. Look at Massachusetts. Look at Virginia. Are they efficient states? He was for letting a separation take place if they desired it. He had rather there be two confederacies than one founded on any other principle than an equality of votes in the Senate.

Jonathan Dayton of New Jersey reiterated that, "The smaller states can never give up their equality. For himself he would in no event yield that security for their rights."

Rufus King of Massachusetts had a "firm belief that Massachusetts would never be prevailed on to yield to an equality of votes."

James Madison of Virginia, a staunch opponent of equal votes for the states in either branch of Congress explained that:

If a proper foundation of government was destroyed by substituting an equality in place of a proportional representation, no proper superstructure would be raised....

The evil instead of being cured by time,
would increase with every new state that
should be admitted, as they must all be
admitted on the principle of equality...the
perpetuity it would give to the preponder-
ance of the northern against the southern
scale was a serious consideration. It seems
now to be pretty well understood that the
real difference of interests lay, not between the
large and small but between the n(orthern)
and southern states. The institution of slavery and its consequences formed the line of
discrimination. There were five states in the
South, eight on the northern side of this line.
Should a proportional representation take
place it is true, the northern side would still
outnumber the other; but not in the same
degree at this time; and every day would
tend toward an equilibrium.

And James Wilson of Pennsylvania reminded the
Convention that:

The great fault of the existing confederacy is
its inactivity. It has never been a complaint
against Congress that they governed over-
much. The complaint has been that they
have governed too little. To remedy this
defect we were sent here....Will not our constituents say we sent you here to form an
efficient government and you have given us

one more complex indeed, but having all the
weakness of the former government?

While this inconclusive squabbling continued in
Philadelphia, the problem of slavery which threatened the
existence of the union at the Convention in Philadelphia
was being resolved at the Congress in New York.

# Chapter II

# A Slave-Free
# Northwest Territory

While the Constitutional Convention in Philadelphia staggered to a "dead stop," the Continental Congress in New York came to life. The five delegates arriving from the Convention in Philadelphia created a quorum so the Congress could make decisions. On July 9, 1787, the Congress returned to the land ordinance that it had considered back in May. The ordinance, which related to the entire western territory, was referred to a new committee consisting of Richard Henry Lee and Edward Carrington from Virginia, Nathan Dane from Massachusetts, Melancton Smith of New York, and John Kean of South Carolina.[1]

Nathan Dane, the drafter of the ordinance, described what happened next in a letter to Rufus King of Massachusetts three days after the event:[2]

> There appears to be a disposition to do business and the arrival of R. H. Lee is of considerable importance. I think his character serves, at least in some degree, to check the effects of the feeble habits and lax mode of thinking of some of his countrymen. We have

been employed about several objects, the principal of which have been the government
enclosed and the Ohio purchase; the former
you will see is completed, and the latter will
probably be completed tomorrow. We met
several times and at last agreed on some principles—at least Lee, Smith, and myself.[3] We
found ourselves rather pressed. The Ohio
Company appeared to purchase a large tract of
federal lands—about six or seven millions of
acres—and we wanted to abolish the old system and get a better one for the government of
the country, and we finally found it necessary
to adopt the best system we could get.

The committee took only two days to return with a
much-expanded proposal. Part of one of those two days
was taken up with a meeting by Carrington, King, and
Dane with Manasseh Cutler concerning his proposal from
the Ohio Company to buy land in the territory.[4] This short
time seems hardly enough to develop the conceptions that
went into the Ordinance and reduce them to acceptable
language. This supports the view that the decision about
slavery had been made earlier in Philadelphia, to be implemented in New York.

The draft was prepared by Nathan Dane of Massachusetts, Richard Henry Lee of Virginia, and Melancton
Smith of New York.[5] Smith was both strongly antislavery
and a land speculator who was involved in the arrangement by which the Ohio Company's proposed purchase of
1.3 million acres escalated to 6 or 7 million.[6]

The Dane-Lee-Smith draft of the ordinance was given its first reading on July 11, had its second reading on July 12, and was adopted on July 13.[7] The first critical step taken was to change the name of the ordinance from "An ordinance for the government of the western territory until the same shall be divided into different states" to "An ordinance for the temporary government of the territory of the U.S. NW of the River Ohio."[8]

All previous land ordinances had encompassed all of the territory, north and south of the Ohio, acquired or to be acquired by the United States. This was the first time that a territorial ordinance was limited to the north of the Ohio River. Restricting the land ordinance to the northwest meant that slavery continued to be lawful south of the Ohio.[9] This change is another indication that the decision to protect slavery north of the Ohio had emerged to address the crisis at the Constitutional Convention in Philadelphia.

It appeared to respond to the pressures to create a slave-free northwest arising from both the Convention and the Ohio Company speculators who had been seeking slave-free areas for development since 1783. The draft produced by the new committee contained fourteen significant elements in addition to the provisions already before the Congress, some of which had been considered earlier but had never been organized into a single coherent program.[10] In addition to those rights stated in the earlier draft—jury trial, habeas corpus, and non-discriminatory taxation of non-resident proprietors—the new provisions adopted what we today would call "fundamental rights" as the basis for the territorial government and the state governments that would later emerge.[11]

Dane, on behalf of the committee, moved the provisions of the ordinance one by one. He had not intended to introduce the antislavery provision until the rest of the ordinance had been approved, and even then he was doubtful. He knew that only Massachusetts of the northern states was present, and that all five of the southern states that had a perfect record of opposing every measure that cast doubt on slavery were also present.[12] He thought—with good reason—that the antislavery provision would suffer the same fate as Jefferson's proposal of 1784 and King's proposal in 1785.[13] But, after the rest of the ordinance had been adopted, Dane was surprised, or more likely astounded. He wrote to King:

> When I drew the ordinance (which passed, a few words excepted, as I originally formed it) I had no idea the states would agree to the sixth article, prohibiting slavery, as only Massachusetts of the eastern states was present, and therefore omitted it in the draft; but finding the House favorably disposed on this subject, after we had completed the other parts, I moved the article, which was agreed to without opposition.[14]

His letter states that he heard southern representatives "favorably disposed" about an antislavery provision. We do not have a record of who spoke in favor of the provision, but history points directly at Richard Henry Lee. He had often been the spokesman for Virginia's positions on legislative issues. He was probably supported by fellow

Virginian Edward Carrington, and by the antislavery Melancton Smith of New York. Representatives of the other slave states who had just been informed of the new southern position on slavery may have remained silent. But that was enough for Dane. At that point, he moved the article, "which was agreed to without opposition."

From his letter to King, it is clear that Dane had not been informed of the southern plan. His letter quoted here strongly suggests that the southerners had already agreed among themselves to support the proposal. This collaboration is further evidence that the decision to create a no-slave zone was a serious response to the northerners' concern about slavery at the Philadelphia convention.

Lee and delegates from Philadelphia may not have told Dane about the plan, because they needed time to persuade the southern delegates to give up slavery north of the Ohio River. If their plan had not worked, they would not have been embarrassed by Dane's awareness of their effort. The important point for the southerners in New York was not to debate the proposal, but to adopt it so that the northerners in Philadelphia would understand that they had won a slave-free area north of the Ohio, and perhaps save the union from dissolution.

The prohibition on slavery, including the provision for return of fugitive slaves reads:

> There shall be neither slavery nor involuntary servitude in the said territory, otherwise than in the punishment of crimes whereof the party shall have been duly convicted: provided, always, that any person escaping into the same, from whom labor or service is

lawfully claimed in any one of the original states, such fugitive may be lawfully reclaimed and conveyed to the person claiming his or her labor or service as aforesaid.[15]

Dane's clause was effective immediately, allowing the Ohio Company to encourage northern settlers to go quickly into Ohio country, without fear of having to compete with slave labor or of living in a slave state. In that sense, the ordinance was stronger than the earlier versions proposed by Jefferson and King that allowed slavery in the territory until 1800.[16] At the same time, it was limited to protecting the ownership rights of masters only in the original states. This demonstrates that the clause was essentially copied from King's 1785 proposal that was never voted upon.[17] The clause says nothing about the status of slaves escaping from any new states or territories that might be created in the future. These issues had arisen sharply at the Convention in Philadelphia, but the clause was not modified to consider the future. This suggests the haste in which the provision had been taken from King's proposal.

Dane's antislavery clause would have an immediate impact on persons who were considering bringing slaves into the territory. Their property would be at risk. Given the choice, slave owners would—and did—go into the southwest or across the Mississippi where their "property" was secure.[18] Thus the clause—by its existence rather than its administration—was to some extent self-executing.[19]

The ordinance passed only because of the votes of the southern slave-holding states. The eight states voting for the ordinance were Massachusetts, New York, New Jersey, Delaware, Virginia, North Carolina, South Carolina, and Georgia. The ordinance was adopted with equal votes from non-slave states and from all of the major slave states.[20] Seven votes were needed for passage. If only two of the slave states had voted no, been divided, or had not appeared, the ordinance would not have passed. Three years earlier, Virginia and South Carolina had voted against Jefferson's antislavery amendment, and North Carolina was divided, which meant a "no" vote.[21] Two years earlier, Virginia, the Carolinas, and Georgia had opposed even considering King's 1785 motion to impose a prospective limitation on slavery. Thus three of the slave states, Virginia, North Carolina, and South Carolina, changed their votes from 1784, and those states plus Georgia changed their votes from 1785 to assure the creation of a "free" northwest. Had the slave states maintained the positions they held in 1784 and 1785, the ordinance would have failed.

Virginia played a crucial role in the adoption of the ordinance. Two Virginia delegates (Lee and Hardy) had voted against consideration of King's motion in 1785. In 1787, Lee had changed his vote of 1785, and Carrington had replaced Hardy.[25] Virginia supported a stronger antislavery resolution in 1787 than the one it had opposed in 1785.[26]

In addition to the fugitive slave clause copied from King's 1785 proposal, there were other provisions in the new ordinance that were sweeteners for gathering support from the southern delegates. The statement supporting freedom to navigate the Mississippi would help the southwesterners in their opposition to a proposed treaty that would have

## Voting by States, Individuals on Antislavery 1784, 1785, and 1787

| | 1784[22] Vote on Jefferson's Slavery Clause | 1785[23] Vote to Refer King's Motion to Committee | 1787[24] Vote on Northwest Ordinance |
|---|---|---|---|
| | YES | YES | YES |
| NH | Foster, Blanchard | Foster, Long | Absent |
| MASS | Gerry, Partridge | Holton, King | Holton, Dane |
| RI | Ellery, Howell | Ellery, Howell | Absent |
| CT | Sherman, Wadsworth | Cook, Johnson | Absent |
| NY | de Witt, Paine | W. Livingstone, Platt | Smith, Haring, (Yates-N) |
| NJ | Dick ** | Beatty, Cadwallader | Clarke, Scheurman, Stewart |
| DEL | Absent | Absent | Kearny, Mitchell |
| PA | Mifflin, Montgomery, Hand | Gardner, W. Henry | Absent |
| | NO | NO | YES |
| MD | McHenry, Stone | McHenry, J. Henry, Hindman | Absent |
| VA | Hardy, Mercer (TJ-Y) | Hardy, Lee (Grayson-Y) | Carrington, Lee, Grayson |
| NC | Spaight, Williamson Y* | Spaight, Sitgraves | Blount, Hawkins |
| SC | Read, Beresford | Bull, Pinckney | Kean, Huger |
| GA | Absent | Houstoun | Few, Pierce |

*No state vote because delegates split evenly.

** Vote did not count; state needed two to vote.

allowed Spain to close the Mississippi at New Orleans for many years.[27] The proposal for justice for the Native Americans may have helped to bring Benjamin Hawkins of North Carolina on board. Hawkins had vast experience in negotiating with the Native Americans, and would later become an "Indian Agent" for the southwest territory.

Nathan Dane of Massachusetts and Edward Carrington of Virginia believed that the initial settlers of the northwest territory would be New Englanders. Dane wrote:

> I think the number of free inhabitants, sixty thousand, which are requisite for the admission of a new state into the confederacy, is too small; but having divided the whole into three states, this number appears to me to be less important. Each state in the common course of things must become important soon after it shall have that number of inhabitants. The eastern state of the three [Ohio] will probably be the first, and more important than the rest, and will no doubt be settled chiefly by eastern people; and there is, I think, full and equal chance of its adopting eastern politics.[28]

The term "eastern politics" included opposition to slavery.[29] The Northwest Ordinance was and is considered the finest hour for the often maligned Continental Congress, and uncertainty concerning the reasons for its adoption still exists.

Credit has been claimed for Nathan Dane of Massachusetts who drafted it, for Timothy Pickering who promoted it, for Thomas Jefferson who drafted the 1784 ordinance, and for Manasseh Cutler of the Ohio Company who lobbied for land in the Ohio region.[30] Dane wrote that Richard Henry Lee was of "considerable importance" in shaping the proposal. They all represented forces at work in forging conditions for the ordinance, but none of them have been credited with the underlying concept of adopting an ordinance applying only to the land north of the Ohio.

Duncan MacLeod, in his penetrating analysis in *Slavery, Race, and the American Revolution,* ultimately considered that the ordinance was a sort of "accident" because its passage did not fit the pattern of prior or subsequent events.[31] Some historians consider the Northwest Ordinance to have been a "tacit agreement," or an unintended policy, permitting slavery south of the Ohio.[32] But there was nothing tacit about it. Both supporters and opponents of slavery understood—and acted upon the understanding— that slavery was lawful in all the territory of the United States unless and until a government altered its status.[33] As Edward Coles said in 1856:

> As drafted, the Northwest Ordinance assured both North and South of a political balance between slave and free states. It not only prohibited slavery in the northwest, but guaranteed its continued vitality in the southwest.[34]

In fact, the Northwest Ordinance was a perfect fit to the pattern of events at the Constitutional Convention in Philadelphia. It accurately addressed the fear of the northerners that they would have to compete with slave labor as they went west—a fear that could have split the union.

William Grayson of Virginia, in a letter to James Monroe in August, 1787, suggested both economic and political reasons why the South agreed to the division.[35] One economic reason was to prevent slave-labor competition in growing tobacco and indigo north of the Ohio; another was to enhance the value of Virginia lands on the south side of the Ohio.[36] One political reason may have included the desirability of securing the return of fugitive slaves. But Grayson says nothing one way or the other about the major political reason: getting the North to accept the "Connecticut compromise" counting three-fifths of the slaves as "population" entitled to representation in the House. The three-fifths rule also assured the South that there would be no more short-term efforts by the North to challenge slavery.[37]

Historian Staughton Lynd has clearly outlined the relationship between the Convention and the Congress as it relates to the Northwest Ordinance in *Class Conflict, Slavery, and the United States Constitution.*[38] His analysis suggests that North and South each expected the ordinance to benefit their political interests and were prepared to gamble on future developments. He also argues that slavery in the northwest might have been given up by the South at the Constitutional Convention then in progress in Philadelphia, in exchange for counting slaves as three-fifths of a person in establishing representation in the House of Representatives.[39] But the three-fifths rule had already been agreed to by the Committee on July 3, before the southern contingent left for Philadelphia. While that agreement was not final, it was the key to holding the nation together and was bound to be given substantial weight by the delegates.

Yet Lynd may have been correct in another sense. The outrage expressed at slavery at the Convention after June 30 was at least in part the fear that slavery would extend into the Ohio country and foreclose development by individual farmers. This concern was most likely recognized by Benjamin Franklin or Richard Henry Lee shortly after Madison made his "it's about slavery" speech on June 30. Once the northern fears of the expansion of slavery to their west were removed, they agreed to go along with the three-fifths rule.

Lynd's interpretation underestimates the importance to the North of the prospect of being enclosed in a nation of slavery, a concern expressed repeatedly at the Convention from June 30 to July 14.[40] The agreement reflected in the ordinance was to draw a line between slave and free territory and the states that would emerge from it—a profound decision which limited the operation of the three-fifths rule to states that were south of the Ohio River, and would later be extended to the west after the Louisiana Purchase.

Lynd's analysis depends on a showing that the Convention in Philadelphia was aware of the details of the Northwest Ordinance by July 12, when the Convention approved the three-fifths formula.[41] Legal historian Paul Finkelman has pointed out that the travelers from New York to Philadelphia, who Lynd relies on as carriers of the news, could not have done so, because the antislavery provision of the ordinance was not introduced until the 13 of July.[42]

When the genesis of the antislavery clause in the North-west Ordinance is found to have been in Philadelphia, not New York, problems of timing are avoided. The crucial date for Congressional action in New York was July 13. Information on the action reached Philadelphia late July 14 or early July 15. The relevant Convention action in reliance on the Northwest Ordinance took place July 16 with the adoption of the Connecticut compromise. That compromise included the adoption, without debate, of the three-fifths rule. The Convention adjourned after a brief discussion of other matters.[43]

When they first came to the Constitutional Convention in Philadelphia, southern states planned to vigorously protect their interest in slavery.[44] Their starting point was the pro-slavery position that had been written into the Articles of Confederation through the privileges and immunities clause and later confirmed in the 1784 ordinance. The status quo treated slavery as lawful and protected in all the territories.

The Virginia plan did not change the anti-*Somerset* provision of the privileges and immunities clause of the Articles. Later in the Convention, the southern states successfully included three-fifths of their slaves in determining how many representatives a state was entitled to in the House of Representatives.[45] They postponed the abolition of the slave trade for twenty years by proposing a requirement of a two-thirds majority for legislation regulating commerce, and then surrendering the demand as a compromise.[46] They also secured federal assistance in the case of slave rebellions, and the right to the return of fugitive slaves, thus continuing their repudiation of the rule in the *Somerset* case.[47] In the course of the debates, southern delegates repeatedly threatened to walk out if their terms were not met.[48]

Yet in New York, they agreed to the antislavery status of the northwest territory, and the free states they knew would emerge from it. The key point the southern delegates gained by supporting the ordinance was that they satisfied the northern demand for a slave-free territory. The territory was divided along the line that Ellsworth had suggested on June 29. The North then accepted the Connecticut compromise and the union was saved. The emergence of new states in the territory south of the Ohio would protect southern slavery interests in the Senate, while the three-fifths rule would protect them in the House by giving greater weight to white voters in the South than to white voters in the North.

Other reasons have been given for the willingness of the South to give up on slavery in the northwest. In winter climates, slavery was not viewed as cost effective as in the South. While this condition was not prohibitive along the Ohio, it would make slavery less cost effective further north. The northwest territory was a big headache for the country, as it had been for Britain. Virginia had ceded her western lands to the Continental Congress in 1783, in part to get out of, or resolve, the tangle of claims which had developed there, along with Indian troubles and foreign intrigue.[49]

Some southerners may have believed that the antislavery clause would weaken the northwest territory relative to the South by curtailing the use of slave labor. In addition, they may have believed Monroe's report on the poor quality of lands in the territory so that that they were not overly interested or concerned.[50]

Paul Finkelman, a widely recognized student of the Northwest Ordinance, has concluded,

> The vigorous defense of slavery by the Deep South delegates to the Convention stands in contrast to the adoption of [the antislavery provision] of the ordinance, if that article is seen as "antislavery." However, it is likely that the Deep South delegates in Congress thought that the article would protect slavery where it was and allow it to spread to the southwest; thus they may have seen the article as pro-slavery, or at least as protective of slavery.[51]

Historian Charles Beard noted that the southern interests were different from those of the North:

> The third group of landed proprietors were the slave holders. It seems curious at first glance that the representatives of southern states which sold raw materials and wanted competition in shipping were willing to join a union that subjected them to commercial regulations devised immediately in behalf of northern interests....An examination of the records shows that they were aware of this apparent incongruity, but that there were overbalancing compensations to be secured in a strong federal government....The southern planter was also as much concerned with

slave revolts as the creditor in Massachusetts was concerned in putting down Shays's "desperate debtors," and therefore supported the national government as an agency to suppress such revolts.[52]

Certainly the southerners would not want restless, rebellious, poor, antislavery Yankees to burst out of New England and come south.[53] Despite the stated fears about slave revolts, the only real rebellion that the Virginians had ever faced came from poor whites, not blacks.[54] Bacon's rebellion of 1676 was undertaken, said the official version, by a white "rabble of the basest sort of people, whose condition was such as by a change could not admit of worse."[55]

But Nathanial Bacon himself was well born and came to Virginia with enough money to build a house and buy a plantation. At the time, Governor William Berkeley was trying to placate Native American tribes in the area to reduce attacks on colonists. Bacon's approach was to attack and kill Native Americans to reduce the danger to the colonists. Many of the settlers agreed with Bacon. This brought him in conflict with the governor. Bacon accused him of misconduct and marched on the capital with a band of settlers. Thereafter, when much maneuvering had taken place between the Berkeley and Bacon factions, Bacon burned Jamestown to the ground. He died and his rebellion sputtered out after more killing and burning.[56]

The fears of white revolt in Virginia led to the formalization and expansion of race slavery. The reports of Shays's Rebellion in 1786, coupled with similar expressions of debtor discontent in the middle colonies and in Virginia itself, must have rekindled memories of Bacon's rebellion, and the extensive damage that poor whites could do if aroused. Better that the Yankees keep their antislavery and other "antisocial" attitudes north of the Ohio.

This was no hypothetical risk. Northerners were already "invading" the South. The white population of the lower South increased dramatically between 1750 and 1780. Historian Jack Greene observes, "A substantial part of the astonishing white-population growth among the lower southern states was, like that of Virginia, the result of immigration from the northern states."[57] This population shift was noted by southern representatives at the Constitutional Convention.

Channeling the Yankees northwestward created little risk that the northwest territory would rapidly spawn new states in that area because of Monroe's reports about the barren quality of the land.

Leaving the northwest slave-free would have other advantages. Antislavery southerners like Edward Coles and free blacks might migrate to the territory.[58] Southerners may have viewed the territory as a safety valve or dumping ground for antislavery sentiment, protecting slavery from erosion from within as well as invasion from without.[59] The expansion of slavery south of the Ohio would be less troubled by southern antislavery ideas.[60] This thought of using the territory as a kind of Siberia was not unusual. In 1801, at the legislature's request, Governor Monroe wrote to President Jefferson about the possibility of purchasing "lands outside the state"—including lands in the northwest territory—to send persons "obnoxious to the laws or dangerous to the peace of society."[61] Jefferson asked in response, "Should we be willing to have such a colony in contact with us?" He had a different view of the future. He anticipated continental expansion of "a people speaking the same language, governed in similar forms and by similar laws; nor can we contemplate with satisfaction either blot or mixture on that surface."[62]

This prospect of the northwest as a safety valve for anti-slavery feeling might explain the pleasure that Edward Carrington took in telling James Monroe how the Yankees were going to move into the northwest territory. And why Manasseh Cutler used the argument that Yankees would settle the northwest to persuade his southern friends to support the land deal; and why Richard Henry Lee was proud of the "strong toned" government of the Northwest Ordinance.

The channeling of New England antislavery people north of the Ohio protected the institution of slavery in the rest of the country. This could be accomplished while keeping the constitution free of antislavery taint, and building into it numerous protections for slavery interests. This was the real pro-slavery interest in the summer of 1787, which Madison crystallized on June 30 when he defined the primary difference between the states as not size but slavery.

This channeling of antislavery people to the North had consequences on the ground. Antislavery supporters would prefer the "free air" of the northwest territory on religious, ideological, and practical economic grounds, including the avoidance of slave competition and its depreciation of the value of white labor. They would—over time—create a society that viewed slavery as wrong. Slave owners, in turn, would not risk their property northwest of the Ohio when they could go elsewhere.[63]

Abraham Lincoln maintained that the ordinance diverted settlers to Missouri between 1810 and 1820. "The number of slaves in Missouri increased by 7,211, while in Illinois in the same ten years, they decreased by 51."[64] Lincoln made this comment while refuting Steven Douglas's claim that the Northwest Ordinance did not prevent slavery from moving into a western territory. Therefore, although slave owners did settle in southern Ohio, Indiana, and Illinois, they did not become sufficiently influential to overturn the ordinance. But the risk of an antislavery northwest was a distant one in 1787, while the Ellsworth-Morris threat to split the union at the Convention in Philadelphia was immediate.

These considerations converged to identify the fundamental reason why southerners supported the slavery prohibition in the Northwest Ordinance. It is the same reason which led them into the Revolution—the protection of the institution of slavery—in light of the post-Revolutionary War conditions. Creating a free area north of the Ohio kept Yankees in the north while protecting slavery interests in the south. The result was the creation of the largest slave-free area in the western world.

This then, was the mutual modification by North and South of the arrangement of 1774 between John Adams and the southern gentlemen.[65] The unlimited pro-slavery arrangement of 1774 was changed by mutual agreement between southern and northern interests and sealed by the unanimous vote of the Continental Congress for the Northwest Ordinance.[66] With the territory divided between slave and free areas, the states could remain united. A principle was established that addressed the slavery issue for eighty years: a Congressionally drawn line between slave and free states would maintain a balance of power in the national government.

Placing the conclusion concerning the future of slavery in the ordinance instead of the constitution had an additional significant effect; it enhanced the likelihood of adoption of the constitution. It reduced the emphasis on the issue of slavery in both North and South. Antislavery northerners would not attack the pro-slavery elements in the constitution as heavily; advocates for slavery would be given comfort by the pro-slavery provisions, and not be overly concerned with expansion of slavery into the North.[67] It served to stabilize the nation until 1850, long after the British had freed the slaves in the West Indies.

The ordinance was the foundation of the Connecticut Compromise in which the states were given equal votes in the Senate while in the House, slave-state power was enhanced by counting three-fifths of the slaves toward state representation. This balance of interests achieved what Madison had first sought at the Convention on June 30, when he identified the struggle as between slave and non-slave states.

Ironically, the division of the nation over slavery hardened some whites' perceptions that blacks were their economic enemies because their cheap labor diminished the worth of white labor. Where physical labor was the primary necessity for survival, not to mention prosperity, the difference in labor value of whites and blacks was the difference between bare subsistence and some level of comfort.

This explains, at least in part, why whites in the South fought so hard to keep their one or two slaves, and why whites in the North were so adamant in their opposition to slavery. There is no "sole cause" of the social phenomena of black exploitation and subordination. But the division of the union in 1787, which provided the first extension of human rights to blacks, simultaneously sharpened race-based difficulties that confront us to this day.

John Adams recognized that the two documents—the Constitution and the Northwest Ordinance—constituted a single new system of government. In the fall of 1787 he wrote:

> In the course of last summer, two authorities have appeared....The first is an ordinance of Congress of the 13th of July, 1787, for the government of the territory of the United States northwest of the river Ohio. The second is the report of the convention at Philadelphia of the 17th of September, 1787....The new system, which seems admirably calculated to unite their interests and affections, and bring them to an uniformity of principles and sentiments, is equally well combined to unite their wills and forces as a single nation; a result of accommodation cannot be supposed to reach the ideas of perfection of any one.[68]

The Northwest Ordinance was not an accident, or an independent fortuitous event, or the result of cool weather.

It was an extraordinary act of statesmanship in a situation that otherwise would have produced the dissolution of the union, resulting in two or three nations competing for territory and resources. At least one of those nations would have maintained slavery into an indefinite future. The British probably anticipated such a prospect when they turned the huge and ungoverned territory over to the United States.

The various compromises of the founding fathers produced a single nation. The price slaves paid for the maintenance of that nation was nearly a hundred more years of slavery, and another hundred years of subordination to white "superiority." Their descendants—indeed, all citizens—should understand the price they paid for our liberties.

# Chapter 12

# Cementing the Bargain: Ratification by Virginia and the First Congress

The Northwest Ordinance was adopted on Friday, July 13, 1787. The ninety-mile trip from New York to Philadelphia took a day and a half by a coach service called "the flying machine."[1] Therefore, news that the ordinance had been adopted in New York reached Philadelphia by late Saturday, July 14, or early Sunday, July 15.

By Sunday afternoon, the northern delegates in Philadelphia knew that slavery had been prohibited in the northwest territory. They may have caucused that day to decide whether to end their objections to the three-fifths rule that they had resisted so vigorously the previous week. We do know that on Monday morning, the sixteenth of July, the Connecticut compromise was adopted. States would have equal representation in the Senate, and in the House they would be represented in proportion to their population plus three-fifths of their slaves. Northerners had abandoned their objections of the previous weeks.

If Franklin or Lee, or anyone else, had discussed with the northerners the possibility that the no-slavery clause in the Northwest Ordinance would be adopted by the Congress, the northerners would have had time to think about how to respond. If—as seems more likely—the southerners had decided to adopt the ordinance to show their good faith without prior discussion with the northerners, then the northerners would have had little time to decide what to do. Either way, it was decision time for them. The interests of their constituents in a no-slavery zone in which to settle—and their personal interests—won out.

The arrival of the news about the Northwest Ordinance changed the tone of the Convention from the snarling hostility of June 29 through July 14. Now it was calm and business-like. Historian Catherine Drinker Bowen, among others, has attributed this change in tone to a cooling breeze; but northern tempers about slavery were so hot in the previous week that it is unlikely that a breeze could have calmed them.[2] The extent to which slavery could expand in the West was just as important to the North on Monday, July 16, as it had been on Saturday, July 14, when it was discussed by the Convention.[3]

The northern tempers cooled on Monday, July 16, because they had won equal votes in the Senate and a huge slave-free area where their constituents could go west without facing plantation owners grown rich from slave labor or slaves whose presence threatened their jobs and wage level. Whatever other factors may have been at work in producing the Northwest Ordinance—and there were many—the overriding concern, as expressed by Timothy Pickering of

Massachusetts in 1785, was to prevent this threat to white workers from spreading throughout the new nation.

To be sure, the emerging abolitionist movement, the inconsistency of slavery with the principles of the Revolution, a rise in religious sensibilities, the manipulations of land speculators, and the ambitions of political figures contributed to the outcome. But these are soft variables— difficult to measure and weigh. In a world where most work for most people was physical labor, the presence of black labor that was free to its owners had chilling consequences for white workers in the northern tier of states. The adoption of the Northwest Ordinance in Philadelphia is the only viable explanation for the decision of the northern states to give up their attacks on the three-fifths rule.

The Connecticut compromise for equal votes in the Senate and whites plus three-fifths of the slaves in the House passed five to four.[4] Connecticut voted for it, despite earlier threats to secede. New Jersey, Delaware, Maryland, and North Carolina supported it. The opponents were Pennsylvania, Virginia, South Carolina, and Georgia, all of whom were opposed to the equality of votes in the Senate.[5] New York was absent, but Virginia governor Edmund Randolph noted that if New York had been present, the vote would have been six to four in favor.[6] On the other hand, if Massachusetts had voted against it, instead of being divided, it would have been five to five, and as a tie would have lost.

After the vote, Governor Randolph of Virginia appeared to be disconcerted. He asked for an adjournment so that "the large states might consider the steps proper to be taken in the present solemn crisis of the business, and that the small states might also deliberate on the means of conciliation."[7]

Patterson, whose New Jersey plan had succeeded with respect to the Senate, considered Randolph's statement as a threat by the large states to walk out of the Convention and end the Confederation. Patterson told Randolph that "No conciliation could be admissible on the part of the smaller states on any other ground than that of an equality of votes in the second branch [Senate]. If Mr. Randolph would reduce to form his motion for an adjournment *sine die*, he [Patterson] would second it with all his heart."[8] An indefinite adjournment—without a date to reconvene—would mean the end of the Convention and the Union.

Randolph hastily backed away from this interpretation of his statement. He "had never entertained an idea of an adjournment *sine die*, and was sorry that his meaning had been so readily and strangely interpreted. He had in view merely an adjournment till tomorrow in order that some conciliatory experiment might if possible be devised."

Randolph denied threatening a walk-out. Patterson became more gracious. He seconded the motion for a day's adjournment. The states divided five to five on the adjournment question.

Then cooler heads prevailed. Elbridge Gerry said Massachusetts, which had voted "no" on adjournment, would change its vote because "they saw no new ground of compromise, but as it seemed to be the opinion of so many states that a trial should be made, the state would now concur in the adjournment."[9]

John Rutledge of South Carolina, a state that had also opposed the adjournment, could

> see no chance of a compromise. The little
> states were fixt....All that the large states
> had to do was to decide whether they would
> yield or not....Had we not better keep the
> govt. up a little longer, hoping that another
> convention will supply our omissions, than
> abandon everything to hazard. Our con-
> stituents will be very little satisfied with us if
> we take the latter course.[10]

The motion to adjourn "til tomorrow" was adopted
seven to two with one divided. Massachusetts and South
Carolina had changed their votes.

A hastily organized caucus of members from the larger
states and some from the smaller states met the next morning, before the Convention session began. At this meeting,
the states that had opposed equal votes in the Senate were
indecisive and vague, and could not agree on a strategy to
oppose the result. Madison, who had fought the equality of
votes in the Senate with all his skill, was unhappy to report
this conclusion, but report it he did.

> The result of this consultation satisfied the
> smaller states that they had nothing to
> apprehend from a union of the larger, in any
> plan whatever against the equality of votes
> in the Senate.[11]

In the Convention that morning, the opponents of equal
representation in the Senate opened a new front by questioning how much power to give a Congress that would not

be entirely elected by proportional representation as they had wished. From that point forward, the Convention settled down to business. As historian Lance Banning put it, "The bargain of July 16 assured that the Convention would succeed."[12] By July 26, it adjourned so that a committee of detail could begin to shape the issues that had been resolved in the previous days. The Convention reconvened on August 6, and began to work through the report of the committee. That report structured the rest of the Convention's work. The discussion at the Convention became more technical and less emotional. Slavery related issues were discussed on August 21, 22, 25, and September 10.[13] Some harsh words were exchanged, but the level of contention and dissatisfaction expressed in early July never resurfaced. The slavery issues were interspersed with other matters as the Convention moved toward its conclusion. These issues never dominated the way that they had in early July.

On Tuesday, August 21, toward the end of the day, the Convention voted to prohibit taxes on exported goods. Luther Martin of Maryland proposed a provision to permit a prohibition or tax on the import of slaves because the three-fifths rule would encourage such importation.[14] Nobody else was interested. John Rutledge of South Carolina said, "The true question at present is whether the southern states shall or shall not be parties to the union."[15]

Oliver Ellsworth of Connecticut, who had been prepared to leave the union over the three-fifths rule before the Northwest Ordinance was passed, now took a different view. "Let every state import what it pleases. The morality or wisdom of slavery are considerations belonging to the states themselves."[16]

Charles Pinckney from South Carolina seconded Rutledge. "South Carolina can never receive a plan if it prohibits the slave trade. In every proposed extension of the powers of Congress, that state has expressly and watchfully excepted that of meddling with the importation of Negroes."[17]

The next day, August 22, the discussion continued. Roger Sherman joined his Connecticut colleague Ellsworth in opposing any change in the situation of the three-fifths rule, because "the abolition of slavery seemed to be going on in the U.S. and the good sense of the several states would probably by degrees complete it."[18]

George Mason of Virginia repeated the long-held Virginia position that the international slave trade should be subject to restriction. Elsworth repeated his "let us not intermeddle" speech of the previous day. Charles Pinckney of South Carolina said that the southern states needed the discretion to decide whether to stop importing slaves, because "South Carolina and Georgia cannot do without slaves."[19]

In the end, the Convention voted to refer to a committee issues concerning whether there should be restrictions on the slave trade and whether restrictions on foreign commerce should require a two-thirds vote. Gouverneur Morris from Pennsylvania recommended committing both issues to a committee because "these things may form a bargain among the northern and southern states."[20] The vote to refer the issues was nine to two.

The Convention was now adept at referring difficult matters to a committee and going forward with the easier issues. On August 22, these difficult issues included ex post facto laws (making criminal laws retroactive) and bills of attainder (legislative determination of individual guilt).

The threats of South Carolina delegates to walk out did not generate the heat of July 2 through 14. Almost all members of the Convention were now in a mood to complete their work. The walk-out threats by the southerners were not severe enough to interrupt the decision-making process.

August 23 was taken up with totally different matters. On August 24, the committee reported, recommending that the slave trade be allowed to continue until the year 1800 and that a requirement of a two-thirds vote on regulation of commerce be eliminated.[21] This bargain was put off to be considered on August 25, and the Convention proceeded with other business. On August 25, General Pinckney moved that the slave trade be allowed to continue until 1808. The motion passed by seven votes to four.[22] Morris, with tongue in cheek, wanted to name North Carolina, South Carolina, and Georgia as the beneficiaries of this extension, but he withdrew the proposal after a trio of negative comments.[23] The Convention adjourned until Monday, August 27. That day was taken up with details of the judicial system. The discussion was carried over into Tuesday, August 28, followed by voting on several other less controversial issues. These included the provision dealing with privileges and immunities of residents of one state when they entered another state.[24]

The privileges and immunities clause in the Articles of Confederation was reshaped to conform with the agreement to exclude slaves from the northwest territory. The

Articles had allowed "the removal of property imported into any state to any other state of which the owner is an inhabitant."[25] The notion that a slave owner from Virginia could buy land in Ohio and bring his slaves up to work it, taking them back when the snow fell so they could continue to do useful work, was inconsistent with the concept of a slave-free northwest territory. This clause was neatly snipped from the Articles without debate or explanation.[26] The clause as adopted read:

> The citizens of each state shall be entitled to all privileges and immunities of citizens in the several states.[27]

General Pinckney objected, wishing to continue the Articles version of the privileges and immunities clause. Madison's notes brushed this effort off as saying he "seemed to wish some provision be included in favor of property in slaves."[28]

This deletion was consistent with the agreement that the Ohio River would be the dividing line between slave and free states. Pinckney may have been attempting to improve the agreement, but the committee on detail ignored his concern. This decision completed the understanding which had been reached earlier concerning the no-slave status of the northwest territory. This change in the privileges and immunities clause made clear that the master's right to take a slave into a non-slave state and then force him to return south—guaranteed in the Articles—was not a privilege or immunity of a citizen of the United States. This clause coupled with the fugitive-slave clause created a distinction between slaves who escaped from a slave state and were subject to recapture, and slaves who had been brought into a free state by their masters and could not be compelled to return.

At the end of same day, Tuesday, August 28, 1787, Butler and Pinckney from South Carolina suggested including fugitive slaves and servants in the extradition clause relating to returning criminals to the state where a crime was committed, but Sherman of Connecticut pointed out that there was "no more propriety in the public seizing and surrendering a slave or servant than a horse."[29] Butler withdrew his proposal to rephrase it.

On Wednesday, August 29, the package deal concerning the number of votes needed to regulate commerce and the duration of the slave trade was adopted. The slave trade was allowed to continue for twenty years, until 1808.[30] The effort to require a two-thirds vote for regulation of commerce was rejected, meaning that a simple majority would be sufficient to adopt controls on commerce. Both provisions were adopted without dissent.

The provision dealing with fugitive slaves was more complex. The Northwest Ordinance had adopted King's draft fugitive slave clause of 1785 without substantial change. It applied only to slaves "from whom labor or service is lawfully claimed in any one of the original states." The word "lawfully" was deleted and the limitation to slaves escaping from the original states was removed, making the provision applicable to slaves escaping states which might be created later.[31]

No person held to service or labor in one

state, under the laws thereof, escaping into
another, shall, in consequence of any law or
regulation therein, be discharged from such
service or labor, but shall be delivered up on
claim of the party to whom such service or
labor may be due.[32]

This clause was also adopted without discussion. By
1787, the fugitive-slave issue would become important, as
slaves began escaping north and the northern states were
not helpful concerning their return.[33] The fugitive-slave
clause satisfied both northern and southern economic
interests. Southerners might expect the clause to help get
some of their runaway slaves back or discourage them
from seeking freedom in the first place. The clause also
assured northerners, concerned that former slaves would
drive down labor rates, that they would not have to compete with so many escaped slaves seeking jobs that whites
would otherwise hold.[34]

Nevertheless, the continuous efforts of slaves to escape
across the line of the Ohio River, and of slave catchers to
repossess them, served in the nineteenth century to sharpen
the distance and increase the hostility between the settlers of
slave states and those of free states. The antislavery mood in
the northern states during the nineteenth century politicized
a number of situations where slave owners sought to use the
judicial process to recover their "property."[35]

Thus the Constitution plus the Northwest Ordinance
drew a line, not only between slave and free territories but
between states which in the future might be created. It
continued the subordination of free-state law to that of the

slave states but only with respect to fugitives. The case of a slave who had come to a free state or territory with his master and refused to return—the issue in the *Somerset* case—presumably would be subject to the law of the jurisdiction in which the question of freedom was raised. This was the rule announced in Somerset's case. The United States Supreme Court in the *Dred Scott* case of 1857 disavowed the distinction between slave and free states drawn in the Northwest Ordinance with respect to black slaves. It held that slavery was lawful everywhere in the country. This decision all but guaranteed that a civil war would follow.

The final reference to slavery at the Convention came on September 10, in a discussion of the method of amending the Constitution:

> Mr. Rutledge said he never could agree to give a power by which the articles relating to slaves might be altered by the states not interested in that property and prejudiced against it. In order to obviate this objection, these words were added...'provided that no amendments which may be made prior to the year 1808, shall in any manner affect' [the extension of the slave trade until 1808].[36]

The interaction between the Convention and the Congress illuminates the role of Manasseh Cutler of Massachusetts, the agent for the Ohio Company, which had been seeking extensive lands in the northwest territory since 1783. Cutler was a distinguished clergyman, a military chaplain during the Revolution, a doctor, and a scientist. Ohio Company speculators, including many former soldiers, had been seeking land in the northwest since 1783 to encourage migration from the crowded North. They petitioned Congress for land again in 1787.

Cutler made a trip to both New York and Philadelphia in July of 1787. He arrived in New York on July 5, presented letters of introduction to members of Congress on July 6, attended meetings with the committee that was considering the Ohio Company proposition, saw the sights, and met extensively with people both in and out of Congress who could aid in his project.[37] On July 10, while awaiting the report of the committee drafting a revised Northwest Ordinance, a committee composed of Carrington, King, Dane, and Bension reported favorably on the Ohio Company's request to buy land in the territories from the Congress. All except Bension were also members of the committee that would recommend the Northwest Ordinance.

Cutler then went to Philadelphia for five days where he met with many of the delegates to the Constitutional Convention. He was hustling the most important people in the nation over the terms of the land deal which he hoped to make with the Congress. He had thought the ordinance issue was largely settled when he left New York. The remaining question involved the terms on which the land deal would be made, and the personnel who would govern the northwest territory.

Cutler and Congress engaged in hard bargaining after his return to New York from Philadelphia on July 19. On July 23, Congress passed a bill setting terms for an agreement with the Ohio Company which were not favorable enough for Cutler. He reacted by threatening to take his money and credit and buy lands then held by some of the states. He also dropped General Samuel Holden Parsons as the Company's candidate for governor of the territory, and threw his support to Congressional president Arthur St. Clair, a Scottish-born Revolutionary War soldier who had moved to Pennsylvania. Cutler's diary suggests that his decision to drop Parsons in favor of St. Clair was well received by his "southern friends," and smoothed the way for the contract. St. Clair's views were well known to southerners whom he had served with under General Nathanael Greene in the Revolution. They may have seen him as more "flexible" toward southern interests than General Parsons, a puritanical New Englander, was likely to be.

Once it was assured that St. Clair would become governor of the territory, he used his influence to gain support for the contract with the Ohio Company. St. Clair's later pro-slavery interpretation of the Northwest Ordinance may have been anticipated by his southern supporters for the governorship. St. Clair lobbied the northeastern delegates to support the proposed deal, and on July 27, Congress adopted more favorable terms, enabling the Ohio Company to buy millions more acres of land than it had originally sought.[38]

The haste in which this newly modeled Northwest Ordinance was adopted is attributable to the Congress's desire for the land deal to go through. The inclusion of such fundamental matters as slavery would have caused at least raised eyebrows, unless some such matters had been agreed upon beforehand by those in Philadelphia who found the ordinance compatible with the protection of slavery.

The agreement to divide the federal territory into slave and free areas was ratified by the Virginia legislature in 1788, and by the First Congress under the Constitution in 1789 and 1790.[39]

In December, 1788, after the Constitution had been ratified, Virginia had an opportunity to invalidate, or at least thoroughly confuse the legality of the Northwest Ordinance. In 1783, Virginia had ceded the northwest territory to the federal government, on condition that ten states be created in the territory north of the Ohio River in accordance with a plan developed by Jefferson. But by 1786, on the basis of a recommendation from Monroe, Congress concluded that this division was impractical.[40] It asked Virginia to modify its cession agreement to allow between three and five states in the territory. Congress included the three to five state proviso in the Northwest Ordinance, and, after its adoption, sent it to Virginia with a request that Virginia ratify the change. Edward Carrington, who had voted for the ordinance as a delegate to the Continental Congress had no doubt that Virginia would do so. He reported to Jefferson on October 23, 1788:

> The western territory belonging to the United States has more effectually received the attention of Congress during this session than it ever did before. Enclosed you will receive the ordinance for establishing a temporary government there, and providing for its more easy passage into permanent state governments. Under the old arrangements the

country might upon the whole have become
very populous, and yet be inadmissable to the
rights of state government, which would have
been disgusting to them and ultimately inconvenient for the empire. The new arrangement
depends on the accession of Virginia which
there can be no doubt of obtaining.[41]

Virginia did so on December 30, 1788. The Virginia legislation recited the provision of the Northwest Ordinance
which required that the constitutions and governments be
formed in conformity to the principles contained in the
ordinance—which included the no-slavery clause. The
Virginia legislature, knowing that these principles included
a prohibition on slavery, "ratified and confirmed" the
Northwest Ordinance.[42]

Both Congress and the Virginia legislature assumed that
a modification of the cession agreement was necessary to
effectuate the ordinance. Although the formal legal relation
between the cession agreement and the ordinance was
never determined, it was assumed that Virginia had veto
power over the ordinance. While the vote of the Virginia
delegates to the Constitutional Convention in support of
the ordinance might have been considered idiosyncratic or
accidental by some historians, the ratification by the legislature most certainly was done with full knowledge of its
antislavery character. The absence of debate about the matter in Virginia suggests that the division of the territory had
been agreed to on grounds understood and accepted by the
Virginians.[43]

On August 7, 1789, the First Congress sitting under the

new Constitution adopted as Chapter VIII of the Statutes of the United States, appearing in 1 Stat. 50, "An act to provide for the government of the territory northwest of the river Ohio." The introductory clause read:

> Whereas in order that the ordinance of the United States in Congress assembled, for the government of the territory northwest of the river Ohio may continue to have full effect, it is requisite that certain provisions should be made, so as to adapt the same to the present Constitution of the United States.

Those provisions required the governor to report to the president rather than Congress, provided for presidential appointment and removal of officers with senatorial advice and consent, and for the secretary to act in the absence of the governor. There was no debate on this implicit ratification of the ordinance, which brought it into line with the new Constitution by redefining the chain of authority stipulated in the Articles of Confederation.[44]

The same Congress, in 1790, again ratified the Northwest Ordinance by making it applicable to territories south of the Ohio, with one fundamental difference—slavery was permitted. This difference is further evidence of the understanding that the Northwest Ordinance drew a line on slavery in the United States. The language used to accomplish this result was as obscure as that used in the Constitution concerning slavery.

> The inhabitants...shall enjoy all the

privileges, benefits, and advantages set forth in the ordinance of the late Congress for the government of the territory...northwest of the river Ohio. And the government of the said territory shall be similar to that which is now exercised in the territory northwest of the Ohio; except so far as is otherwise provided in an act of Congress of the present session, entitled "An act to accept a cession of the claims of the state of North Carolina to a certain district of western territory." [45]

The act accepting cession from North Carolina had been approved on April 2, 1790.[46] It approved the "deed of cession" from North Carolina that contained the following condition:

The territory so ceded shall be laid out and formed into a state or states, containing a suitable extent of territory, the inhabitants of which shall enjoy all the privileges, benefits, and advantages set forth in [the Northwest Ordinance]...**provided always that no regulation made or to be made by Congress shall tend to emancipate slaves.**[47] (emphasis added)

When the cession act was considered in the House of Representatives on March 26, 1790, the Annals of the Congress reported that:

A condition in the Act of Cession, relative to the emancipation of slaves, that Congress should not (as in the act for the government of the western territory) provide for their freedom occasioned some debate; an amendment was prepared and debated, but not adopted.[48]

With these few words, the First Congress under the Constitution confirmed that the line between slave and free territories had been drawn at the Ohio. It also decided, in response to a petition by Ben Franklin on behalf of the Pennsylvania Society for the Abolition of Slavery, that

Congress have no authority to interfere in the emancipation of slaves, or in the treatment of them within any of the states; it remaining with the several states alone to provide any regulations therein, which humanity and true policy may require.[49]

But the territories were different. There, Congress could and did regulate slavery, until the political will failed in 1854. In the Kansas-Nebraska Act, Congress declared that popular sovereignty would decide whether a state would be free or slave. The Civil War was then only seven years away.[50]

Whatever the problems and shortcomings in the northwest in connection with slavery in future years, the founding fathers had enacted the first blanket prohibition of slavery in the history of the world covering an area of two hundred sixty thousand square miles, or one-third of the land area of the United States at that time.[51] This was agreed to by the South for the same reason that had motivated their assumption of the leadership of the Revolution in 1774; the protection of slavery under the changed conditions and attitudes about slavery that had emerged since 1774 when John Adams made the deal to protect slavery at the beginning of the Revolution.

# Chapter 13

# How Then Should We View the Founding Fathers?

From 1787 on, the story of the interpretation and administration of the Northwest Ordinance is confused. In the early nineteenth century, political figures paid homage to the ordinance as a reflection of the higher law of the Magna Carta and the Declaration of Independence. Ultimately the Free Soil Party and the Republican Party emerged.[1] At the same time, administrators, judges, and congressional committees narrowly construed the antislavery provision, slave owners evaded or ignored it, and in 1857 the Supreme Court declared it to have no legal effect.[2] Nonetheless, the ordinance worked to channel pro-slavery settlers south and west of the territory, and encouraged those who were antislavery to settle in it.[3]

Indeed, it is impossible to imagine the Civil War without the Northwest Ordinance. Ohio, Indiana, and Illinois would have become slave states without it—it was a near thing.[4] The North could not have pursued a war without those states.

Beyond that, a Lincoln would not have emerged from a slave state. Lincoln's father, a farmer in Kentucky, crossed the Ohio into Indiana in 1816 when Lincoln was seven, partly because of religious objections to slavery, partly because he did not want to compete with slave labor, and partly because, by virtue of the Northwest Ordinance, land titles were clearer in the territory than where the southern land occupancy system had generated uncertainty.[5]

The enforcers of the Northwest Ordinance were real-estate speculators with lands in Kentucky and west of the Mississippi, who advised people moving west that the ordinance would prevent them from using or obtaining slaves, so they should steer clear of the territory. The result was that, while southern Ohio, Indiana, and Illinois were settled in part by Virginians and later Kentuckians, they never achieved the political mass that would enable them to overturn the antislavery principles of the ordinance, although they tried. Meanwhile the prospect of a slave-free state attracted those who opposed slavery.

One such person drawn to the territory because of the antislavery provision in the Illinois constitution was the extraordinary Virginia aristocrat Edward Coles. From an old Virginia family, Coles was a cousin of Dolley Madison and served for six years as President James Madison's secretary.

He took Thomas Jefferson's Declaration of Independence seriously. In 1814, six years after the end of Jefferson's presidency, he initiated a famous correspondence.[6]

He wrote to Jefferson:

My object is to entreat and beseech you to exert your knowledge and influence in devising and getting into operation some plan for the gradual emancipation of slavery....In the calm of this retirement you might, most beneficially to society, and with much addition to your own fame...put into complete practice those hallowed principles contained in that renowned Declaration, of which you were the immortal author.

Jefferson replied in a long letter, which can be summed up in the following:

No, I have overlived the generation with which mutual labors and perils begat mutual confidence and influence. This enterprise is for the young, for those who can follow it up and bear it through to consummation. It shall have all my prayers, and these are the only weapons of an old man.

Coles wrote back:

Your time of life I had not considered an obstacle to the undertaking. Doctor Franklin, to whom, by the way, Pennsylvania owes her own early riddance of the evils of slavery, was as actively and as usefully employed on as arduous duties after he had passed your age as he had ever been at any period in his life.

These brief extracts hardly do justice to the courtly and polite exchange between Coles and Jefferson. Coles carried out his plan, moved to Illinois, freed his slaves, gave them one hundred sixty acres each, and offered supportive activities while they adjusted to their new-found freedom. He was elected governor and successfully fought off a call to repeal the prohibition on slavery in the Illinois Constitution that had been required by the Northwest Ordinance. The vote was 6,822 against and 4,950 in favor. By a margin of 1,872 votes, the people of Illinois confirmed the antislavery provision in their constitution.

Alexis de Tocqueville, in his 1835 visit to America, traveled the Ohio and reported on the result of drawing the line between slavery and freedom, in a way somewhat akin to the recent Western view of the Iron Curtain:

> Upon the left bank of the stream the population is sparse; from time to time one discerns a troop of slaves loitering in the half-desert fields; the primeval forest reappears at every turn; society seems to be asleep, man to be idle, and nature alone offers a scene of activity and life. From the right bank, on the contrary, a confused hum is heard, which proclaims afar the presence of industry; the fields are covered with abundant harvests; the elegance of the dwellings announces the taste and activity of the laborers; and man appears to be in the enjoyment of that wealth and contentment which is the reward of labor.[7]

True or apocryphal, the Northwest Ordinance, by creating a slave-free area, broke the power of slavery. A populace evolved in the area who, because they did not exploit slave labor, were not blinded by self-interest into ignoring its evils.

The history of the United States from the Northwest Ordinance to the Civil War revolved around the principle of 1787 that Congress would divide the nation into slave and free areas and states. The details changed as the United States expanded to the west. With the Louisiana Purchase in 1803, the territory of the country more than doubled and there was no limitation on slavery in the new lands. In 1820, as a part of a deal known as the Missouri Compromise, Missouri was allowed to come in as a slave state while Maine came in as a free state, and the no-slave zone of the northwest territory was continued west of the Mississippi. In 1854, the national political will broke down; Congress left the choice of free or slave territory to be determined by the people on the ground. "Popular sovereignty" meant competition that was sometimes bloody between supporters of free states and those of slave states. The spirit of compromise and political accommodation which had held the country together for eighty years (1774–1854) had lost its vitality. The result was a substitution of war for politics.

The Supreme Court, in the *Dred Scott* decision of 1857, delivered the *coup de gras* to the political compromise over slavery in the Constitution and Northwest Ordinance of 1787, holding that Congress did not have the power to draw any line between free and slave states.[8] War was inevitable, unless slavery was accepted as the nationwide institution it had been between 1774 and 1787. By the 1850s, northern antislavery attitudes, strengthened by the experience of life under the Northwest Ordinance, made that impossible. The *Dred Scott* decision also made compromise by the South impossible, because the South had won the right to extend slavery where it wished. Therefore, it would no longer compromise.

The Civil War was in part due to Chief Justice Taney's failure in *Dred Scott* to appreciate two major events. The first was Mansfield's decision in the *Somerset* case. No one reading that decision could have written that Negroes had been regarded, as Taney wrote,

> So far inferior that they had no rights which
> the white man was bound to respect....And in
> no nation was this opinion more firmly fixed
> or more uniformly acted upon than by the
> English government and English people.[9]

Taney simply ignored Somerset's case in stating his conclusion about the English law.[10] It is still standard practice to rely on the English law background to understand and explain the context of American legal decisions. Taney's second error was in ignoring the understanding of 1787, which was confirmed by eight states at the Continental Congress, by the Constitutional Convention, by Virginia's amending its act of cession, and by the First Congress in 1789–1790, which sharpened the line between slave and free territories.

Ultimately, the Civil War resulted from the southern decision to try for a second time to preserve slavery by seceding from a government which challenged it. Secession from Britain had worked the first time, extending slavery an additional thirty years beyond its abolition in the British Empire.

This dream of a southern slave empire fueled the secessionist movement.[11] The dream ended at Gettysburg and Vicksburg in early July, 1863, the anniversary month of the Declaration of Independence, the Northwest Ordinance, and the French Declaration of the Rights of Man, which many Americans viewed as an expansion of the colonial revolution against British monarchy.

The "soldiers of the Northwest Ordinance" assured the outcome of the battles that were the turning point in the war.[12] At Gettysburg, the Iron Brigade from Wisconsin, Ohio, Indiana, and Michigan (formerly parts of the northwest territory) saved the cemetery ridge for the Union Army on the first day.[13] On the second day, the First Minnesota Regiment of 262 men plugged a gap in the cemetery ridge line that was attacked by 1,600 Alabamians.[14] On the third day, Michigan cavalry prevented Stuart's Confederate cavalry from supporting Picket's charge.[15] In the same month, Vicksburg surrendered to troops of General Ulysses S. Grant—a descendant of a Scot who had settled in Massachusetts in 1630. Grant was born in Ohio after it had become the first state to be carved out of the northwest territory.[16] While he was forcing General Robert E. Lee toward the Appomattox court house on April 9, 1865, three U.S. Colored Infantry Regiments from the Twenty-Fifth U.S. Army Corps, the first army corps made up of black soldiers, were among the seventeen regiments that blocked Lee's escape route to the west. Of the nearly one hundred eighty thousand black troops that served in the Union Army during the Civil War, at least one hundred thirty-eight thousand were former slaves.[17]

The end of the Civil War meant the end of formal slavery in the United States, but race subordination perpetuated the inferior position of the former slaves and their descendants for a century. This principle was challenged in 1948 when another political figure raised in the "pure air" of the northwest territory—Hubert Humphrey of Minnesota—admonished the Democratic Party to "get out of the shadow of states' rights and walk forthrightly into the sunshine of human rights."[18] Southerners seceded a third time, this time from the Democratic Party. But their efforts to maintain the remnants of slavery were frustrated in 1964 by two other political figures from the northwest territory, Congressman William McCullough of Ohio and Senator Everett Dirksen of Illinois, who led conservative Republicans to support the Civil Rights Act of 1964.[19] The act was given substantive content by yet another northwest territory descendant, Warren Burger of Minnesota, chief justice of the United States Supreme Court, in a 1971 opinion which reverberates to this day.[20] His opinion held that the Civil Rights Act was violated by employment practices that screened out a higher proportion of minorities than of whites and were not justified by job-related considerations. This one decision has played a major role in the substantial improvement in both minority and female employment opportunities since then.

The issues of race and slavery played an integral part in the foundation of the republic in 1774 and we have born the brunt of the compromises made to achieve a union ever since. The Declaration of Independence articulated—even if it was not fully pursued or even intended—a vision of equality which has continuously reminded, chided, inspired, and motivated us to seek what we might become.

Benjamin Franklin began the compromises with his solution to the deadlock in Philadelphia that saved the unity of the nation by establishing a principle of freedom that was applied to a third of the territory of the United States. But he did not stop there. In his last foray into public policy, he became president of the Pennsylvania Society for the Abolition of Slavery, and designed the first American Affirmative Action Plan to accompany the abolition of slavery. Reading it today, Franklin appears very much ahead of his time. In 1789, on behalf of the society, he wrote the following policy statement:

> Slavery is such an atrocious debasement of human nature that its very extirpation, if not performed with solicitous care, may sometimes open a source of serious evils....To instruct, to advise, to qualify those who have been restored to freedom, for the exercise and enjoyment of civil liberty, to promote in them habits of industry, to furnish them with employment suited to their age, sex, talents, and other circumstances, and to procure their children an education calculated for their future situation in life; these are the great outlines of the annexed plan.

The plan had four components, each to be carried out by a committee of the Pennsylvania Society for the Abolition of Slavery.[21]

The first component was a committee to assist with advice, instructions, and protection from wrongs to the former slaves, concern for their morals, and "other friendly services." The second was a committee of guardians to facilitate the training and education of children and young people. The third was a committee on education to influence the children to attend "the schools already established in this city, or form others with this view." And the fourth was a committee of employ, who "shall endeavour to procure constant employment" for laborers and to help them become apprentices in the skilled trades and also "assist in commencing business, such as appears to be qualified for it."

A comparison of Franklin's plan with modern equal opportunity employment and affirmative action programs will show the similarity of concern from 1789 to 2005. This comparison demonstrates that these issues have always been actively before the American people in one political form or another. The United States has discussed these issues longer, agonized over them more, legislated about them more, and fought about them more than any other country on earth. We solved the slavery question in blood, one hundred and thirty years ago, and forty years ago embarked on the effort to apply the political concept of equality to social and economic reality. Our struggles demonstrate the difficulties involved. We are the world's repository of experience in the difficulty of that endeavor.

How then should we view the founding fathers? Historian Gary Nash is highly critical. They should have let South Carolina and Georgia go in 1787. The rest of the nation did not need them. Therefore, the compromises on slavery were unnecessary to the union. Legal historian Paul Finkelman accuses Jefferson of "making a covenant with death."[23] Historian William Freehling accuses him of prolonged and unnecessary abdication concerning slavery.[24]

Nevertheless, they did settle many principles in their day in ways which we have good cause to applaud. They freed the world from the domination of monarchy, struggled toward a notion of democracy which is still unfolding, embraced principles of intellectual, political, and religious liberty, and made the first inroads on exploitive empire in adopting the "equal-footing" principle for new states. Measured against the magnitude of what they attempted, they succeeded greatly and are to be honored for it. Jefferson deserves particular attention for excluding the word "property" from the Declaration of Independence. Had he included it, it might have sanctified human slavery into an indefinite future. Its substitute, "pursuit of happiness," is wonderfully open-textured. It encompasses both private greed and the public happiness of participating in a just society. The quest for a just society reaches far back beyond the Scottish philosophers who were Jefferson's intellectual mentors, back to the Old Testament's command that "there shall be one law unto you, and unto the stranger who dwelleth within thy gates, for ye were strangers in the land of Egypt."[25] The quotation from James Madison toward the close of this book emphasizes that the driving influence of even the wisest wealthy slave owning political figure, was to widen those gates of which the Old Testament spoke to embrace a larger community.

But the founders did all this on the backs of generations of slaves. By their own standards, they were failures in dealing with slavery. Their actions were based on their view of race. Black slavery was hereditary—white indentured servitude was temporary.

We should honor the men and women of the past for their virtues. Their imperfections and failures both liberate and obligate us to be as creative as they were to mold new—and better—forms of social life. We are as free to shape the principles which they announced to our needs as they shaped eighteenth-century principles to theirs. We are not bit players trapped in a world drama where the greatest achievements took place long before our birth.

We are heirs to the American passion to struggle with the relation between liberty and equality that began in Philadelphia in September, 1774. We have addressed the race problem in a more forthright way than at any time since the Civil War. Our generation has spent forty years struggling to apply the Civil Rights acts of the 1960s which first recognized the right of people of color (and women) to full participation in economic and social affairs. Implementing these acts has sorely tested us all. Our difficulties enable us to better understand the difficulties which confronted those who made the decisions in 1774 and 1787. As they struggled to achieve a new vision of their world, we are doing so in ours. The founders—through the decisions of 1774 through 1787—created tensions that have defined our politics and policies for more than two hundred thirty years.

Understanding that the Revolution was fought, in part, to protect slavery reveals that the southerners who fought the Civil War to preserve the arrangement of 1787 were partly correct: the Constitution, viewed alone, supported slavery. We should acknowledge that fact and perhaps relieve resentments that persist to this day. But by the same token, the Northwest Ordinance banned slavery from a third of our territory. The Constitution would not have been adopted without the ordinance. The burden of continuing to address the race-slavery issue was passed on to succeeding generations, and remains with us today.

Fifty years ago, Gunnar Myrdal called our internal tensions over race the "American Dilemma," but "passion" is perhaps a more expressive term.[26] Jefferson struggled with the race-slavery issue all his life, and summed up his perception in 1820: "We have the wolf by the ear, and we can neither hold him, nor safely let him go."[27] He also succinctly spelled out the roots of our struggle with the "wolf" in his last letter before his death on July 4, 1826. These words, too, still shape the American psyche. Jefferson was too ill to come to Washington to celebrate the fiftieth anniversary of the Declaration of Independence. As he looked back over the half century, he was pleased that the sentiments in the Declaration still commanded the allegiance of his countrymen. He believed that the Declaration continued to be:

> the signal arousing men to…the palpable truth, that the mass of mankind has not been born with saddles on their backs, nor a favored few booted and spurred, ready to ride them.[28]

The first American revolution protected slavery; the second—the Civil War—destroyed it, but exposed a racism that maintained the subordination of black people. The third revolution—the post-World War II revolution—seeks substantive opportunity. All of these revolutions involved questions of race and equality. The difficulties in this, our national project, are enormous and confusing, and the results uncertain. As Lincoln said, "We simply must begin with and mold from disorganized and discordant elements. Nor is it a small additional embarrassment that we...differ among ourselves as to the mode, manner, and measure of reconstruction." The contemporary concern about affirmative action and reverse discrimination continues the American passion to pursue the relation between liberty and equality which began in Philadelphia in September, 1774. We still struggle with the wolf.

The curtain of history can be raised to illuminate the agreement to protect slavery in September, 1774, when representatives of the North and South first met. Without that agreement, there would have been no union of North and South. British power might well have overwhelmed those who sought freedom. But the agreement made in 1774 was amended in 1787 to divide the nation. The division was made to last as long as the political, economic, and social forces permitted. The framers in Philadelphia understood that the future of the nation would be influenced by growth to the west, and they considered that restricting slavery to the lands south of the Ohio was essential for the union to hold together. They could not know that their compromises toward the end of the eighteenth century would lead a president eighty years later to conclude that "a house divided against itself cannot stand." [29] Lincoln led the Civil War to end the institution that had been largely responsible for the birth of the nation.

It is wrong to impute ultimate wisdom to the framers of our country's political system. Theirs was the wisdom of time and place, and their concepts of individual freedom and religious liberty, rooted in an agricultural economy and sustained on the backs of slaves, were of great value. Their world was built on an optimistic assumption; that their successors would deal with the world that they faced with the same conviction and willingness to compromise that they had shown. What is significant about their original intent is the willingness to compromise to achieve basic and important objectives in the shadow of well-recognized realities and to trust much to the future judgment of our people. This is the defining characteristic of our collective drama.

The notion that these leaders—who had lived in their lifetimes under at least four different governments—wished to freeze the concepts they developed in the hurly-burly of current events is nonsense. What they expected of successive generations was that the inheritors of the system of freedom and democracy that they built would act with as much wisdom for their own time as they had shown in shepherding the nation into being. The Constitution was not created to be a straightjacket; it is a framework for a living engagement with the contemporary problems.

Our nation was born partly to protect race slavery, and grew to maturity with a decision to limit that slavery. We have a collective responsibility to view this history from our own perspective. While personal guilt is not in question, personal responsibility for the condition of people of color continues. Whites are the beneficiaries of the totality of the decisions made by our founders. Where, in the light of more modern views, they erred, we have the same obligation they assumed; to build in our time a society that better accords with our fundamental values than the one that we inherited.

They chose to fight a rigid society that was not responsive to their needs. They sought to create a society that would be more flexible and responsive and they succeeded. The value of their success lies in our continued willingness to address today's problems with the same spirit. Madison summed this up best in the *Federalist* 14, responding to the argument that the nation was too vast to be governed by a republic:

> Why is the experiment of an extended republic to be rejected, merely because it may comprise what is new? Is it not the glory of the people of America, that, whilst they have paid a decent regard to the opinions of former times and other nations, they have not suffered a blind veneration for antiquity, for custom, or for names, to overrule the suggestions of their own good sense, the knowledge of their own situation, and the lessons of their own experience?...They pursued a new and more noble course. They accomplished a revolution which has no parallel in the annals of human society. They reared the fabrics of governments which have no model on the face of the globe. They formed the design of a great Confederacy, which it is incumbent on their successors to improve and perpetuate.[30]

In this spirit, it is our opportunity to address the resonances of slavery that are still heard in the land. The Civil Rights Act of 1964 marked our most recent sustained effort toward a more equal society. At the first anniversary of that act, President Lyndon Johnson, at Howard University—probably without knowing it—sounded eerily like Benjamin Franklin in 1789.

> Freedom is the right to share, share fully and equally, in American society—to vote, to hold a job, to enter a public place, to go to school.…But freedom is not enough. You do not wipe away the scars of centuries by saying: now you are free to go where you want, and do as you desire, and choose the leaders you please. You do not take a person who, for years, has been hobbled by chains and liberate him, bring him up to the starting line of a race, and then say, "You are free to compete with all the others," and still justly believe that you have been completely fair.
>
> Thus it is not enough just to open the gates of opportunity. All our citizens must have the ability to walk through those gates.…We seek not just freedom but opportunity. We seek not just legal equity but human ability, not just equality as a right and a theory but equality as a fact and equality as a result.[31]

President Johnson's sentiment was echoed in 1990 by Justice Sandra Day O'Connor of the United States Supreme Court:

> As a nation we aspire to ensure that equality defines all citizens' daily experience and opportunities as well as the protection afforded to them under the law.[32]

While we have made measurable progress in improving opportunities, we still need to address these issues in the spirit of Benjamin Franklin.[33] Our posterity should be able to look back and conclude that we accepted Madison's obligation to "improve and perpetuate" the society that the founding fathers—and their successors over two centuries—bequeathed us. The phrase "improve and perpetuate" may appear internally inconsistent, but it is not. It acknowledges that values of the Declaration infuse our lives with obligations to each other, to those who came before and will come after, to enhance those values that—in our view—will make the pursuit of happiness—which includes living in a just society—a genuine human option.

# In Memoriam

Ruth and I first began this book about slavery after we visited the mansion in Northern Virginia that belonged to Robert E. Lee. We wandered the sweeping lawns and the luxurious rooms—what had once been the great wealth of the Southern Aristocracy, most of it based on slavery. It was in the rooms of that mansion that the Lees had conspired with Jefferson to overthrow the British government. We wondered why the scions of the successful planter slaveholder families would bite the hand that had brought them such wealth. We continued our research over the years, and at the behest of our literary agent, Ronald Goldfarb, we completed one more revision in December of 2003. In January 2004, Ruth died in an automobile accident. In the spring, while I was struggling with memories of our marriage of fifty-one years, Ron urged me to complete the manuscript. As I did so, I felt that Ruth was by my side, and we were still working together.

Her spirit and her life come alive in the "Requiem for Ruth Blumrosen" written by our dear friend Barbara Chase-Riboud:

# Requiem for Ruth Blumrosen

I will leave your white house and tranquil garden
Let life be empty and bright.
                    -Anna Andreyevna Akhmatova

I
I think about you to the point of tears,
Catch the hundreds of intonations of your voice,
The self-taught justice of your smile,
The many allées of your brilliant mind,
The bottomless reservoir of sweetness.
How could you end so suddenly?
Drowning out the sound of my own voice speaking
With the crack of hot steel and plate glass
And the shriek of shattered dreams?
It is so absurd I almost laugh crazily,
Into the bitter virgin silence you have left behind,
Polite to the end, closing the door softly
On unforeseen evil, everything upside-down forever,
In secret places that you never showed me,
Laughing together in passing.

II
Thus you bear my heart away chilled,
Amongst the peonies which bloomed yesterday,

In Memoriam

Where only my tears live and my fear reflected
In the mirror of serene Gulf waters where patiently
I wait each day for one last conversation, one last kiss,
In that bronze twilight between being and not being,
And the melancholy frustration of a loved one's
Cancelled rendezvous. I can't be angry.
For I wasn't there; only grief and darkness were there,
In my place, deep and velvety and above all,
Incomprehensible as are other people's dreams, as is,
A distant light-house or a burden in an outstretched palm,
I don't even recognize my own wailing voice,
Or the unsolvable riddle burning like a night lamp
Before an eternal door, eternally closed.

III
Your home is now the waters of the Gulf of Mexico
Grown silent from the sun's bright blaze.
Your limpid countenance and tender eyes
Watch from its depths the long day extinguished
By violence and the even longer night when penguins
Dance on shore in a grove of singing nightingales
And illegal aliens take flight for the border.
But you are quiet, resplendent in moonlight and salty
      mist,
Your judicial eyes are closed wide open.
Your lips curve in an arc at our reckless rovings
And incessant murmurings because: you are quiet.
Dark blue drifts over the sea's lacquer.
My Requiem is no longer sorrowful, but radiant,
A copper penny thrown over my shoulder, slicing
The satin surface, a silver coffin, pure swan.

## IV

Rest. Rest. Rest, my love, my Ruth,
Leave our sobbing and our prayers
Facing your magnificent smile
How bright the lunar eyes and relentless far-off gaze
That has come to rest on the doorstoop of Paradise.
Glancing back she cries: "I will wait"
Which like a wax seal on the heart, unique,
    valedictory,
Unforgettable, erases all remaining memory of the
    event,
Forgiving all with a wave of her tawny hand so that
Each day becomes a Remembrance Day. And she can't
    return!
But even beyond Lethe, I shall take her with me,
Hold to the living outline of her soul: "I will wait" she
    cries,
A sacred reproach from the one who died to those who
    cannot
Imagine her death, which is neither a magnificat of
    roses nor a
Host of Archangels, but a gracious acquittal of the
    living.

Barbara Chase-Riboud
*Rome, March 19, 2004*

Barbara Chase-Riboud is a Carl Sandburg Prize–winning poet and the author of five acclaimed, widely translated historical novels, *Sally Hemings*, *Valide: A Novel of a Harem*, *Echo of Lions*, *The President's Daughter*, and *Hottentot Venus*. Her major sculpture, *Africa Rising*, is in the Federal Building in downtown Manhattan, near the African Burial Ground.

# Bibliography
# of Works Cited

Adams, Charles Francis. *The Works of John Adams*, Vol. X. Boston: Little, Brown, 1856

Alden, John R. *A History of the American Revolution*. New York: Alfred A. Knopf, 1969

Andrews, Charles M. *The Colonial Background of the American Revolution*. New Haven: Yale University Press, 1924

Arendt, Hannah. *On Revolution*. New York: Penguin, 1990

Bailyn, Bernard. *The Ordeal of Thomas Hutchinson*. Cambridge, MA: Belknap Press, 1974

Ballagh, James Curtis, Ed. *A History of Slavery in Virginia*. Baltimore, MD: Johns Hopkins University Press, 1902, Reprinted 1968

Bancroft, George. *History of the United States, IV*. New York: Little, Brown, 1854

Banning, Lance. *The Sacred Fire of Liberty: James Madison and the Founding of the Federal Republic*. Ithaca: Cornell University Press, 1995

Barrett, Jay. A. *Evolution of the Ordinance of 1787*. New York: Knickerbocker Press, 1891; Reprinted in Dale Van Every. *The First American Frontier*. Arno Press, 1977

Blackstone, William. *Commentaries on the Laws of England: A Facsimile of the First Edition of 1765-1769*. Vol. 1. Chicago: University of Chicago Press, 1979

Blackstone, William. *Commentaries on the Laws of England 1768-69*. Ed. 3. Oxford: Clarendon Press, 1768–1769

Bowen, Catherine Drinker. *Miracle at Philadelphia: The Story of the Constitutional Convention, May to September, 1787*. Boston: Little, Brown, 1986

Bradley, Patricia. *Slavery, Propaganda, and the American Revolution*. Jackson, MS: University Press of Mississippi, 1998

Brands, H. W. *The First American: The Life and Times of Benjamin Franklin.* New York: Doubleday & Co., 2000

Breen, T. H. *Tobacco Culture: The Mentality of the Great Tidewater Planters on the Eve of Revolution.* Princeton: Princeton University Press, 2001

Brodsky, Alyn. *Benjamin Rush: Patriot and Physician.* New York: St. Martin's Press, 2004

Burnett, Edmund Cody. *The Continental Congress.* New York: MacMillan & Co, 1941

Butterfield, L. H., Ed. *The Adams Papers: Diary and Autobiography of John Adams.* Vol. 1–3. Cambridge, MA: Belknap Press, 1961

Cappon, Lester J., Ed. *The Adams–Jefferson Letters: The Complete Correspondence Between Thomas Jefferson and Abigail and John Adams.* Chapel Hill: University of North Carolina Press, 1959

Carter, Clarence, Ed., *The Territorial Papers Of The United States,* Vol. II. U.S. Government Printing Office, 1934

Chamberlain, Mellen, LLD. *John Adams: The Statesman of the American Revolution.* Cambridge: Houghton, Mifflin & Co., 1898

Chitwood, Oliver Perry. *Richard Henry Lee: Statesman of the Revolution.* Morgantown: West Virginia University Foundation, 1967

Collier, Christopher and James Lincoln Collier. *Decision in Philadelphia: The Constitutional Convention of 1787.* New York: Ballantine Books, 1986

Commager, Henry Steele, ed. *Documents of American History.* 9th ed. New York: Appleton Century Crafts, 1971

Cutler, William Parker and Julia Perkins Cutler, Eds., *Journals and Correspondence of Rev. Manasseh Cutler, LLD.* Vol. 1. Original, 1888; Reprinted, Athens, Ohio: Ohio University Press, 1987

Davis, David Brion. *The Problem of Slavery in the Age of Revolution, 1770–1823.* Ithaca: Cornell University Press, 1975

Draper, Theodore. *A Struggle for Power: The American Revolution.* New York: Random House, 1996

Dumond, Dwight Lowell. *Antislavery: The Crusade for Freedom in America.* University of Michigan Press, 1961

Egnal, Marc. *A Mighty Empire: The Origins of the American Revolution.* Ithaca: Cornell University Press, 1988

# Bibliography

Ellis, Joseph. *American Sphinx: The Character of Thomas Jefferson*. New York: Alfred A. Alfred A. Knopf, 1996

Ernst, Robert. *Rufus King: American Federalist*. Chapel Hill: University of North Carolina Press, 1968

Farrand, Max. *The Framing of the Constitution of the United States*. New Haven: Yale University Press, 1913

Farrand, Max. *The Records of the Federal Convention of 1787*. New Haven: Yale University Press, 1911, Revised 1966

Fehrenbacher, Donald E. *The Dred Scott Case: Its Significance in American Law and Politics*. Oxford: Oxford University Press, 1978

Fehrenbacher, Donald E. *The Slaveholding Republic: An Account of the United States Government's Relations to Slavery*. Oxford: Oxford University Press, 2001

Ferling, John. *John Adams: A Life*. New York: Henry Holt & Co., 1992

Ferling, John. *A Leap in the Dark: The Struggle to Create the American Republic*. Oxford: Oxford University Press, 2003

Ferling, John, *Setting the World Ablaze: Washington, Adams, Jefferson, and the American Revolution*. Oxford: Oxford University Press, 2000

Fielding, Sir John. *Extracts from Such of the Penal Laws, as Particularly Relate to the Peace and Good Order of the Metropolis*. London, 1762

Finkelman, Paul. *An Imperfect Union: Slavery, Federalism, and Comity*. Chapel Hill: University of North Carolina Press, 1981

Finkelman, Paul. "Slavery and Bondage in the Empire of Liberty," In Frederich D. Williams, Ed., *The Northwest Ordinance: Essays on Its Formation, Provisions, and Legacy*. East Lansing, MI: Michigan State University Press, 1988

Finkelman, Paul. "Slavery and the Constitutional Convention; Making a Covenant with Death," in *Beyond Confederation: Origins of the Constitution and American National Identity*. Richard Beeman, Stephen Botein, and Edward C. Carter II, Eds. Chapel Hill: University of North Carolina Press, 1987

Flournoy, H. W. Ed., *Calendar of Virginia State Papers, May 16, 1795 to December 31, 1798, Embracing the Letters and Proceedings of the Committee of Correspondence and Inquiry of Virginia and the Other Colonies from March 12, 1773 to April 7, 1775*. Vol. VIII, 1890, Reprinted 1968

Foner, Philip, ed. *Basic Writings of Thomas Jefferson*. New York: Willey Book Co., 1944

Foner, Philip. *History of Black Americans from Africa to the Emergence of the Cotton Kingdom*. Westdort, CN: Greenwood Press, 1975

Freehling, William. *The Road to Disunion: Secessionists at Bay 1776–1854*. Oxford: Oxford University Press, 1990

Fryer, Peter. *Staying Power: The History of Black People in Britain*. Pluto Press, 1984. www. eastlondon history.com/wilkes.htm

Gerzina, Gretchen Holbrook. *Black London*. New Brunswick, NJ: Rutgers University Press, 1995

Gipson, Lawrence Henry. *The Coming of the Revolution*. New York: Torchbook, 1962

Goebel Jr., Julius. *Cases and Materials on the Development of Legal Institutions*. Brattleboro, VT: Vermont Printing Co.,1946

Greene, Jack P., Ed. *Negotiated Authorities: Essays in Colonial Political and Constitutional History*. Charlottesville, VA: University of Virginia Press,1994

Greene, Jack P. *Understanding the American Revolution: Issues and Actors*. Charlottesville, VA: University of Virginia Press, 1995

Grigsby, Hugh Blair. *The Virginia Convention of 1776*. New York: Da Capo Press, 1969

Halliday, E. M. *Understanding Thomas Jefferson*. New York: HarperCollins, 2001

Henretta, James A. "Wealth and Social Structure." In *Colonial British America*, edited by Jack P. Greene and J. R. Pole. Baltimore, MD: Johns Hopkins University Press, 1984

Higginbotham Jr., A. Leon. *In the Matter of Color*. Oxford: Oxford University Press, 1978

Hildreth, Richard. *The History of the United States of America*. Vol. II, New York: Harper & Bros., 1880

Hutson, James, Ed., *Supplement to Max Farrand's The Records of the Federal Convention of 1787*. New Haven: Yale University Press, 1987

Isaac, Rhys. *Landon Carter's Uneasy Kingdom: Revolution and Rebellions on a Virginia Plantation*. Oxford: Oxford University Press, 2004

Isaacson, Walter. *Benjamin Franklin: An American Life*. New York: Simon & Schuster, 2003

Jefferson, Thomas. *Works of Thomas Jefferson*, edited by Paul Leicester Ford. Vol. I. New York: G. P. Putnam's Sons, 1904

# Bibliography

Jensen, Merrill. *The Articles of Confederation: An Interpretation of the Social-Constitutional History of the American Revolution 1774–1781.* Madison: University of Wisconsin Press, 1959

*Journals of the Continental Congress, 1774-1789.* Washington, D.C.: U.S. Government Printing Office, 1904–37

Lindsay, Arnette G. "Diplomatic Relations Between the United States and Great Britain Bearing on the Return of Negro Slaves, 1783–1828." *Journal of Negro History.* Vol. 5. (October, 1920); http://dinsdoc.com/lindsay-1.htm

Lynd, Staughton. *Class Conflict, Slavery, and the United States Constitution.* Indianapolis, IN: Bobbs-Merrill, 1767

MacLeod, Duncan. *Slavery, Race and the American Revolution.* London: Cambridge University Press, 1974

Maier, Pauline. *American Scripture: Making the Declaration of Independence.* New York: Alfred A. Knopf, 1997

Maier, Pauline. *From Resistance to Revolution.* New York: Random House, 1972

Maier, Pauline. *The Old Revolutionaries: Political Lives in the Age of Samuel Adams.* New York: W.W. Norton & Company, 1980

Mayer, Henry. *A Son of Thunder: Patrick Henry and the American Republic.* Charlottesville: University Press of Virginia, 1991

Mays, David John. *Edmund Pendleton, 1721–1803: A Biography.* Vol. I, II, New Haven: Harvard University Press, 1952

McCullough, David. *John Adams.* New York: Simon & Schuster, 2001

McGaughy, J. Kent. *Richard Henry Lee of Virginia.* Lanham, MD: Rowman & Littlefield, 2004

Middlekauff, Robert. *The Glorious Cause.* Oxford University Press, 1985

Miller, John C. *Origins of the American Revolution.* Palo Alto, CA: Stanford University Press, 1943, 1991

Morgan, Edmund S. *American Slavery, American Freedom: The Ordeal of Colonial Virginia.* New York: W.W. Norton & Co., 1975

Morgan, Edmund S. *The Birth of the Republic 1763–1789.* 3d Ed. Chicago: University of Chicago Press, 1992

Morris, Richard. *The Forging of the Union 1781–1789.* Cambridge: Harper and Row, 1987

Morrison, Samuel Eliot. *The Oxford History of the American People*. Vol. 1. New York: Meridian, 1964

Nagel, Paul C. *The Lees of Virginia: Seven Generations of an American Family*. Oxford: Oxford University Press, 1990

Nash, Gary B. *Race and Revolution*. Madison: Madison House, 1990

Nevins, Allan. *The American States During and After the Revolution, 1775–1789*. New York: MacMillan Company, 1924

Oakes, James. *The Ruling Race: A History of American Slaveholders*. New York: Norton & Co., 1998

Oldham, James. *The Mansfield Manuscripts and the Growth of English Law in the 18th Century*. Vol. II. Chapel Hill: University of North Carolina Press, 1992

Oldham, James. "New Light on Mansfield and Slavery." *The Journal of British Studies* Vol. 27, No. 1 (Jan. 1988)

Onuf, Peter S. *Statehood and Union: A History of the Northwest Ordinance*. Bloomington: Indiana University Press, 1987

Peabody, Sue. *There Are No Slaves in France: The Political Culture of Race and Slavery in the Ancient Regime*. Oxford: Oxford University Press, 1996

Rakove, Jack N. *The Beginnings of National Politics: An Interpretive History of the Continental Congress*. New York: Alfred A. Knopf, 1979

Rakove, Jack N. *Original Meanings: Politics and Ideas in the Making of the Constitution*. New York: Alfred A. Knopf, 1996

Randall, Willard Sterne. *Thomas Jefferson: A Life*. New York: Harper Perennial, 1994

Reid, John Phillip. *Constitutional History of the American Revolution*. Vol. IV, Madison: University of Wisconsin Press, 1993

Robinson, Donald L. *Slavery in the Structure of American Politics 1765–1820*. New York: Harcourt Brace Jovanovich, 1971

Rogers, Jr., George, and David R. Chesnutt, Eds., *The Papers of Henry Laurens*. Vol. 1, 7, 8, 9. Columbia: University of South Carolina Press, 1979–81

Rutland, Robert A., Ed. *The Papers of George Mason*. Vol. 1. Chapel Hill: University of North Carolina Press, 1970

Shyllon, F. O. *Black Slaves in Britain*. London: Oxford University Press, 1974

Smith, Paul H., Ed. *Letters of Delegates to Congress, 1774–1879*. Vol. 1, 7, 8. Washington, DC: Library of Congress, 1976

# Bibliography

Statuary, David P. *Shays's Rebellion: The Making of an Agrarian Insurrection.* Amherst: University of Massachusetts Press, 1980

Story, Joseph. *Commentaries of the Constitution of the United States.* Original, 1833; Reprinted, Carolina Academic Press, 1987

Sutton, Robert P. *Revolution to Secession: Constitution Making in the Old Dominion.* Charlottesville, VA: University of Virginia Press, 1989

Tarter, Brent and Robert Scribner, Eds. *Revolutionary Virginia: The Road to Independence.* Charlottesville, VA: University of Virginia Press, 1983

Thorpe, Francis Newton. *The Federal and State Constitutions, Colonial Charters, and Other Organic Laws of the States, Territories, and Colonies Now or Heretofore Forming the United States of America.* Vol. 1–3, 5–7. Washington, D.C.: Government Printing Office, 1909

Washburne, E. B. *Sketch of Edward Coles, Second Governor of Illinois, and of the Slavery Struggle of 1823–1824.* Original, 1882. Reprinted, New York: Negro Universities Press, 1969

Weiner, Mark. *Black Trials: Citizenship from the Beginnings of Slavery to the End of the Caste.* New York: Alfred A. Knopf, forthcoming. Ch. 3

Weiner, Mark. "New Biographical Evidence on Somerset's Case." 23 *Slavery and Abolition Journal* (April, 2002)

Wiecek, William M. *The Sources of Antislavery Constitutionalism in America, 1760–1848.* Ithaca: Cornell University Press, 1977

Williams, Frederick D., Ed. *Northwest Ordinance: Essays on Its Formulation, Provisions, and Legacy.* Lansing: Michigan State University Press, 1989

Wills, Gary. *Inventing America: Jefferson's Declaration of Independence.* New York: Doubleday, 1978

Wills, Gary. *Negro President: Jefferson and the Slave Power.* New York: Houghton Mifflin, 2003

Wood, Gordon S. *The Americanization of Benjamin Franklin.* New York: Penguin Press, 2004

Wood, Gordon S. *The Radicalism of the American Revolution.* Vintage Books, 1993

# Notes

CHAPTER I
SOMERSET'S JOURNEY SPARKS THE AMERICAN REVOLUTION

1. Details of the lives of Somerset and Stewart have recently been unearthed by our colleague Mark Weiner in "New Biographical Evidence in Somerset's Case": 121–36; and in *Black Trials*. Weiner has reported that the correct spelling of Stewart's name is Steuart, but the conventional spelling has been retained.

2. Weiner, *Black Trials*, 77

3. Gerzina, *Black London*, 1–68

4. Fielding, *Extracts from Penal Laws*, 142–144

5. Gerzina, *Black London*, passim

6. Fryer, *Staying Power*, 71–72 . See www. eastlondon history.com/wilkes.htm

7. Weiner, *Black Trials*, 79; Gerzina, *Black London*, 90–132

8. See Wiecek, *Antislavery Constitutionalism*, 20–61; Shyllon, *Black Slaves in Britain*. Oldham, *Mansfield Manuscripts* 1221–45

9. Landon Carter, the owner of the most slaves in Virginia, expressed similar feelings in his diary when some of his trusted slaves left to join the British in 1776. Isaac, *Landon Carter's Uneasy Kingdom*, 3–15

10. Habeas corpus is an ancient form of order requiring a person to explain to the court the reasons for the detention of another person.

11. Blackstone, *Commentaries (1765)*, 123, repeated on 412. Blackstone modified this statement in his 1768–69 revision by adding at the end that, "the master's rights to his service may possibly still continue." Blackstone, *Commentaries (1768–69)*, 424–425. See Wiecek, *Antislavery Constitutionalism*, 27

12. Mansfield was hated in the colonies after 1765 when he rejected the colonial claim of "no taxation without representation" by stating that the colonies were fully subject to the will of Parliament in all matters. During debate on the repeal of the Stamp Act and adoption of Declaratory Act, he took the position that the colonists were subject to the power of Parliament without limitation, and that there was no difference between internal and external taxes and that "when the supreme power abdicates, the government is dissolved." Gipson, *Coming of the Revolution*, 113–114. See Bernard Bailyn, *The Ideological Origins of the American Revolution* (Cambridge, MA: Harvard University Press, 1967) 200–202 on the English attitude toward Par-

liament as reflected by Blackstone. See Beverly Zweiben, *How Blackstone Lost the Colonies* (Garland Publishing Co., 1990), suggesting that Blackstone's assertion of Parliamentary supremacy bore some responsibility for hardening the position of the British government.

13. Davis, *Problem of Slavery,* 488-501, discusses the *Somerset* decision as part of an emerging free-labor philosophy. See Gipson, *The Coming of the Revolution,* 7, for a general perspective on the period in England.

14. Oldham, "New Light on Mansfield" 45-65 at 48

15. Gerzina, *Black London,* 88-89

16. Ibid. 66–67

17. Ibid. 120, quoting Granville Sharp, New York Historical Society, 186

18. *Somerset v. Stewart,* Howell's State Trials, Vol. 20, 1, 80 (1771–7).

19. Edward Fiddes, "Lord Mansfield, and the *Somerset* Case," *Law Quarterly Review* 50, (1934), 508–509

20. *General Evening Post,* May 26, 1772 , p. 4, col. 3 (p. 2 of May 28 section). Stewart acknowledged that the West Indian planters and merchants had taken over control of the case. Davis, *Problem of Slavery,* 480–81n20.

21. Howell's State Trials, Vol. 20, 82 (1771–7). There is some dispute over the exact language used in Mansfield's opinion. See Oldham, "New Light on Mansfield." The dispute does not affect the point that the decision was interpreted at the time as freeing the slaves in England. A clear summary of the uncertain status of slaves in England prior to the Somerset decision appears in Higginbotham, *In the Matter of Color,* 313–355. The restrictive interpretations of the decision of *Somerset* in England after the 1780s are discussed at 356–358.

22. Contents of the British papers and magazines are described in Gerzina, *Black London,* 130. Contents of the American colonial papers are discussed in Chapter 2. The initial interpretations of the decision by other courts in Britain confirmed the breadth of the ruling. Two opinions of lower British courts, one in 1773 and one in 1776, were preserved by Sharp. A lower court decision in 1773, Cay and Crichton, Prerogative Court, May 11, 1773, held that an executor of an estate need not report a slave as property of his dead master. The High Court of Admiralty decided that one who had been wrongly held as a slave aboard ship was entitled to recover from his master the value of his services, since the state of slavery did not exist. *Rogers alias Riggs v. Jones,* High Court of Admiralty, June 29, 1776. The *Rogers* decision posed an additional threat to slave owners; the possibility of back-pay liability to the slaves that were freed by the *Somerset* decision. Reports of both cases appear as appendices 10 and 11 to Granville Sharp, "The Just Limitation of Slavery," (1776), which appears in "Tracts on Slavery, Including Just Limitations of Slavery in the Laws of God, References to and Extracts from Mansfield's judgment, etc," by Granville Sharp. Vol. 23 of a collection of pamphlets bound by Thomas Binns, London, in the 1830s, in possession of Antislavery International, 4 Stableyard Broomgrove Road, London, SW9,9tl. Scottish law followed this broad interpretation of *Somerset.* Wiecek, *Antislavery Constitutionalism,* 33

23. Fielding, *Extracts from Penal Laws,* 3.

24. See Gerzina, *Black London,* 123–132, 165–204 for a discussion of the post-*Somerset* issues concerning slavery in England.

25. Benjamin Franklin, "The Somerset Case and the Slave Trade," London Chronicle, June 20, 1772.
26. Oldham, "New Light on Mansfield," 65–66.
27. Fryer, *Staying Power*, 203–207, describes how British slaves emancipated themselves by walking away from their masters.
28. Edward Ball, *Slaves in the Family* (New York: Farrar, Straus & Giroux, 1998) 218

CHAPTER 2
THE TINDERBOX

1. Bradley, *Slavery, Propaganda,* 68–80 provided the basis for the following table.

NEWSPAPER COVERAGE OF *SOMERSET* IN THE COLONIES 1772

| Colony/Paper | Number of items | Date of first entry |
|---|---|---|
| MASSACHUSETTS | | |
| Boston Gazette | 1 | Sept. 21 |
| Massachusetts Spy | 4 | Aug. 27 |
| Mercury | 1 | |
| Boston Post Boy | 4 | July 27 |
| Massachusetts Gaxette & Boston News Letter | 4 | |
| Essex Gazette Salem [no #] | 4 | Aug. 25 |
| | | |
| PENNSYLVANIA | | |
| Chronicle | 2 | Aug. 22 |
| Pennsylvania Journal | 1 | Sept. 2 |
| Pennsylvania Packet | 2 | Aug. 3 |
| Pennsylvania Gazette | 2 | Aug. 12 |
| | | |
| RHODE ISLAND | | |
| Providence Gazette | 5 | Feb. 17 |
| Newport Mercury | 3 | Aug. 3 |
| | | |
| NEW YORK | | |
| New York Journal | 3 | Apr. 30 |
| | | |
| NEW HAMPSHIRE | | |
| Gazette | | |
| | | |
| VIRGINIA | | |
| Gazette (P & D) | 5 | May 7 |
| Gazette (Rind) | 1 | Nov. 12 |
| | | |
| SOUTH CAROLINA | | |
| Gazette | 1 | Aug. 13 |
| S. C. and American Gazette | | Aug. 3 |

2. Wiecek, *Antislavery Constitutionalism,* 40
3. *South Carolina Gazette and Country Journal,* Tuesday, Sept. 15, 1772
4. Ibid. September 22, 1772
5. All of the early charters contained restrictions on colonial legislation which echoed these statutes prohibiting legislation which was repugnant or contrary to, and permitting legislation which was agreeable to, the laws of England. The charters are collected in Thorpe, *Federal and State Constitutions.* The Virginia charter appears in Vol. 7, p. 3806; North Carolina charter at Vol. 5, 2755; Georgia charter at Vol. 2, p. 770. The Maryland charter of 1632 required laws to "be consonant to reason and be not repugnant nor contrary, but (so far as conveniently may be done) agreeable to the laws...of England." Vol. 2 p. 1681. Similar statements appear in the charters of Pennsylvania, vol. 5 p. 3038; Massachusetts (1620) Vol. 3, p. 1833, (1629) vol. 3, p. 1833, (1691) Vol. 3, p. 1882; New Jersey (1664) Vol. 5, p. 2538, (1712) Vol. 5, p. 1712; Rhode Island (1663) Vol. 6, 3215; Connecticut (1662) Vol. 1, p. 533.
6. Those in Virginia would have remembered the extensive litigation involving a Virginia law that allowed debtors to pay debts based on an artificially low value of tobacco, adopted because of the skyrocketing value of tobacco due to a bad crop in 1758. The clergy, whose salary had previously been fixed at the weight of tobacco, were—along with other creditors—denied the benefit of the increase in price. They appealed to the board of trade to invalidate the law as inconsistent with the previously fixed rate.

   The Board of Trade eventually concluded that the law was disallowed but was not clear on whether the disallowance was retroactive to cover the period of the parsons' complaint. The parsons then sued in local courts to recover their loss. Some were thrown out on grounds that the disallowance was not retroactive, but one court held that the law was retroactive. It then empanelled a jury to determine how much the parsons should recover. This case was Patrick Henry's introduction to Virginia politics. He was so persuasive that the parsons should be treated like all other creditors that the jury awarded one cent in damages. Mayer, *Son of Thunder,* 59–66; Goebel, *Cases and Materials,* 80–81. Randall, *Thomas Jefferson,* 160–167 suggests that Jefferson's thinking about the relation between Britain and the colonies had crystallized while working on a case that involved parliamentary control over divorce
7. South Carolina act regarding payment of monies, 1770; New York omnibus act adopting English statutes, 1770; New Jersey inheritance law, 1771. In 1772 the Privy Council struck down a North Carolina anti-riot act, and a Dominica act regarding tax bills. Goebel, *Cases and Materials,* 72n102.
8. Brands, *First American,* 363–370
9. Chitwood, *Richard Henry Lee,* 36–37; McGaughy, *Richard Henry Lee of Virginia,* 77–78
10. McGaughy, *Richard Henry Lee of Virginia,* 77–78
11. Bailyn, *The Ordeal of Thomas Hutchinson,* 365–369
12. The Declaratory Act of 1766 asserted:

    "that the said colonies and plantations in America have been, are, and of right ought to be, subordinate unto and dependent upon the imperial crown and Parliament of Great Britain, and that the King's majesty, by and with the advice and consent of the lords spiritual and temporal, and commons of Great Britain, in Parliament assembled, had, hath, and of right ought to have, full power and authority to make laws and statutes of sufficient force and validity to bind the colonies and people of America, subjects of the crown of Great Britain, in all cases whatsoever." Commager, *Documents*, 60

13. Morrison *Oxford History*, 256–258
14. Rakove, *National Politics*, 4
15. Jefferson, "Autobiography," in Foner, *Basic Writings of Thomas Jefferson*, 411–12
16. McCullough, *John Adams*, 67
17. Maier, *From Resistance to Revolution*, 220–26, describes the continuing efforts to keep the public focused on British misdeeds during this period.
18. Ferling, *Leap in the Dark*, 68–70
19. "uneasy truce," Alden, *History of the American Revolution*, 125. "quiet years," Egnal, *A Mighty Empire*, 247–269. "In reality, for most of the last three years [1770–1773] the government paid little attention to the colonies....[Lord] North was content to let colonial affairs drift, as long as they drifted quietly." Middlekauff, *Glorious Cause*, 208–209.
20. Andrews, *Colonial Background*, 152, "The years from 1770 to 1773 were a time of comparative calm. Business revived, commercial prosperity returned, the moderates had the situation well in hand, and the Sons of Liberty, who had greeted the collapse of the non-importation movement with vexation of spirit, were for the moment discredited and under a cloud."

    See also, Miller, "The Decline of the Revolutionary Movement," *Origins of the American Revolution*, 315–325; Robert McCluer Calhoon, *Revolutionary America: An Interpretive Overview* (Harcourt, Brace, Jovanovich, 1976) 52, "time of quiet in imperial colonial relations."
21. Hildreth, *History of the United States*, 567
22. Greene, *Negotiated Authorities*, 259–318
23. Ibid. 240–241
24. Rogers, *Papers of Henry Laurens*, 435–6. Dunning was Stewart's lawyer in the *Somerset* case. See Davis, *Problem of Slavery*, 472,493–94, 498
25. Laurens may have obsessed over the *Somerset* decision. On September 21, 1773, the *South Carolina Country Journal* published an advertisement for four slaves who had run away from the plantation of Henry Laurens in September and December 1772, "the following NEW NEGROES, viz. SOMERSET, his country name Massery, about 5 feet 8 or 9 inches high, slim, long visage, and very black, of the Mandingo country." Rogers, *Papers of Henry Laurens*, Vol. 7, 109
26. Laurens' opposition to slavery was stated in 1776. "I abhor slavery," he wrote in a letter to his son John of August 14, 1776 and indicated his intention to begin manumission of his hundreds of slaves. Philip M. Hamer Ed. *Papers of Henry Laurens*, (Columbia, SC: University of SC Press, 1979) Vol. 1 99–100
27. Lindsay, "Diplomatic Relations," 391–419
28. Rogers, *Papers of Henry Laurens*, v8,464. See letters from Laurens to Appleby, 464; to Appleby, 466; to J. Clay, 468n6. Laurens evidently kept his own black servant with him in England.

29. "Mass Hist. Soc. Proceedings XLIII," in Davis, *Problem of Slavery*, 494n44

30. *Virginia Gazette* (P & O) June 30, 1774

31. See discussion in Finkelman, *Imperfect Union*, 39, "It is clear that this quotation [slavery is so odious] was widely circulated and believed in Britain and America. Americans and Englishmen, including the knowledgeable Granville Sharp, interpreted *Somerset* as ending slavery in England." See also, Wiecek, *Antislavery Constitutionalism*, 20–39

32. The relation between slavery and land values is discussed in Oakes, *Ruling Race*, 12–14 [pre-Revolution], 73 [post-Revolutionary period]

33. Henretta, "Wealth and Social Structure," 273–742

34. Morgan, *American Slavery, American Freedom*, 295-315

35. Ibid. 344, 380–381, 386

36. Breen, *Tobacco Culture*, 161–175

37. See text at notes, 25, 50, 51

38. Ferling, *Setting the World Ablaze*, 64–91, notes the parallel development of Adams's and Jefferson's concepts of colonial freedom.

39. Jefferson, "Autobiography," in Ford, *Works*, 9–10.

40. Chamberlain, *John Adams*, 58

41. Butterfield, *Diary and Autobiography*, Vol. 2, 75

42. The Adams had five children. Abigail Amelia Adams (1765–1813), John Quincy Adams, who also served one term as president (1767–1848), Susanna Adams (1768–1770), Charles Adams (1770–1832), and Thomas Adams(1772-1832)

43. Bailyn, *Ordeal of Thomas Hutchinson*, 196–220

44. Halliday, *Understanding Thomas Jefferson*, 31–43

45. Randall, *Thomas Jefferson,* 163–67.

46. Goebel, *Cases and Materials*, 72

47. Thomas Jefferson, "A Summary View of the Rights of British America" (Avalon Project, Yale Law School) www.yale.edu/lawweb/avalon/jeff-summ.htm "Our ancestors, before their emigration to America, were the free inhabitants of the British dominions in Europe, and possessed a right which nature has given to all men, of departing from the country in which chance, not choice, has placed them, of going in quest of new habitations, and of there establishing new societies, under such laws and regulations as to them shall seem most likely to promote public happiness....America was conquered, and her settlements made, and firmly established, at the expense of individuals and not of the British public. Their own blood was spilt in acquiring lands for their settlement, their own fortunes expended in making that settlement effectual; for themselves they fought, for themselves they conquered, and for themselves alone they have right to hold. Not a shilling was ever issued from the public treasures of his majesty, or his ancestors, for their assistance, till of very late times, after the colonies had become established on a firm and permanent footing....That settlements having been thus effected in the wilds of America, the emigrants thought proper to adopt that system of laws under which they had hitherto lived in the mother country, and to continue their union with her by submitting themselves to the same common sovereign, who was thereby made the central link connecting the several parts of the empire thus newly multiplied."

48. Adams view was that if "sovereignty" was unitary, so that England either had complete control over the colonies or none at all, the answer was "none" because Britain never claimed the right to enslave the colonies. See Chapter 5.

49. Lord Mansfield, in the parliamentary debate over repeal of the Stamp Act in 1766 said that nothing "could be more fatal to the peace of the colonies at any time, than the Parliament giving up its authority over them; for in such a case there must be an entire dissolution of government. Considering how the colonies are composed, it is easy to foresee there would be no end of feuds and factions among the several separate governments, when once there shall be no one government here or there of sufficient force or authority to decide their mutual differences; and, government being dissolved, nothing remains but that the colonies must either change their constitution and take some new form of government, or fall under some foreign power....Proceed, then, my Lords, with spirit and firmness; and when you have established your authority, it will be time to show your lenity. The Americans...are a very good people and I wish them exceedingly well; but they are heated and inflamed...in the words of Maurice, prince of Orange, concerning the Hollanders, 'God bless the industrious, frugal, and well-meaning, but easily deluded people.'" http://balrog.sdsu.edu/~putman/410a/parldebates.htm

50. See Peabody, *There Are No Slaves in France*

51. Hildreth, *History of the United States*, Vol. II, 567, defined the problems the colonial lawyers had with the repugnancy laws after the *Somerset* decision declared slavery "odious" and not recognized as common law in his 1846 book. Hildreth had marshaled the evidence necessary to conclude that the South had joined the Revolution to protect slavery, but he did not reach that conclusion. Such a conclusion at the time would have supported southern claims that slavery was protected by the Constitution, a conclusion that Hildreth would not have wished to support. Hildreth's antislavery position is explained in his *Despotism in America: An Inquiry into the Nature and Results, and Legal Basis of the Slave-Holding System in the United States* (Boston: A. Kelley Publishers, 1970) 177–218. He argued that *Somerset* plus the repugnancy clauses invalidated slavery in the colonies before the Revolution.

52. See Wood, *Americanization of Benjamin Franklin*, 70–72

## CHAPTER 3
## VIRGINIA RESPONDS TO THE *Somerset* DECISION

1. Breen, *Tobacco Culture*, 32–37

2. Oakes, *Ruling Race*, 180

3. Breen, *Tobacco Culture*, 15–39, discusses the thesis that some Virginian planters sought independence as a way of avoiding payment of their debts to British merchants. Breen finds that an oversimplification, but notes that starting in 1772, the issue of planter debt, which had been a private matter, became politicized. "Neither the transition away from tobacco nor the rising level of indebtedness caused the great planters to support the Revolution. These experiences did, however, help determine how the tidewater gentlemen ultimately perceived the constitutional issues of the day." (at 161). Breen does not mention the *Somerset* case.

4. The Slave, Grace, 2 Haggard Admiralty (G.B.) 94, 1827.

5. Fryer, *Staying Power*, 71–72

6. Breen, *Tobacco Culture*, 20–3, 58–9, 60, 65, 69, 87, 89

7. See Chapter 1

8. Not long! In the Cape area of South Africa in 1812, the British enacted restrictions on the de facto slavery status of bushmen, and set up a special court, nicknamed the "Black Circuit," to assure their enforcement. When a "bushman" named Booy sought to enforce his rights, and his master refused, the resulting battle at Slaughters Nek led to the hanging of five Boers, laid the foundation for the Boer separation, the Boer War, and ultimately apartheid. Allister Sparks, *The Mind of South Africa*, (New York: Alfred A. Knopf, 1990) 91-96

9. In contrast, France had created conditions during the eighteenth century in which slave owners could bring their slaves to France for certain purposes, and keep them there for limited periods of time. See Peabody, *There Are No Slaves in France.*

10. Ben Franklin may have suggested something of this sort to the British while he was the colonial agent for Pennsylvania, Massachusetts, and Georgia. Isaacson, *Benjamin Franklin*, 158–161

11. "I seek for the liberty and constitution of this kingdom no further back than the [Glorious] Revolution. There I take my stand." Quoted in Reid, *Constitutional History*, 171–72. Mansfield was a protector of parliamentary supremacy vis a vis the king, and therefore opposed the view of the colonies that they were connected with the king, not parliament. Reid suggests that Mansfield's position was necessary to prevent the king from controlling a major source of revenue and influence, which would not be subject to Parliament. Reid, *Constitutional History*, 163–173

12. Wood, *Radicalism of the American Revolution*, 169–189

13. Cappon, *Adams–Jefferson Letters*, 455

14. Isaacson, *Benjamin Franklin*, 158–161

15. Higginbotham, *In the Matter of Color*, 19–150. Bradley, *Slavery, Propaganda*, points out that the northern press, by its continual reporting of criminal activities of slaves, helped create an atmosphere of distrust and distaste for blacks in Massachusetts and elsewhere, even as criticism of slavery was becoming more common.

16. Foner, *History of Black Americans*, 295

17. Robinson, *Structure of American Politics*, 34-86

18. Ellis, *American Sphinx*, 29–36

19. Burnett, *Continental Congress*, 16

20. Jefferson, "Autobiography," in Ford, *Works*, 9–10

21. Discussed in Chapter 7

22. Washburne, *Sketch of Edward Coles*, 21–31

23. Chitwood, *Richard Henry Lee*, 18–19

24. Henry Mayer, *Son of Thunder*, 168–69

25. Stanley Elkins and Eric McKitrick, *The Age of Federalism* (Oxford University Press, 1993) 203–04

26. MacLeod, *Slavery, Race*, 31–61, at 32 notes that "the objection [to the slave trade] arose principally from a concern for the white community and not from a concern for the Negro."

27. MacLeod, *Slavery, Race*, 44

28. Jefferson, "Letter to Edward Coles," August 25, 1814: "In the first or second session of the legislature after I became a member, I drew this subject [of slavery] to the attention of Col. Bland, one of the oldest, ablest, & most respected members, and he undertook to move for certain moderate extensions of the protection of the laws to these people. I seconded his motion, and, as a younger member, was more spared in the debate; but he was denounced as an enemy of his country, & was treated with the grossest indecorum." Washburne, *Sketch of Edward Coles*, 25

29. Ellis, *American Sphinx*, 89. See Ellis's index under "Jefferson, conflict avoidance by"

30. See Peter Kolchin, *American Slavery, 1619-1877* (New York: Hill and Wange, 1993) 37–38; Richard S. Dunn, "Servants and Slaves: The Recruitment and Employment of Labor," in Jack P. Greene and J. R. Pole, Eds., *Colonial British America* (Baltimore: Johns Hopkins University Press, 1984) 157, 164–69, 175–76.

31. Morgan, *American Slavery, American Freedom*, 301

32. Henretta, "Wealth and Social Structure," 273–74

33. Rhys Isaac, *Transformation of Virginia, 1740–1790* (Chapel Hill, NC: University of NC Press, 1982) 247-248

34. Ballagh, *History of Slavery in Virginia*, 22

35. Bancroft, *History of the United States, IV*, 413–15

36. See Freehling, *Road to Disunion*, 214–16

37. Greene, "Foundations of Political Power in the Virginia House of Burgesses, 1720–1776," in Greene, *Negotiated Authorities*, 238–58, 259–318, for an analysis of the political culture of mid-eighteenth-century Virginia.

38. See Chapter 7.

39. See Clinton Rossiter and Richard Bland, "The Whig in America," 10 *William & Mary Quarterly*, 3d series (Jan.1953) 33–79 at 38

40. Chapter 2

41. See Mays, *Edmund Pendleton*, Vol. II, 3–17

42. Mays, *Edmund Pendleton* Vol. I, 268

43. Mayer, *Son of Thunder*, 243

44. Mays, *Edmund Pendleton*, Vol. II, 11. Grigsby, *Virginia Convention*, 44–55

45. Draper, *Struggle for Power*, 381

46. Isaacson, *Benjamin Franklin*, 271–78

47. Butterfield, *Diary and Autobiography*. The episode is examined closely in Bailyn, *Ordeal of Thomas Hutchinson*, 221–59. Bailyn, examining all the facts—which were not available to Franklin or Adams—acquits Hutchinson of the wrongdoing as seen by the people of Massachusetts.

48. Ferling, *John Adams* , 81. See 80–84 for Ferling's discussion of the different positions taken by historians as to when Adams became so committed, and why he picked the Hutchinson letters episode as the last event that committed Adams.

CHAPTER 4
THE VIRGINIA RESOLUTION UNITES THE COLONIES AND
LEADS TO THE FIRST CONTINENTAL CONGRESS IN 1774

1. John Pendleton Kennedy, Ed., *Journal of the House of Burgesses of Virginia*, Volume 1773–1776, (Richmond, VA, 1905–15) 28

2. See Ch. 3

3. Morgan, *Birth of the Republic,* 56. Samuel Adams developed such committees within the towns of Massachusetts in 1772, but it was Virginia's version that united the colonies, ending the British assumption that they could not work together.

4. This information, not available to the colonials in 1772 or 1773, is available to us at http://gaspee.org/index.htm#Analysis. Details of the Gaspee Days Parade Saturday, June 11, 2005 are available at http://www.gaspee.com/GaspeeDaysParade.html.

5. Andrews, *Colonial Background,* 153

6. Flournoy, "Calender," 27–65

7. Morgan, *Birth of the Republic,* 58–59; Ferling, *Leap in the Dark,* 91–93

8. Ferling, *Leap in the Dark,* 101–103

9. Ibid. 103–108

10. Wills, *Inventing America,* 26-27, describes the "tea party" as "an arduous undertaking, full of military risk and sheer physical problems."

11. Draper, *Struggle for Power,* 441. "For the British government, the Continental Congress was illegal. That it could not be prevented from meeting showed how far the decline of British power had gone."

12. Draper, *Struggle for Power,* 417

13. Reid *Constitutional History,* Vol. IV, 11

14. Flournoy, "Calender," 10

15. Ibid. 68

16. Morris, *Forging of the Union,* 77–79, charts the method of election of the delegates: Pennsylvania and Rhode Island selected its delegates by the assembly; the Connecticut assembly chose the committee of correspondence; the Delaware speaker called assembly when the governor declined to act; Maryland, extralegal committees appointed by counties; Massachusetts, general court in defiance of governor; New Hampshire, extralegal meeting of town deputies; New Jersey, extralegal committee appointed by counties; New York, extralegal committee elected in New York City and County, endorsed by some other counties; Suffolk and Orange Counties sent their own delegates; South Carolina, extralegal general meeting, later ratified by assembly; Virginia, provincial convention of county delegates.

17. The Virginia instructions to delegates of Aug. 1, 1774, stated in part: "The original constitution of the American colonies possessing their assemblies with the sole right of directing their internal polity, it is absolutely destructive of the end of their institution that their legislatures should be suspended or prevented, by hasty dissolutions, from exercising their legislative powers." Commager, *Documents of American History,* 78

    *Polity* is defined in *Oxford English Dictionary,* (2d ed. 1989) as (1) civil organization (as a condition); civil order. Administration of a state; civil government (as a process or course of action), quoting Jefferson's "Summary View": "sole right of directing their internal polity." (2) a particular form of political organization: a form of government.

    *Policy* is defined as "a course of action adopted and pursued by a government, party ruler, or statesman, etc. any course of action adopted as advantageous or expedient." Whether the two terms are generally interchangeable, it is clear that the institution of slavery was so integral to the southern economy that a decision respecting it would be embraced by either term.

18. Julian P. Boyd, Ed., *Papers of Thomas Jefferson* (Princeton University Press, 1950) Vol. 1, 121–37. For a critique of the accuracy of Jefferson's factual statement in his summary view, see Wills, *Inventing America*, 27–28

19. "Virginia Instructions to the Delegates to the Continental Congress, August 1, 1774," Commager, *Documents of American History*, 78

20. Arendt, *On Revolution*, 119. Hannah Arendt understood that the objection to taxation without representation was not revolutionary until the southerners demanded independence from Parliament.

21. British politician Edmund Burke, in 1775, and American historian Edmund Morgan, in 1975, drew this same conclusion. Burke emphasized the attachment to liberty by whites in the South arising from the presence of slavery. "In Virginia and the Carolinas, they have a vast multitude of slaves....Those who are free are by far the most proud and jealous of their freedom. Freedom to them is not only an enjoyment, but a kind of rank and privilege....Those people...are much more strongly...attached to liberty, than those to the northward." Edmund Burke to Parliament, March 22, 1775. Cook, Albert S., ed. Vol. II, Speech on Conciliation with America (New York: Longman's, Greenard Co., 1913) 123-24.

    Morgan concluded that: "Virginians may have had a special appreciation of the freedom dear to republicans, because they saw every day what life without it could be like." Morgan, *American Slavery, American Freedom*, 376

## Chapter 5
## John Adams Supports the South on Slavery

1. Butterfield, *Diary and Autobiography*, 96n1. The delegates had been appointed by the General Court sitting in Salem.

2. Rakove, *National Politics*, 108. Maier, *Old Revolutionaries*, 3-50

3. Butterfield, *Diary and Autobiography*, 104

4. Ibid.106

5. Ibid.109

6. Ibid.112

7. Brodsky, *Benjamin Rush*

8. Ferling, *Leap in the Dark*, 48–50

9. Butterfield, *Diary and Autobiography*, 114, 115n2. See David Freeman Hawke, *Benjamin Rush: Revolutionary Gadfly*, (City: Bobbs-Merrill, 1971) 116–17

10. Butterfield, *Diary and Autobiography*, 114

11. Ibid. 116

12. Ibid. 136

13. Ibid. 126

14. Phyllis Lee Levin, *Abigail Adams: A Biography* (New York: St. Martin's Griffin, 2001) 36

15. Morgan, *Birth of the Republic*, 63–64

16. Butterfield, *Diary and Autobiography*, 119. (discussed in Chapter 3)

17. "John Adams to William Tudor, Sept. 19, 1774," in Smith, *Letters of Delegates to Congress*, 129–30

18. Joseph Ellis. *Passionate Sage: The Character and Legacy of John Adams* (New York: N. W. Norton & Co., 1993) 39.

19. Smith, *Letters of Delegates to Congress*, 178

20. Butterfield, *Diary and Autobiography*, 120
21. Ferling, *Leap in the Dark*, 114n5
22. Butterfield, *Diary and Autobiography*, 120
23. See Chapter 10
24. See Higginbotham, *In the Matter of Color*, 19–150
25. Foner, *History of Black Americans*, 295. Writs of assistance were general warrants enabling customs officers to search on suspicion alone.
26. Ibid.
27. Grigsby, *Virginia Convention*, 66–67
28. Ferling, *Leap in the Dark*, 41. In 1780, while lieutenant governor of South Carolina, Gadsden successfully recommended that Charleston be surrendered to the British. Buchanan, *The Road to Guilford Court House: The American Revolution in South Carolina* (New York: John Wiley & Sons, 1997) 66, 69
29. Butterfield, *Diary and Autobiography*, v1, 133. Sept. 14, 1774. The words following the quotation, "This I deny," were Adams's views of Gadsden's analysis.
30. Adams, "Letter to William Tudor, June 1, 1818."*The Works of John Adams*, 315.
31. Adams, "Letter to Robert Evans, June 8, 1819."*The Works of John Adams*, 380. Frederick M. Binder, *The Color Problem in Early National America as Viewed by John Adams, Jefferson, and Jackson*, (The Hague: Mouton Press, 1968) 11–31, discusses Adams's views in considerable detail, but does not mention the quotations in the text.
32. See Benjamin Quarles, *The Negro in the American Revolution*, (Chapel Hill: University of NC Press, 1961) esp. 47n53.
33. Henry Wiencek, *An Imperfect God: George Washington, His Slaves, and the Creation of America* (New York: Farrar, Straus & Giroux, 2003) 215.
34. Smith, *Letters of Delegates to Congress*, 217
35. Robinson, *Structure of American Politics*, 114–115
36. See Chapter 4 note 17
37. Brodsky, *Benjamin Rush*, 352-356
38. Discussed in Chapters 10 and 11
39. Cappon, *Adams–Jefferson Letters*, 548
40. Ibid. 549
41. Ibid. 551
42. Ibid. 569–70
43. Ibid. 571. This attitude explains his compiler's comment that Adams seemed disinterested in the slavery issue. Robert J. Taylor, Ed., *Papers of John Adams*, Vol. III, May 1775–January 1776 (Cambridge: Belknap Press, 1979) xvi–xvii. Historian Theodore Draper's view was that the American elite "wanted freedom from British subjugation without social travail and transformation," Draper, *Struggle for Power*, 516
44. See Nash, *Race and Revolution*, 25–50
45. Lester H. Cohen, "Creating a Usable Future: The Revolutionary Historians and the National Past," in Jack P. Greene, Ed., *The American Revolution: Its Character and Limits* ( New York: NYU Press, 1989) 309–330
46. Ellis, *American Sphinx*, 267, suggests that Adams's position presupposed a reciprocal obligation on the "southern gentlemen" to effect a policy of gradual emancipation. The existence of such an understanding seems unlikely in the Revolutionary years, and was explicitly denied by General Pinckney

of South Carolina at the Constitutional convention. "General Pinckney thought himself bound to declare candidly that he did not think S. Carolina would stop her importations of slaves in any short time, but only stop them occasionally as she does now." Rutledge of South Carolina agreed. "If the convention thinks that N.C., S.C., and Georgia will ever agree to the plan, unless their right to import slaves be untouched, the expectation is vain. The people of those states will never be such fools as to give up so important an interest." Farrand, *Records*, Vol. 2, 373, Aug. 22, 1787.

47. Richard Brookheiser, *America's First Dynasty*, (New York: Simon & Schuster, 2002)198

48. McCullough, *John Adams*, 545, describes Adams as "the farmer's son who despised slavery," in contrasting him to Jefferson, and also quotes Adams's "confession" that he had deferred to the South on the issues of slavery, at 633, but does not draw any conclusions from that "confession" about Adams's role concerning slavery during his active years.

49. Burnett, *The Continental Congress*, 225-227

50. "Letter to John Holmes, April 22, 1820," in Ford, *Works of Thomas Jefferson*, 158

51. Jensen, *Articles of Confederation*, 146–47

52. Morgan, *Birth of the Republic*, 96–97

53. Rakove, *National Politics*, 3–20

54. John Adams, to Benjamin Rush, July 23, 1806. John A. Schultz and Douglas Adair, Eds., *The Spur of Fame: Dialogues of John Adams and Benjamin Rush, 1805–1813* (San Marino, CA: The Huntington Library, 1966) 61

55. Cappon, *Adams–Jefferson Letters*, 451, July 15, 1815.

56. Ibid. 452

57. Ibid. 455.

58. Quoted in Fritz Hirschfeld, *George Washington and Slavery: A Documentary Portrayal* (Columbia, MO: University of Missouri Press, 1997) 121

## CHAPTER 6
## THE COLONIES CLAIM INDEPENDENCE FROM PARLIAMENT

1 Rakove, *National Politics*, 27–35

2. "Instructions for the Deputies appointed to meet in General Congress on the Part of this Colony, 6 August 1774," Commager, *Documents of American History*. http://www.ushistory.org/declaration/related/instr.htm

3. Rakove, *National Politics*, 33

4. The Suffolk Resolves were prepared by Joseph Warren in a convention in Suffolk County condemning Parliament and a "licentious minister," declaring all British appointed officers who did not resign enemies of the people, calling for armed militias, and stoppage of all commerce with Britain. They were approved by the Congress around September 16, as an expression of "wisdom and fortitude." See Draper, *Struggle for Power*, 429

5. Draper, *Struggle for Power*, 426–440. Ferling, *Leap in the Dark*, 109–122 describes in more detail the action at the Congress. The Declaration adopted on October 14 is available on the web at the Avalon Project of Yale Law School, http://www.yale.edu/lawweb/avalon/resolves.htm

6. Butterfield, *Diary and Autobiography*, Vol. 3, 310

7. Butterfield, *Diary and Autobiography*, Vol. 3, 308-310.

8. See Ch.4

9. Smith, *Letters of Delegates to Congress*, 44. The editorial note establishes that the document is either John Rutledge's proposed resolution to the committee, or James Duane's notes on a Rutledge proposal. This suggests that the linkage of the two concepts originated with Rutledge, and was taken up by Duane. It had earlier been believed the draft was by Duane. See Morgan, *Birth of the Republic*, 65

10. Draper, *Struggle for Power*, 265. The initial combination of "internal polity and taxation" appeared in the Virginia House of Burgesses' petition of 1764, repeated in the Virginia resolves of May 29, 1765. Edmund S. Morgan and Helen M. Morgan, Eds., *The Stamp Act Crisis: Prologue to Revolution* (Chapel Hill: University of NC Press, 1962)

11. See Richard Barry, *Mr. Rutledge of South Carolina* (New York: Duell, Sloan and Pieve, 1942) for an account that identifies qualities of political sagacity in Rutledge's actions.

12. Smith, *Letters of Delegates to Congress*, 39,40, 42. See Morgan, *Birth of the Republic*, 65

13. Butterfield, *Diary and Autobiography*, 308–310

14. The committee to state the rights of the colonies was established by the Congress on Tuesday, Sept. 6, 1774. JCC, 26. On Wednesday, Sept. 7, the Congress appointed two from each colony for the committee. On Friday, Sept. 9, the committee, "met, agreed to found our rights upon the laws of nature, the principles of the English Constitution & charters & compacts; ordered a sub. comee. to draw up a state of rights." Smith, *Letters of Delegates to Congress*, 56. On Sept. 14, the subcommittee met, and reported to the Great Committee which appointed the next morning, the Sept. 15 for a consideration of the report.

15. It appears that the Great Committee considered the report on rights on Sept. 15, 16, 19, 20, and 21, and reported to the Congress on Sept. 22. Sept. 24, 26, and 27 were devoted by Congress to developing the non-importation principle. Thus, as of Sept. 28, when Galloway's plan was presented, Congress had before it the report of the Great Committee which included the language which Adams had drafted.

16. Adams may have intended to include the presentation of Galloway's Plan of Union, proposed on Sept. 28, as an attack on his draft.

17. This provision is essentially in accord with the Virginia instructions to its delegates to the Continental Congress. See Chapter 4

18 Adams suggested that the italicized language was the critical issue, by indicating that it was the point of Rutledge's interest. This language would not have been disputed by New York commercial interests who wished to continue British control of shipping, or by those like Galloway who preferred to retain British dominated legislative jurisdiction over the colonies, as much as the boldfaced language declaring independence from Parliament.

19. See Chapter 2

20. See Chapter 5

21. There is evidence that Adams was aware of Rutledge's proposal at the time he prepared Article IV. Rutledge's proposal consisted of three paragraphs. The short middle paragraph contained one sentence: "We do not however admit into this collection [of English statutes and common law] but absolutely reject the statutes of Henry the VIII and Edward VI respecting treasons and misprisions of treason." Adams's diary for Sept. 13, 1774, the

day before the subcommittee report was submitted to the great committee, notes, " 1 & 2. Phil. & Mary. C. 10. ss. 7." The editors note: "The British statute cited is 'An acte whereby certayne offenses bee made tresons,'" Butterfield, *Diary and Autobiography*, 1554–55. The references of both Rutledge and Adams to treason in connection with what became Article IV suggest that they understood the risks that the adoption of the Article entailed. "Direct evidence," in the form of writings by the delegates concerning their desire for independence in 1774, does not exist, and for a good reason. The delegates were concerned about being prosecuted for treason. John Adams's diary, on Tuesday, Sept. 13, the day this deal was struck with Rutledge and the sub-committee, contains a citation to the British treason statute, as does Rutledge's own proposal.

22. Hugh Williamson, "The Plea of the Colonies on Charges Brought Against Them by Lord Mansfield and Others in a Letter to His Lordship" (London, 1775) 8. Williamson in a paper printed in London in early 1775, argued against the idea that "an abstract theorem, a general declaration, [the Declaratory Act] has given more offense to the Americans than all the injuries they have received." He pointed out that "as members of the British empire, they have enjoyed, till the beginnings of the present controversy, (a few impolitic and unprofitable restrictions excepted) as much liberty as was consistent with civil government, or as much as they could possibly expect under a new form....What would tempt such people to become independent?" (at 16-17)

He concluded that "life and property were at the disposal of men who knew them not, who were not touched by their calamities; of men who were to gain by their loss and prosper by their adversity," (at 13-14) and that taxation without representation was the "sole cause" of the present war (at 27).

23. Don Cook, *The Long Fuse: How England Lost the American Colonies, 1760–1785* (New York: Atlantic Monthly Press, 1995) 199
24. We observed the same approach among white southerners in Louisiana in 1961 with respect to racial segregation, and white South Africans in 1987 concerning apartheid.
25. See Chapter 4
26. Jensen, *Articles of Confederation*, 118–19, says that this nascent "states' rights" position was shared in 1776 by both "radicals" and "conservatives."
27. Butterfield, *Diary and Autobiography*, 309
28. Merrill Jensen, *Commentary to Randolph Greenfield Adams: Political Ideas of the American Revolution; Britannic-American Contributions to the Problem of Imperial Organization*, 3d Ed., (New York: Barnes & Noble, 1958) 24
29. Laurence Henry Gipson, *The Triumphant Empire*, Vol. XIII (New York: Knopf, 1974) 198
30. Draper, *Struggle for Power*, 518
31. A Parliament that, for example, might abolish slavery, as the British Parliament did in 1833.
32. John Phillip Reid, *Constitutional History*
33. See Ferling, *Leap in the Dark*, 116–120, reporting Galloway's speech and analyzing his plan.

34. The jurisdiction is described by Galloway. Smith, *Letters of Delegates to Congress*, 118

35. Smith, *Letters of Delegates to Congress*, 118. There is an inconsistency in Galloway's referring to the "present constitution and powers of regulating and governing its own internal police in all cases whatsoever." In 1774, the term "present constitution and powers" of the colonies were subject to invalidation under two circumstances: (1) if the British Parliament exercised its jurisdiction under the Declaratory Act and (2) if they were not consistent with the common law, which included the *Somerset* decision. The phrase "in all cases whatsoever" is the language of the British Declaratory Act of 1766, which claimed total parliamentary authority over the colonies. It was precisely the matter at issue between the colonists pursuing the Virginia instructions and the empire. Galloway's use of both phrases in the same sentence may have been intended to patch over this basic difference without resolving it, or to appear to give enhanced powers to the colonial legislatures, while leaving them subject to both the king and Parliament.

36. The wedding of the British and American parliaments might also have made more certain that English common law would apply in America.

37. See Wills, *Inventing America*, 36–39

38. See Chapter 4 note 17

39. This is from John Adams's notes of the debates, Smith, *Letters of Delegates to Congress*, 109,111; Patrick Henry comment on 111

40. It is ironic that a strong central government, in which U.S. senators were to be selected by state legislators, was proposed by Virginians at the Constitutional Convention of 1787.

41. This point is noted, though not explored in relation to slavery by John Ferling, *The Loyalist Mind: Joseph Galloway and the American Revolution* (University Park, PA: Penn. State University Press, 1977) 30

42. Two other provisions of the declaration of 1774 also conflicted with the Galloway Plan. Article VII provides that the colonies are entitled to "all the immunities and privileges...secured by their several codes of provincial laws." This is a demand for recognition of provincial laws, including the slave codes, as the kind of "positive law" referred to by Mansfield in *Somerset*. It is inconsistent with any supervisory legislative power in any parliament, privy council, or the courts.

    Article X of the declaration states that "the exercise of legislative power in the several colonies, by a council appointed during pleasure, by the crown, is unconstitutional, dangerous, and destructive to the freedom of American legislation." Burnett characterizes this clause as "in effect, a criticism of a principal feature of the Galloway plan of union." Burnett, *The Continental Congress*, 54

43. Draper, *Struggle for Power*, 429–30. Galloway had been a follower of Benjamin Franklin. Franklin's Albany Plan of Union in 1755 failed because the colonies thought it gave them too little discretion, and the British thought it gave them too much.

44. Butterfield, *Diary and Autobiography*, Vol. 2, 140. Note 1 on 141, "To this first intimate contact between John Adams and his fellow delegates on the one hand, and the silent member from Virginia [Washington] much has been attributed, probably justly. With little doubt it markedly

influenced Washington's view of the conduct of the leaders of the patriotic movement in Massachusetts."

45. W. W. Abbot and Dorothy Twohig, Eds., *The Papers of George Washington*, Colonial Series, Vol. 10 (Charlottesville: University of Virginia Press, 1995)161, 171–72

46. Butterfield, *Diary and Autobiography*, 151. It was a little surprising that Massachusetts was divided since John Adams drafted the article and his cousin Samuel Adams was also a delegate, unless Massachusetts was staying in the background as Rush had suggested.

47. Butterfield, *Diary and Autobiography*, Vol. 1, 152n2

48. Galloway's complaints appear in Smith, *Letters of Delegates to Congress*, 113-117

49. John Locke, *Two Treatises on Government* (Original, 1690., New York: Macmillan Publishing Co, 1947)

CHAPTER 7
THE IMMORTAL AMBIGUITY: "ALL MEN ARE CREATED EQUAL"

1. Mayer, *Son of Thunder*, 249–257

2. http://collections.ic.gc.ca/blackloyalists/documents/official/virginia_response.htm

3. Miller, *Origins of the American Revolution*, 478. It also confirmed that many slaves were aware of the *Somerset* decision, and believed that the British were telling the truth when they offered freedom.

4. Samuel Johnson, *Taxation No Tyranny: An Answer to the Resolutions and Address of the American Congress* (1775)

5. Rhys Isaac, *Landon Carter's Uneasy Kingdom*, 3–15

6. http://collections.ic.gc.ca/blackloyalists/documents/official/virginia_response.htm

7. Maier, *American Scripture*, 13

8. Draper, *Struggle for Power*, 459–479

9. Maier, *American Scripture*, 63

10. Ibid. 98–105

11. Jefferson, "Thomas Jefferson to Richard Henry Lee, May 8, 1825," in Ford, *Works*, Vol. 16, 118

12. See Chapter 3

13. See Rutland, *Papers of George Mason*, cxi-cxxvi

14. Maier, *American Scripture*, 87

15. Maier, *American Scripture*, 269n62. Rutland, *Papers of George Mason*, 274

16. Tarter, "Appendix, Monday, May 27, 1776," *Revolutionary Virginia*, Vol. VII, Part I. 271, 276. Maier, *American Scripture*, 133–35, suggests that this is the language that Jefferson modified in drafting the Declaration of Independence.

17. Tarter, *Revolutionary Virginia*, Vol. VII, Part 2, 454

18. Mays, *Edmund Pendleton*, 121

19. Mays, Edmund Pendleton Vol. II, 121

20. Maier, *American Scripture*, 269n62, "The Committee draft, it seems, was far more widely circulated and more influential than that finally adopted by the Virginia Convention."

21. Ibid.

22. Published in Philadelphia on June 12. Maier *American Scripture*,126

23. Memo of H. Carrington, 9 Sept. 1851. Tarter, *Revolutionary Virginia*, 454
24. The Convention sat as a committee of the whole. This description of the process of adoption of the Virginia Declaration of Rights relies heavily on Tarter, *Revolutionary Virginia*, Vol. VII, part 1, 276 and Vol. VII, part 2, 454–455. See Maier, *American Scripture*, 193
25. Tarter, "Appendix, Monday, May 27, 1776," *Revolutionary Virginia*, Vol. VII Part I, 271, 276
26. Ellis, *American Sphinx*, 55–56. Maier, *American Scripture*, 125–26
27. Maier, *American Scripture*, 99
28. Ibid. 100
29. Mayer, *Son of Thunder*, 205–206.
30. Maier, *American Scripture*, 135–136, suggests otherwise. "The opening assertion of 'self-evident' truths concern men in a 'state of nature' before government was established." But the establishment of a government is an exercise in political judgment, not a philosophic treatise. The same is true of Mason's draft of the Virginia Declaration of Rights. Both documents speak to present political principles. Pendleton's addition of the qualifying phrase "when they enter a state of society" was understood as carving out an exception from these principles, so that they would not apply to black slaves.
31. *JCC* Vol. 5, 1079; Jefferson, "Autobiography," in Ford, *Works*, 44-45
32. *JCC* Vol. 5, 1080
33. Joseph Ellis, *American Sphinx*, 56, "Jefferson was probably aware of the contradiction between his own version of the natural rights philosophy and the institution of slavery. By dropping any reference to 'property' he blurred the contradiction."
34. Fredrika Teute Schmidt and Barbara Ripel Wilhelm, "Early Pro-Slavery Petitions in Virginia," 30 *William and Mary Quarterly*, 133 (1973) 140; Lunenberg County, 161 signatures.
35. Washburne, *Sketch of Edward Coles*, 25
36. Wills, *Inventing America*
37. The suggestion made by Howard Mumford Jones that Jefferson had imperfectly recalled the language of the Virginia declaration is implausible, in light of the importance which he attached to his drafting assignment. This assignment recognized his stature among the leadership, and was a springboard to his later influence. We know he took the assignment very seriously and kept a careful record of changes made in his draft, thereby expressing his displeasure at the tinkering done by the Congress. See Wills, *Inventing America*, 230. Wills also describes the efforts Jefferson made to preserve "his" Declaration and noted that Jefferson had urged Lafayette to delete the term "property" from his draft declaration of Human Rights for France.

     Wills's explanation is that Jefferson was not so much influenced by Locke as by the Scottish philosopher Francis Hutcheson, whose philosophy emphasized the "right of exchange…not the right of retention." (Ibid. 231). Wills demonstrates not only that Jefferson followed Hutcheson's approach to the organization of social values, but also that Jefferson himself had a persistent concern that real property rights, as then understood, could stultify social development and prevent the emergence of wide-scale land ownership. Thus he opposed primogenitor and entail, and supported free alienation of land.

38. Maier, *American Scripture*, 134
39. For example, Wills, *Inventing America*; Davis, *Problem of Slavery*; Maier, *American Scriptures*; Becker, *The Declaration of Independence: A Study in the History of Political Ideas* (New York: Knopf, 1942)
40. Jefferson had included the words "inherent and" before "unalienable rights." Congress removed them.
    http://www.ushistory.org/declaration/document/congress.htm
41. "Original Rough Draft of the Declaration of Independence," *Papers of Thomas Jefferson*, Vol. 1 (1760–1776) Julian P. Boyd, Ed. (Princeton: Princeton University Press, 1950) 243–47.
    http://www.constitution.org/tj/doi_rough.htm
42. Ellis, *American Sphinx*, 51–52, treats this section as an attempted absolution of colonial responsibility for slavery. MacLeod, *Slavery, Race*, 32–33, also notes that the British support for the slave trade was an important part of the "southern defense of its institutions." He concludes, "If for no other reason than that the trade depended upon a market, the reaction was illogical."
43. Jefferson, "Autobiography," in Ford, *Works*, 28
44. Ellis, *American Sphinx*, 52
45. Higginbotham, *In the Matter of Color*, 371. The states reviewed are in addition to Virginia, Massachusetts, New York, South Carolina, Georgia, and Pennsylvania.

CHAPTER 8
THE ARTICLES OF CONFEDERATION REJECT *Somerset* AND PROTECT SLAVERY

1. Dickinson was asked to prepare a draft. Burnett, *Continental Congress*, 213–229, describes the debates on the articles during 1776. He concludes that Dickinson was much influenced by Benjamin Franklin's plan of 1775. Franklin's plan, however, concluded differently. It did not give general authority to a central government.
2. Ferling, *Leap in the Dark*, 70
3. Jensen, *Articles of Confederation*, 254–262 (Dickinson Draft); 263–270 (as adopted). Dickinson refused to sign the Declaration of Independence and did not participate in the deliberations after July 4, 1776.
4. Jensen, *Articles of Confederation*, 259, ¶2. This statement of authority is tucked in the middle of Article XVII, possibly to avoid immediate attention by a reader.
5. Jensen, *Articles of Confederation*, 254
6. Ibid. 259, ¶1
7. See Chapter 6 note 35
8. For the Declaratory Act of 1766, see Ch. 2 at note 12
9. For the Galloway Plan, see Chapter 6 at note 35
10. Smith, *Letters of Delegates*, Vol. 4, 338; Jensen, *Articles of Confederation*, 139
11. Jack N. Rakove, *National Politics*, 164–176
12. Burke's position is set forth in a letter of April 29, 1777, Smith, *Letters of Delegates*, Vol. 3, 671–73. Virginia and Pennsylvania expected to be the most important states in the new confederation, along with Massachusetts. On Burke's contributions to the debate on the Articles, see Morris, *Forging of the Union*, 87–91

13. Jensen, *Articles of Confederation*, 175 describes the "weakening" of the powers of the federal government which had been proposed by Dickinson.

14. Art. II, Jensen, *Articles of Confederation*, 263

15. See Burnett, *Continental Congress*, 237–39

16. See Morris, *Forging of the Union*, 80–91

17. Jensen, *Articles of Confederation*, Art. XIII, 270, Unanimity to amend. Art. 9, ¶6, 269, Nine states required for some issues, seven for all others.

18. John Russell Bartlett, Ed., *Records of the Colony of Rhode Island*, Vol. III (Providence: A. C. Green, 1856–65) 251-253

19. It applied only to slaves thereafter brought into the colony. It exempted travelers who took their slaves with them when they left and slaves of "inhabitants of either of the British Colonies, islands or plantations" who entered the colony "with an intention to settle or reside, for a number of years." It also excluded slaves whose owners had brought them from Africa and been unable to sell them elsewhere, if the owner would post a £100 bond to guarantee their removal within a year. This clause was deleted in 1784, thus prohibiting slave trading in Rhode Island. The same act provided for manumission of persons born after March of that year. A 1779 act prohibited slaves from being sold out of the state against their consent. These acts taken together make clear that the abolitionist tone of the preamble of the 1774 act was tempered by a recognition of the rights of existing slave owners in Rhode Island, and a desire to permit slave owners to come to the colony, which they did. MacLeod, *Slavery, Race*, 32

20. Jensen, *Articles of Confederation*, 255. "Art VI. The inhabitants of each colony shall henceforth always have the same rights, liberties, privileges, immunities, and advantages in the other colonies which the said Inhabitants now have, in all cases whatever, except in those provided for by the next following Article.

    "Art. VII. The inhabitants of each colony shall enjoy all the rights, liberties, privileges, immunities, and advantages in trade, navigation, and commerce, in any other colony, and in going to and from the same from and to any part of the world, which the natives of such colony [or any commercial society, established by its authority] shall enjoy."

21. The draft mentioned "white" inhabitants only in reference to the contributions of each colony for war and general welfare, which was to be in proportion to the number of inhabitants, except Indians not taxed, pursuant to a triennial census which would distinguish white inhabitants (Art. XI); and in reference to the quota of troops from each colony which was to be proportioned to the number of white inhabitants. (Art. XVIII ¶2). Jensen, *Articles of Confederation*

22. See Burnett, *Continental Congress*, 248–254

23. See Chapter 2 at note 28. He was not cautious enough with his papers. While on a mission to France, his ship was intercepted by the British who seized a batch of his papers that did not sink when tossed overboard. As a result, he spent considerable time in the Tower of London. After Yorktown, he was exchanged for Lord Cornwallis. He was appointed as a commissioner to negotiate the Treaty of Paris that ended the Revolutionary War. His only contribution, before he died, was to insist on a provision in the treaty that would require Britain to return the slaves that they

had taken. That provision created great difficulties in its implementation. See Lindsay, "Diplomatic Relations," 391–419

24. In 1774, he had written that, "Entering into the African trade is so repugnant to my disposition & my plan for future life that it seems as if nothing but dire necessity could drive me to it." However, in the same letter, which turned down a request for a partnership relation, he offered to go surety for Mr. John Lewis Gervais, and to obtain "several cargoes of Negroes," if he had not thought that these would be "injurious to your interest." Rogers, "Henry Laurens to John Lewis Gervais, Feb. 5, 1774,"*Papers of Henry Laurens*, Vol. 9, 263–64

Henry Laurens's purported distaste for the trade is also inconsistent with his going surety for John Hopton in the amount of ten thousand pounds sterling, " In order the more effectively to enable you to make offers and accept the sale of African cargoes....We think you in all respects capable of rendering as good accounts of sales for Negroes as any gentleman in Charles Town of your age and experience." Ibid. Vol. 7, 488–89

While Laurens turned down Gervais's request to become his partner in the African trade, he helped find Gervais a partner and offered to back him in such a venture. Ibid. Vol. 8, 496–98; 516–518, 528–30

25. Gregory D. Massey, *John Laurens and the American Revolution* (Columbia: University of South Carolina Press, 2000)

26. "I abhor slavery," he wrote in a letter to his son James on August 14, 1776, and indicated his intention to begin manumission of his hundreds of slaves. Rogers, *Papers of Henry Laurens*, Vol. 1 99–100

27. See Chapter 2

28. *JCC*, Vol. 8, 885

29. Ibid. 888–89. The drafts contained some language variations on the privilege and immunities clause. One version provided:

"The citizens of every state, going to reside in another state, shall be entitled to all the rights and privileges of natural born free citizens of the state to which they go to reside; *and the people of each state shall have free egress and regress for their persons and property to and from every other state, without hindrance, molestation, or imposition of any kind.* Provided that if merchandise of any sort be imported for the purposes of traffick within any state, that the person so importing shall be liable to the same impost and duties as the people of the state are by law liable to where such importations are made, and none other." [emphasis added]

30. "The free inhabitants of each of these states—paupers, vagabonds, and fugitives from justice excepted—shall be entitled to all privileges and immunities of free citizens in the [respective] several states; and the people of each state shall have free ingress and regress to and from any other state, and shall enjoy therein all the privileges of trade and commerce, subject to the same duties, impositions, and restrictions as the inhabitants thereof respectively." Nov. 14, 1777, *JCC* Vol. 8, 907. "Respective" appeared in the draft as adopted, on Nov. 13. Ibid. 899 "Several" replaced it in the final version. Congress also adopted a rendition and a full faith and credit clause relating to the "records, acts, and judicial proceedings of the courts and magistrates of every other state."

31. One technical holding in the *Somerset* decision was that the law of the jurisdiction in which the slave was held determined whether the slave owner

could send him out of that jurisdiction against his will. Lord Mansfield found there was no "positive law" in Britain permitting the slave owner to take such an action. A similar decision could come from a state where slavery was permitted without specific statutory authorization.

32. *JCC* Vol. 8, 907. The final version was adopted November 14.

33. Charles Warren, *The Making of the Constitution*, (Boston: Little Brown & Co., 1929) 561

34. This version made specific Dickinson's draft's provision for "free egress and regress for their persons and property." See Chapter 8 note 30. The general issues of trade and commerce and the taxation of merchants were both encompassed elegantly in the Nov. 11 draft. There seems no occasion to change the general right to move "persons and property" to the more specific "right of removal" language of Nov. 13 other than to emphasize the rejection of the rule in the *Somerset* case.

35. Wiecek, *Antislavery Constitutionalism*, 59

36. The same provision, Art. IV of the Articles, that repudiated the *Somerset* decision included the following language: "If any person guilty of, or charged with, treason, felony, or other high misdemeanor in any state, shall flee from justice, and be found in any of the united states, he shall, upon demand of the governor or executive power of the state from which he fled, be delivered up and removed to the state having jurisdiction of his offense." The next sentence required that "full faith and credit" be given by each state to "the records, acts, and judicial proceedings" of courts in every other state. If escaping from slavery constituted a "felony or high misdemeanor" and a charge was filed with a state court, this provision would require a state in which the slave was found to return him to the charging state.

37. The anti-*Somerset* clause specifically encompassed the slave brought into the jurisdiction by the master, but it might also encompass the slave who escaped into the jurisdiction. The master might plead that he had entered the jurisdiction with the intent to reside, and "found" his escaped slave there and was entitled under the Articles to take him out. The situation of the escaped slave became more important as the slaves learned of the existence of free states, commencing in 1780 with the gradual emancipation law of Pennsylvania.

The Articles did not contain any equivalent to the supremacy clause in Art. VI Sec. 2 of the Constitution. Therefore the legal significance of this section is not clear. The Articles were in effect only between 1781 and 1789, so there was not time to develop a jurisprudence through state courts. The Articles were ratified by each state legislature and therefore would appear to be binding on the state courts as enactments of the state legislature. The experience of ratification by a legislature led the drafters of the Constitution to propose ratification by specially elected conventions so that the Constitution would be recognized as "higher law" that state statutes. Rakove, *Original Meanings*, 94-130.

38. Fehrenbacher, *Dred Scott Case*, 22, discussed the interpretation of the fugitive slave act of 1793 in *Prigg v. Pennsylvania*. "The slaveholder...carried the law of his own state with him when he pursued a fugitive into a free state. The implications of such extraterritoriality were startling, though [Justice]Story left them unexplored. His ruling had the effect, for instance,

of compelling free states to accept the slave-state principle that a black or mulatto was a slave unless he could prove otherwise. One-half of the nation must sacrifice its presumption of freedom to the other half's presumption of slavery." See also Arthur R. Landever, "Those Indispensable Articles of Confederation: Stages in Constitutionalism, Passage for the Framers, and Clue to the Nature of the Constitution," 31 *Arizona Law Review* (1989) 79, 87

39. See William Lee Miller, *Arguing About Slavery: John Quincy Adams and the Great Battle in the United States Congress* (New York: Vintage Books, 1995)

40. Jensen, *Articles of Confederation*, 225–238

41. *JCC* Vol. 26, 114. The settlers were identified as "French and Canadian inhabitants, and other settlers of the Kaskaskies, St. Vincents, and the neighboring villages."

## CHAPTER 9
## THE LURE OF THE WEST: SLAVERY PROTECTED IN THE TERRITORIES

1. Hunter Miller, Ed., *Treaties and Other International Acts of the United States of America*, Volume 2 (Washington, DC: Government Printing Office, 1931) Documents 1–40. Britain had considered this area a headache from the 1760s on. It had discouraged settlements and speculators by a "proclamation line" of 1763, which was supposed to keep speculators and settlers from disturbing the Native American tribes in order to avoid more fighting.

2. *JCC* Vol. 26, 114

3. The Articles did not provide Congress with express power to regulate federal territory. The land cessions to the Congress by the states in the1780s created "federal" territory. See Jensen, *Articles of Confederation*, 185–238, for a discussion of the web of problems surrounding the western lands. Onuf, *Statehood and Union*, examines the way in which the approaches to these problems influenced the Northwest Ordinance of 1787. Acceptance of the cessions by Congress was treated as creating congressional power to control development in the territories. Madison claimed the Northwest Ordinance was not constitutional in the *Federalist* 38, 248–49, (Jan. 15, 1788) "All this has been done; and without the least color of constitutional authority, yet no blame has been whispered; no alarm has been sounded."

4. Nine states were required for ratification of a treaty. Francis Wharton, Avalon Project of Yale Law School, Edited under the Direction of Congress, "Proclamation of Congress Respecting the Definitive Treaty; By the United States in Congress Assembled, Jan. 14, 1784," *The Revolutionary Correspondence of the United States*, Volume VI, Washington, DC: Government Printing Office, 1889.

5. Ibid. Art. XVIII.

6. See Chapter 7

7. Kimberly C. Simmons, JD, *American Jurisprudence* 45, 2d Edition, International Law (St. Paul, MN: West Grou, 2004)

§ 33 "As a matter of strict English usage the term "cession" refers to voluntary surrender of territory or jurisdiction rather than a withdrawal of such jurisdiction by the authority of a superior sovereign. *Cession effects a change of sovereignty over the territory ceded, and a transfer of title to property that is vested in the sovereign making the cession, but it does not affect the property rights of the inhabitants of the territory involved.*" [emphasis added]

8. Wills, *Negro President*, paints the sharpest picture of Pickering as a highly competent, puritanical opponent of slavery on religious grounds.

9. "During the Revolutionary War, the Continental Congress authorized the printing of paper 'money' called 'Continentals,' which depreciated in perceived value [inflated] so quickly and so badly that, soon, they were 'not worth a Continental.'" http://www.geocities.com/tthor.geo/debased-money.html

10. Charles B. Galbreath, *History of Ohio* (American Historical Society, Inc., 1925) 154–57 " 11. That a constitution for the new state be formed by the members of the association previous to their commencing the settlement, two-thirds of the associators present at a meeting duly notified for that purpose agreeing therein. *The total exclusion of slavery from the state to form an essential and irrevocable part of the constitution.*" Ibid. 156. [emphasis added]. See Jay. A. Barrett, *Evolution of the Ordinance*, 7–9

11. See Alden T. Vaughn, *Roots of American Racism*, (New York: Oxford University Press, 1995) 136–174 for a discussion of debate over the origins of racism.

12. Calliope Film Resources. *Shays's Rebellion*. Copyright 2000 CFR. http://www.calliope.org/shays/shays2.html, visited October 19, 2004

13. Statuary, *Shays's Rebellion*, 120–134

14. *JCC*, Vol. 26, 275-79. The plan applied to territory "ceded or to be ceded" to the United States, thus covering territory both north and south of the Ohio river. This was the coverage of all proposed ordinances until 1787. Lynd, *Class Conflict*, 192

15. http://www.yale.edu/lawweb/avalon/presiden/jeffpap.htm.

16. *JCC*, Vol. 26, 247, April 19, 1784. The rules of the Congress required that at least two delegates vote for a measure for the state's vote to count.

17. Randall, *Thomas Jefferson*, 363

18. Prearranged absences at critical junctions in the legislative process are not unknown today.

19. By 1784, Massachusetts had abolished slavery by court decision and Pennsylvania had enacted its gradual emancipation act.

The number of states that might be created north of the Ohio was reduced to three to five. See Barrett, *Evolution of the Ordinance*, 17–27 discussing the number of states, and including a map.

When the territory acquired twenty thousand "free inhabitants," a convention could be called to establish a permanent constitution and government. These states were to be admitted to the union "on equal footing with the said original states" when the population equaled that of the least populous state and upon meeting certain conditions. The states were to: (1) remain in the confederation; (2) be subject to the Articles of Confederation (3) not interfere with U.S. land titles or regulation concerning disposition of U.S. lands (4) pay part of the federal debt apportioned as with the other states; (5) not tax lands or property of the U.S. (6) have a republican government without hereditary titles (7) not to tax non resident proprietors higher than residents; The ordinance was to be a "charter of compact" and "stand as fundamental constitutions between the thirteen original sates and each of the several states newly described." This provision sought to bridge a gap in the power of the Confederacy. The Confederation had no power over territories because none had been provided in the Articles; yet it was necessary to provide for governance for many reasons. The Articles could be amended only by unanimous consent which was never achieved. The voluntary adoption of a "compact" would obscure the want of power. Pinckney at the Convention and Madison in the *Federalist* both considered the NWO to be unconstitutional under the Articles.

20. See Peter S. Onuf, "Settlers, Settlements, and New States," In Jack S. Green, Ed., *The American Revolution: Its Character and Limits* (New York: NYU Press, 1987) 171–96

21. See Freehling, *Road to Disunion*, 138–41. An expression of this concern is found in Timothy Pickering's letter to Rufus King in 1785. See Chapter 9

22. See Chapter 8

23. See Chapter 9

24. See Chapter 9

25. Finkelman, *Slavery and the Founders: Race and Liberty in the Age of Jefferson*, 2ed, 148; Wiecek, *Antislavery Constitutionalism*, 60.

26. Ernst, "Pickering to King, March 8, 1785," *Rufus King*, 54–55

27. See Wills, *Negro President*, 183–93

28. The third possibility, of course, was that Congress expressed no judgment on the slavery issue. This seems unlikely, given that there was existing law about that issue; it was a "two value" proposition—slavery was either legal or illegal.

29. The reasoning assumes, as was true in connection with the slavery issue, that there is no third possibility. The approach taken by Marshall was a variation on the canon "Expressio unius est exclusio alterius," commonly applied when the legislature has chosen one concept over others which are inconsistent with it. Sutherland, *Statutory Construction*, 4e (Willmette, IL: 1984). The "founding fathers" agreed that the Constitution was to be interpreted as if it were legislation, in accordance with the well-known principles of statutory interpretation set forth by Blackstone. See H. Jefferson Powell, "The Original Understanding of Original Intent," from 98 *Harvard L. Rev.* In Jack N. Rakove, Ed., *Interpreting the Constitution: The Debate Over Original Intent* (Boston: Northeastern University Press, 1990) 53. Story agreed; Story, *Commentaries*, 134–148. Blackstone's first edition was well known in the colonies. Volume 1, 59–62, contains general principles of interpretation designed to identify the "intent" of the legislature. Blackstone, *Commentaries*, 59–62

30. See Chapter 8. This restriction had been a part of the southern led effort to protect state supported slavery from external control under the Articles.

31. "Among the enumerated powers, we do not find that of establishing a bank or creating a corporation. But there is no phrase in the instrument which, like the Articles of Confederation, excludes incidental or implied powers; and which requires that everything granted shall be expressly and minutely described. Even the tenth amendment, which was framed for the purpose of quieting the excessive jealousies which had been excited, omits the word 'expressly,' and declares only that the powers 'not dele-

gated to the United Sates, nor prohibited to the states, are reserved to the states or to the people'; thus leaving the question, whether the particular power which may become the subject of contest has been delegated to the one government, or prohibited to the other, to depend on a fair construction of the whole instrument. The men who drew and adopted this amendment had experienced the embarrassments resulting from the insertion of this word in the Articles of Confederation, and probably omitted it to avoid those embarrassments." McCullough at Story, *Commentaries*, adopts this language without attribution, 147. See discussion in Warren, *The Supreme Court in United States History*, (1926) 501. The omission of the term "expressly" from the tenth amendment was discussed in oral argument in McCullough by Mr. Pinckney. "The reservation in the tenth amendment to the Constitution of 'powers not delegated to the United States' is not confined to powers not expressly delegated. Such an amendment was indeed proposed, but it was perceived that it would strip the government of some of its most essential powers and it was rejected." "Landmark Briefs and Arguments of the Supreme Court of the United States," *Constitutional Law*, Vol. 1, 170.

Marshall's doctrine of implied powers was interpreted by John Randolph, Chief Justice of Virginia in 1824 as permitting Congress to "emancipate every slave in the United States." Albert J. Beveridge, *Life of John Marshall*, Vol. IV (Houghton, Mifflin Co., 1919) 308–309, 420

In *Marbury v. Madison*, Marshall used analogous reasoning. He stated "Affirmative words are often, in their operation, negative of other objects than those affirmed."

32. The only background law applicable in light of congressional silence was the anti-*Somerset* provision of the Articles, which protected slavery in all the states. This background law may not have been fully recognized by the historians because it was not supported by case law during the short period of the operation of the Articles. But the very shortness of the period, coupled with the absence of any centralized court, made it unlikely that the Articles would have had an extensive judicial exegesis. It is our two-hundred-plus years' experience with a centralized high court which makes us think that judicial interpretations of the Constitution are crucial to its understanding.

33. When a similar issue arose in Ohio in the nineteenth century, the Circuit Court treated the answer as obvious. One Palmer sought to enjoin the county commissioners from building a drawbridge over the Cuyahoga River on the grounds that it would obstruct navigation, in violation of the "free navigation" clause of the Northwest Ordinance. Defendants argued that the ordinance was inapplicable because the "western reserve" had not been ceded by Connecticut to the federal government until some time after the Ordinance was adopted. Justice McLean, after holding that the drawbridge was not an obstruction within the meaning of the ordinance, concluded:

"That this reserve was, to some extent, subject to the legislation of Connecticut for several years after the date of the ordinance is admitted. But when this territory and the jurisdiction over it were ceded to the United States it became subject to the ordinance, the same as every other part of the northwest territory. Rights acquired under the former laws are governed by those laws. But on its cession to the union, all the laws of the territory, and especially its fundamental law, became the law of the reserve." *Palmer v. Cuyahoga County Commissioners*, 2 Ohio Federal Decisions 264, 266 (1843).

This situation was similar to that of slavery in Virginia at the time of cession to the federal government. Rights to hold slaves acquired under Virginia law remained governed by those laws; on cession to the union, the laws of the territory would apply, but there was no law prohibiting slavery at the time of cession in 1783, and none became applicable until 1787.The deed of cession states that "certain settlers...who have professed themselves citizens of Virginia, shall have their possessions and titles confirmed to them, and be protected in the enjoyment of their rights and liberties." The settlers were identified as "French and Canadian inhabitants, and other settlers of the Kaskaskies, St. Vincents, and the neighboring villages." *JCC* Vol. 26, 114. The possible negative inference that slavery was to be illegal in the vast reach of the territory not mentioned in the cession agreement would not outweigh the underlying Virginia law protecting slavery.

34. "That there shall be neither slavery nor involuntary servitude in any of the states, described in the resolve of Congress of the 23 April, 1784, otherwise than in punishment of crimes, whereof the party shall have been personally guilty: And that this regulation shall be an article of compact, and remain a fundamental principle of the Constitutions between the thirteen original states, and each of the states described in the said resolve of the 23 April, 1784." *JCC*, Vol. 28, 164, March 16, 1785.

The ordinance, which was later adopted, provided for surveys laying out township squares. The proposed land ordinance of 1785, April 12, did address another problem—education in the territories—that would become entwined with the slavery issue in the Northwest Ordinance. *JCC* Vol. 28, 250–4 "There shall be reserved the central section of every township for the maintenance of public schools and the [section] immediately adjoining the same to the northward, for the support of religion, the [profits] arising therefrom in both instances to be applied forever according to the will of the majority of male residents of full age within the same."

35. Votes: Aye NH, MA, RI, CN, NY, NJ, PA, MD (8); No. VA, NC, SC, GA(4). Ernst, *Rufus King*, 55. Counts the votes as 8–3, with Virginia and Carolinas opposing. *JCC* Vol. 28, 164. Ernst also says that eighteen of the twenty-six delegates present supported the motion in committee. (At 55, cites *JCC*, Vol. 28, 164) He adds, "These features (the prospective application and the fugitive slave clause) were designed to win support from the slave states, but Congress still took no action. Recognizing that the committee revisions were unacceptable to the northern delegations, King refrained from pressing the issue. His political sense told him the time was not yet ripe for action. Original motion in "Papers of Constitutional Convention," No. 31, f.327, *National Archives*; He also cites "King to Pickering, Apr. 15, 1785," *King Papers*, N.Y. Hist. Soc.

36. Other members were David Howell [RI] and William Ellery[RI].

37. *JCC*, Vol. 28, 239, April 6, 1785. The Articles appeared to require only seven votes for the adoption of this resolution. The language in boldface in the proviso may have been derived from the Pennsylvania Law of 1780, *1 Laws of the Commonwealth of PA*, 492, 496; *2 Laws of the Commonwealth*

*of PA*, 443-446. 2 *Carey & Bioren's Laws*, 246, Sec. 3, stated: "That all persons, as well Negroes and mulattoes as others, who shall be born within this state from and after the passing of this act shall not be deemed and considered as servants for life or slaves; and that all servitude for life or slavery of children in consequence of the slavery of their mothers, in the case of all children born within this state from and after the passing of this act as aforesaid, shall be and hereby is utterly taken away, extinguished, and forever abolished." Section 11 provided that the act "shall not give any relief or shelter to any absconding or runaway Negro or mulatto slave or servant who has absented himself or shall absent himself from his or her owner, master or mistress, residing in any other state or country, but *such owner, &c., shall have like rights and aid to demand, claim, and take away his slave or servant as he might have had in case this act had not been made.*" [emphasis added] This proviso was repealed in 1826. John Codman Hurd, *The Law of Freedom and Bondage in the United States*, (Original,1862; Reprinted, New York: Negro Universities Press, 1968) 68–69. The proviso may have been intended to comply with the anti-*Somerset* provision of the Articles of Confederation.

38. He initially expected the motion to pass. See "Grayson to Madison, May 1, 1785," Smith, *Letters of Delegates*, Vol. 8, 109–10. At the final debate on the ordinance, at the third reading, May 18–20, 1785, (*JCC*, 375), states present were NH, MASS, CN, NY, NJ, PA, MD, and VA—eight states in all. If seven votes were required to include the anti-slavery clause and MD voted affirmatively, the motion would have passed, with only VA voting against, assuming the previous voting pattern on the motion to consider the King proposal reflected views on the merits. However, MD had voted to consider the King motion by a 2–1 vote. (March 16) If one of those supporters had been absent, MD vote would not have been in the affirmative, and the motion would have lost.

39. The more usual way of accomplishing the result sought by the boldface language would be by repealing the 1784 ordinance. This was done in the Northwest Ordinance of 1787 which repealed the 1784 ordinance only with respect to the northwest territory.

40. Wager Swayne, "Monroe to Jefferson, January 19, 1786," *The Ordinance of 1787 and the War of 1861* (New York: C. G. Burgoyne, 1892) 39

41. *JCC* Vol. 33, 131-35, March 24, 1786; Barrett, *Evolution of the Ordinance*, 33–38. The report was considered by a committee of Congress in March, and again in May, 1786. Another committee made a similar recommendation, and included a plan for territorial government. *JCC* Vol. 30, 251, May 1786.

42. *JCC* Vol. 30, 390-94, July 7, 1786

43. For the view that Monroe never got to the northwest territory, see Jorge M. Robert, "James Monroe and the Three to Five Clause of the Northwest Ordinance," http://www.earlyamerica.com/review/2001_summer_fall/monroe.html

   If this view is correct, it is possible that the letter was intended to lead to a reduction of the North's advantage in any expansion of the union that Jefferson's eight to ten states would have created north of the Ohio River.

44. Members of the Committee were William Samuel Johnson, William Henry, Charles Pinckney, Nathan Dane, and Melancton Smith. *JCC* Vol. 31, 669; Barrett, *Evolution of the Ordinance*, 42–43

45. *JCC* Vol. 31, 669, September 19, 1786.

(1) it applied to all territories; (2) Congress to appoint governor secretary, five judges with common law and chancery jurisdiction; (3) to secure personal liberty and property of inhabitants and other purchasers; (a) preserve habeas corpus and trial by jury (b) intestate succession to children in equal parts regardless of sex; free alienation during life (c) same rules for non-resident proprietors real estate (d) governor commands militia, appoints magistrates, lay out counties and townships (e) free male inhabitants to elect representatives to general assembly, property qualifications for voting and serving (f) mechanics of government (g) inhabitants subject to federal debt, apportioned by same rules as to other states (h) when achieve thirteenth of citizens of original states, to be admitted with congressional consent, on equal footing with original states.

This bill had a second reading on May 9, 1787. *JCC*, Vol. 32, 274-75. Wednesday, May 9, 1787. The draft appearing on 281-3 reflects both the form of the ordinance on May 9, and the form after the debates on May 10 and July 9.

46. It contained the following provisions:

*JCC* Vol. 32, 281, Wednesday, May 9, 1787:

1. Congress to appoint a governor, a secretary, and three judges with common law jurisdiction, following earlier drafts 2. Inhabitants entitled to habeas corpus and trial by jury, as in the September, 1786 draft 3. Governor and judges to adopt such laws of the original states, civil and criminal, as they think best suited, to be effective until the organization of a general assembly, unless disapproved by Congress 4. Governor to be commander in chief of militia, appoint all non-general officers, general officers appointed by Congress, appoint magistrates and civil officers, lay out the territory into counties and townships, as in the 1786 draft 5. When have five thousand free male inhabitants, may elect representatives to a general assembly. Electors to have two years residence and fifty acres freehold or life estate, Representatives to have two hundred acres fee simple, from 1786 draft 6. General assembly to consist of governor, legislative council, and house of representatives; cannot affect lands of United States or tax non-resident proprietor's lands higher than residents, as in 1786 bill. 7. Governor can convene, prorogue, and dissolve assembly, as in 1786 draft 8. Inhabitants subject to part of federal debt apportioned according to common apportionment measure used in other states, as in earlier drafts going back to 1784

On July 9, the bill did not include the provision for the "equal footing" admission of new states when they had one-thirteenth the population of the original states, which had been in the 1786 draft. The "equal footing" issue was before the Constitutional Convention in Philadelphia in early July.

47. H. James Henderson, *Party Politics in the Continental Congress* (NY: McGraw Hill, 1974) 413

## CHAPTER 10
## DEADLOCK OVER SLAVERY IN THE CONSTITUTIONAL CONVENTION

1. See Chapter 8
2. Farrand, *Framing of the Constitution*, 7
3. Statuary, *Shays's Rebellion*, 120–134

4. In addition, the Virginia Delegation included John Blair and James McClurg.
5. Proposals and amendments were made in committee of the whole, subject to the approval by the convention itself, thus not officially committing members until the final vote taken after a committee of detail had polished the language. The actual committee of detail was Gouverneur Morris of Pennsylvania. See Richard Brookhiser, *Gentleman Revolutionary: Governeur Morris, the Rake Who Wrote the Constitution* (New York: Free Press, 2003) 85–93. See Thornton Anderson, *Creating the Constitution: The Convention of 1787 and the First Congress*, 50–58 (University Park, PA: Pennsylvania State University Press, 1993)
6. In 1783, as a result of a compromise proposed by Madison, Congress had adopted the formula that each slave should be counted as three-fifths of a person in measuring the population for valuation purposes. *JCC* Vol. 24, 222-4. The negotiations leading to the formula were described by Madison in his notes of the Congress. *JCC* Vol. 25, 948-9. A committee had recommended that two slaves be rated as equal to one freeman for determining contributions by each state to the federal budget. In the haggling that followed:

Mr. Wolcott was for rating the slaves 4 to 3. Mr. Carrol as 4 to 1. Mr. Williamson wouldn't play. He considered slaves "an encumbrance to society instead of increasing its ability to pay taxes." Mr. Higginson as 4 to 3. Mr. Rutledge would go along with 2 to 1, but believed 3 to 1 was "a juster proportion." Mr. Osgood could not go beyond 4 to 3

A vote was taken on rating them as 3 to 2, and it lost. Voting for it were NH, CN, NJ, PA, DE (5), against were MASS, MD, VA, NC, SC. RI was divided. The southern states plus Massachusetts refused to consider a slave as equal to 66 percent of a free man.

"After some further discussions on the report in which the necessity of some simple and practicable rule of apportionment came fully into view, Mr. Madison said that in order to give a proof of the sincerity of his professions of liberality, he would propose that slaves should be rated as 5 to 3. Mr. Rutledge seconded the motion. Mr. Wilson (PA) said he would sacrifice his opinion to this compromise. Mr. Lee (VA) was against changing the rule, but gave it as his opinion that 2 slaves were not equal to 1 freeman." The vote was yes, NH, NJ, PA, MD, VA, NC, SC. No: RI, CN.
7. Farrand, *Records*, Vol. I, 35-36. The "diversion" of course would have involved an early consideration of not counting slaves to measure representation. For taxation purposes, the slave owners were against counting slaves because that would increase their taxes. The non-slave-holding states supported this approach because it would reduce theirs. The interests of slave states and non-slave states were reversed when applied to the question of representation. In that situation, the southern states would gain enhanced votes by counting slaves, even though slaves could not vote.
8. Ibid. 20, Resolution 2.
9. In the end, the state legislatures selected their senators until the twentieth century.
10. In the debates, the body we know as the House of Representatives was called the first or lower house, and the Senate was called the second house. For convenience, we use the names (House and Senate) later attached to these two bodies.

11. Farrand, *Records*, Vol. I, 193

12. Ibid. 201. See Wills, *Negro President*, 51–61 for a discussion of the origins and consequences of the three-fifths rule.

13. Farrand, *Records*, 193. Six against (MA, PA, VA, NC, SC, GA); five for (CN, NY, NJ, DE, MD). The only proposal then under consideration concerning the makeup of the Senate was that of Virginia, which would allow the House to elect the senators. If the slave states had the benefit of the three-fifths rule in the House, that would enhance their weight in voting for senators. The resolution of these issues was reported to the Convention on June 13, Farrand, *Records*, Vol. I, 227-229. On June 14, Randolph and Patterson moved for a day's adjournment so that the report could be further considered. Farrand, *Records*, Vol. I, 240. The outcome of the consideration was the Patterson plan presented the next day.

14. Farrand, *Records*, Vol. I, 242.

15. Ibid. 313

16. Ibid. 445-6

17. Ibid. 450–452. Isaacson, *Benjamin Franklin*, 445–60, eloquently describes Franklin's role at the Constitutional Convention.

18. Isaacson, *Benjamin Franklin*, 451, 453 (Madison). The convention had no funds for prayer, and did not vote on Franklin's proposal. See Bowen, *Miracle at Philadelphia*, 117–40 for a vivid description of the crucial nature of the debate during this period and the frustration level at the time.

19. Farrand, *Records*, Vol. I, 460-461

20. Ibid. 468–9. The reference to "this part of it" presumably refers to the states south of Pennsylvania. Ellsworth's statement contained the germ of the idea which would grow quickly—dividing the nation "somewhere about" Pennsylvania. The Ohio River, it will be remembered, rises in Pittsburgh, from the conjunction of the Monongahela and the Allegheny. The Ohio River was the southern border of the northwest territory.

21. Ibid. 478

22. Ibid. 475

23. Ferling, *Leap in the Dark*, 281–3, describes them as members of the political elite. "No delegate resembled the activists…of twenty years before. No urban artisans or laborers…were in attendance. Nor had any small farmers…been appointed. Southern yeomen who possessed small farms but no slaves were noticeably absent as well, as were the inhabitants of rustic back country villages." Of course women and blacks remained unrepresented.

24. Farrand, *Records*, Vol. I, 476. According to Yates, on June 29, Madison said, "If there was real danger, I would give the smaller states the defensive weapons—But there is none from that quarter. The great danger to our general government is the great southern and northern interests of the continent, being opposed to each other. Look to the votes in Congress, and most of them stand divided by the geography of the country, not according to the size of the states." Madison's notes are silent about such a comment on that date. Yates may have failed to understand the import of his speech of June 30, or just misdated it.

25. See Nash, *Race and Revolution*, 25–55, for an analysis which suggests that the North did not have to accede to the lower South's demands to maintain slavery and the slave trade at the 1787 Convention.

26. Farrand, *Records*, Vol. I, 486

27. Farrand, *Records*, Vol. II, 9–10

28. Farrand. *Records*, Vol. I, 201

29. See H. James Henderson, *Party Politics in the Continental Congress*, (New York: McGraw-Hill Book Company, 1974) 383–429 discussing various proposals to separate the nation into two or three countries as the Continental Congress demonstrated its failure to address national problems in the post-war period. See also, Calfin C. Jillson, *Constitution Making: Conflict and Consensus in the Federal Convention of 1787*, 64–100 (Agathon Press Inc., 1988) illustrating how the regional differences were openly discussed around the question of representation.

30. Much of the important business of the Philadelphia Convention was done "offstage," in social settings, so that even the diarist's attempt to capture the debates would not identify the currents of views and opinions which circulated. Washington's diary noted frequent dinners and teas with various delegates. Farrand, who compiled the records of the Convention, did not pay attention to such matters. "The social context in which the delegates moved...did not interest Farrand." This "caused him to delete passages about Washington's and other delegates' recreations and amusements in Philadelphia." Hutson, *Supplement to Farrand*, 1n1

31. Farrand, *Records*, Vol. I: May 30, Pinckney, 36; May 31, Pinckney and Rutledge, 53.

32. Ibid. 486

33. Under that plan, the Senate was a smaller body whose members had a longer term, chosen by members of the House from nominees by the state legislature. The difference between the houses was only that the Senate would provide enhanced stability, and perhaps wisdom—another check on the risk of excesses of democracy. Banning, *Sacred Fire*,134–137

34. Farrand, *Records*, Vol. I, 488–9, proposals at 507–8

35. He had proposed that appropriation bills originate only in the House of Representatives. This proposal was included in some subsequent drafts, and a watered down version appears in Art. I Sec. 7 of the Constitution.

36. Jefferson's draft territorial ordinance in 1784 proposed that new states come into the union on an "equal basis" with the original states. See Peter S. Onuf, *Jefferson's Empire: The Language of American Nationhood* (Charlottesville: University of Virginia Press) 67.

37. Luther Martin (MD) reported that the committee established the following week to seek a solution to the small state–large state dispute discussed the likelihood that lightly populated states would increase in population more rapidly than developed ones, and "thereby enormously increase their influence in the national councils." Farrand, *Records*, Vol. IV, 189

38. See Chapter 9 note 40

39. Robert G. Kennedy, *Mr. Jefferson's Lost Cause* (Oxford University Press, 2003)11–16

40. Banning, *American Sphinx*, 68

41. See Chapter 9 note 8

42. Isaacson, *Benjamin Franklin*, 150–1, describes Franklin's calculation of the growth rate of the colonies in 1751.

43. Farrand, *Records*, Vol. I, 509

44. Farrand, *Framing of the Constitution*, 27, 96–7

45. Farrand, *Records*, Vol. I, 511

46. Ibid.
47. Ibid.
48. Ibid. 514
49. Ibid. 515
50. Ibid.
51. Max Farrand, *Framing of the Constitution*, 110, whose volumes *The Records of the Federal Convention* provide the most information about the proceedings of the Constitutional Convention and are relied upon by virtually every scholar, was wrong when he minimized the role of slavery at the convention. "In 1787, slavery was not the important question; it might be said that it was not the moral question that it later became. The proceedings of the federal convention did not become known until the slavery question had grown into the paramount issue of the day. Men naturally were eager to know what the framers of the Constitution had said and done upon this all-absorbing topic. This led to an overemphasis of the slavery question in the convention that has persisted to the present day. As a matter of fact, there was comparatively little said on the subject in the convention. Madison was one of the very few men who seemed to appreciate the real division of interests in this country." Modern scholar Lance Banning, *Sacred Fire*, 549n48, agrees with Farrand. "With most recent students of the convention, I have concluded that slavery itself, although the subject of some bitter words, seldom generated serious, prolonged divisions at the meeting. Most northern delegates were unprepared to challenge the insistence of Georgia and the Carolinas that they would not concur in a unanimous recommendation unless their basic demands were met. The three-fifths formula, familiar from the old Confederation, got the meeting past a number of potential difficulties with relative ease; the old idea that there was an important three-fifths compromise is now universally rejected." Historian Don E. Fehrenbacher, *Dred Scott Case*, 80–1 takes the same approach, while viewing the ordinance and the Constitution separately. Finkelman, "Slavery and the Constitutional Convention" 226–58, has viewed the Northwest Ordinance separately from the Constitutional Convention and has been critical of its draftsmanship because the slavery clause was neither specific enough nor well integrated with the rest of the Ordinance. See his "Slavery and Bondage" in "Empire of Liberty," in Williams, *Northwest Ordinance*, 61–95. His analysis tends to confirm our thesis that the slavery clause was attached in haste because the situation at the Constitutional Convention in Philadelphia required both haste and secretiveness. Similarly, Mark D. Kaplanoff, "The Federal Convention and the Constitution," in Jack P. Green and J. R. Pole, Eds., *The Blackwell Encyclopedia of the American Revolution*, (Cambridge: Blackwell, 1991) 457–70 at 463, says: "Certainly questions relating to slavery were among the most vexatious at the Convention, but the overall importance of slavery in the formation of the Constitution should not be overestimated....The issue did not dominate the proceedings of the Convention nor intrude much into the text of the Constitution." Rakove, *National Politics*, has no separate index category for slavery. His more recent contribution, Rakove, *Original Meanings*, 58–93, has a much more extensive discussion. Lynd, *Class Conflict*, 153–213 sought to move slavery toward a more significant role in the emergence of the nation by connecting the Constitutional Convention and the Northwest

Ordinance. Robinson, *Structure of American Politics*, 41–51, made a similar effort, by connecting slavery to land values.

Our view of Lynd's analysis appears in Chapter 11. Collier, *Decision in Philadelphia*, 204–222 discuss Lynd's detective work in ferreting out the interaction between the Convention and the Congress. They sense there was a deal, but are unsure of its details. They were hesitant to suggest that the North was ready to walk out of the Convention over the slavery question.

52. Only New Jersey and Delaware dissented.

53. Farrand, *Records*, Vol. I, 522–3

54. The Committee also recommended that bills for raising revenue originate in the House and not be subject to amendment in the Senate. This recommendation followed Franklin's earlier proposal to protect the wealthier colonies from having their money spent by the poorer ones, but was later dropped.

55. This enhancement was qualified somewhat in the following week by a change in the initial number of representatives in favor of the "smaller" states.

The small states were NH, RI, CN, NJ, DE, GA (and possibly MD; GA identified with the wealthy slave states). Five of them were clearly anti-slavery. Two committees reported successively on the number of representatives to be allotted initially to each state. Here is how they defined the large and small states:

|     | July 9 | July 10 | Change |
| --- | --- | --- | --- |
| NH | 2 | 3 | +1 |
| MA | 7 | 8 | +1 |
| RI | 1 | 1 | — |
| CN | 4 | 5 | +1 |
| NY | 5 | 6 | +1 |
| NJ | 3 | 4 | +1 |
| PA | 8 | 8 | — |
| DE | 1 | 1 | — |
| MD | 4 | 6 | +2 |
| VA | 9 | 10 | +1 |
| NC | 5 | 5 | — |
| SC | 5 | 5 | — |
| GA | 2 | 3 | +1 |

The states with fewer than five votes on the first and six votes on the second count would be considered relatively small under either count.

The debate on July 10 reflected the efforts of South Carolina to reduce the "northern advantage" by a variety of motions, all of which were defeated. Farrand, *Records*, Vol. I, 566-71.

The enhancement of the voting power of the northern states in the July 10 resolution was in part a response to Patterson's statement of July 9, questioning the initial allocation which took account of slaves. "He could regard Negro slaves in no light but as property. They are not free agents, have no personal liberty, no faculty of acquiring property, but on the contrary are themselves property, and like other property, entirely at

the will of the master. Has a man in Virginia a number of votes in proportion to the number of his slaves? And if Negroes are not represented in
the states to which they belong, why should they be represented in the
general government? What is the true principle of representation? It is an
expedient by which an assembly of certain individuals chosen by the people is substituted in place of the inconvenient meeting of the people themselves. If such a meeting of the people was actually to take place would
the slaves vote? They would not. Why then should they be represented?"
He was also against such an indirect encouragement of the slave trade;
observing that Congress in their act relating to the change of the eighth
article of confederation had been ashamed to use the term "slaves" and
had substituted a description. Farrand, *Records*, Vol. I, 561

56. See his comments in Farrand, *Records,* Vol. I, 463–5: June 29, 485–7; June
30, 529–31; July 5, 551; July 7, 562; July 9, repeating his recommendation
for a compromise of June 30; July 14, Farrand, *Records,* Vol. II, 8–11.

57. Staughton Lynd excepted, historians have not addressed this question
because they assumed that the answer was given by the delegates to the
Continental Congress in New York, and have debated about who, among
them, should get the credit.

58. Chapter 1 note 14

59. See Chapter 10 note 17. The most used proposal was that appropriation
bills should originate in the House of Representatives.

60. Isaacson, *Benjamin Franklin*, 463–7

61. Isaacson, *Benjamin Franklin*, 436–70. Franklin did present a petition to
Congress in 1790, to no avail.

62. See Chapter 12

63. Lynd, "Compromise," in Williams, *Northwest Ordinance*, 187–88, lists the
overlapping membership of the two bodies (Forham, King [MASS], Johnson [CN], Blount [NC], Few, Pierce [GA], and Madison [VA]), and at
207–8, lists those who arrived from Philadelphia in time to take part in
the deliberations leading to the Northwest Ordinance (Blount, Hawkins
[NC], Pierce, Few [GA], Lee [VA]).

64. His explanation of his role in the Hutchinson letters is an example.

65. Isaacson, *Benjamin Franklin*, at index for Richard Henry Lee; Wood,
*Americanization of Benjamin Franklin*, at index for Richard Henry Lee.

66. McGaughy, *Richard Henry Lee of Virginia*,

67. Isaacson *Benjamin Franklin*, 331–32; Wood, *Americanization of Benjamin
Franklin*, 156–57, 189–190, 211, 231, traces the history and longevity of
their animosity.

68. Lynd puts him in New York on July 7. Lynd, "Compromise," in Williams,
*Northwest Ordinance*, 208

69. McGaughy, *Richard Henry Lee of Virginia*, 190

70. See Nagel, *Lees of Virginia*, 131–32

71. See Grigsby, *Virginia Convention*, 143. Others were not so finicky; some fifteen of the fifty-five delegates to the Convention were also members of
the Congress. Lee's opposition to the Constitution may have in part been
generated by his personal commitment to the Continental Congress, and
to his perception that the work of the Constitutional Convention would
be referred to the Congress for a serious review before being sent to the
states. The Convention had been called to recommend amendments to the

Articles, not to create a new system of government. The approach taken by Lee's fellow Virginians in proposing a new structure as well as the ratification process provided in the Constitution itself drastically reduced the role of the Continental Congress and may have induced Lee's opposition to the Constitution. Despite his opposition, he was elected as Virginia's first senator under the Constitution.

72. Jack P. Greene, *Understanding the American Revolution*, 212–24. Other motives might have driven him as well; he was constantly in need of money to support his large family and his participation in public affairs. He had been among the disappointed Virginia land speculators cut off from profit opportunities by the 1763 British prohibition on settlements beyond the Alleghenies.

73. Jack P. Greene *Understanding the American Revolution*, 219

74. Sutton, *Revolution to Secession*, 12–13

75. King's effort had been aroused by Timothy Pickering's desire for a slave-free area north of the Ohio to settle former soldiers from New England. See Chapter 10. Pickering was so strongly anti-slavery that, as a senator from Massachusetts in 1804, he led an abortive secessionist movement of old Federalists in the five New England states and New York and New Jersey. The Federalists were particularly concerned that Jefferson's purchase of the Louisiana territory would "inevitably lessen the weight and influence of the North in the affairs of the nation, augment slave representation, and endanger the Union by stretching boundaries so far as to weaken the country's defenses." Ernst, *Rufus King*, 281–2. Pickering had written to King in March, 1804, expressing his frustration with the situation: "Without a separation, can those [seven northern] states ever rid themselves of Negro presidents and Negro congress, and regain their just weight in the political balance?" Ernst, *Rufus King*, 281

76. Lee's first reported speech in the House of Burgesses in 1759 concluded that slavery was, "dangerous, both to our political and moral interests....Some of our neighboring colonies, though much later than ourselves in point of settlement, are now far before us in improvement; to what, sir, can we attribute this strange, this unhappy truth? The reasons seems to be this: that with their whites, they import arts and agriculture, whilst we, with our blacks, exclude both." Chitwood, *Richard Henry Lee*, 18

77. Chitwood, *Richard Henry Lee*, 19. Richard Henry may well have shared his brother Arthur's views on slavery. In 1767, Arthur published a moral and practical critique of slavery in Rind's *Virginia Gazette*, March 19, reproduced in Nash, *Race and Revolution*, 91–6

78. Chitwood, *Richard Henry Lee*, 211–13

79. Nagel, *Lees of Virginia*, 111. Breen, *Tobacco Culture*, vividly details some of the excesses of the time.

80. Pauline Maier, *Old Revolutionaries*, 164–200

81. John Rhodehamer, Ed., *George Washington: Writings* (New York: Library Classics, 1977) 652

82. Richard Brookhiser, *Founding Father: Rediscovering George Washington* (New York: Simon & Schuster, 1996) 71–3, 131–6

83. Comments of delegates from here to end of Chapter 10: Farrand, *Records*, Vol. I, 578-88; 591-7; 600-606. Farrand, *Records*, Vol. II, 2-11

CHAPTER 11
A SLAVE-FREE NORTHWEST TERRITORY

1. *JCC* Vol. 32, 310. July 11, 1787. The committee consisting of Mr. Edward Carrington, Mr. Nathan Dane, Mr. Richard Henry Lee, Mr. John Kean, and Mr. Melancton Smith to whom the report was referred of a committee touching the temporary government of the western territory reported an ordinance for the government of the United States northwest of the river of Ohio, which was read a first time.

2. Smith, *Letters of Delegates*, Vol. 8, 621–2

3. Melancton Smith was the third member of the committee which recommended the Northwest Ordinance who was credited by Dane with bringing new ideas to bear on the issue. See text of Dane letter, Smith, *Letters of Delegates*, Vol. 8, 621–2. Smith's experience in the next year in securing the ratification of the constitution in New York by adding a condition subsequent seeking a bill of rights illustrates a competence at working through conflicting polycentric problems to achieve a goal of stable government. See Robin Brooks, "Alexander Hamilton, Melancton Smith, and the Ratification of the Constitution in New York," in Kermit Hall, Ed., *The Formation and Ratification of the Constitution* (New York: Garland, 1987) 93–112. On the general approach of the Federalists to ratification, see Rakove, *Original Meanings*, 94–130

4. They, along with Bension, were on a committee to deal with the land purchase.

5. See "Dane's letter to King," Smith, *Letters of Delegates*, Vol. 8, 621–2

6. The additional lands went into the hands of a group headed by speculator William Duer. That group went bankrupt. See Robin Brooks, "Melancton Smith: New York Anti-Federalist, 1774-1798," *1964 PhD Thesis, University Of Rochester*, 64–12,433 (Univ. Of Michigan Dissertation series) 117-43

7. July 13, 1787, *JCC* Vol. 32, 334–43

8. See May 1787, *JCC* Vol. 32, 281. The bracketed and lined words explain the title of the ordinance on May 9, as "An ordinance for the government of the western territory until the same shall be divided into different states." On July 9, the title was "An ordinance for the temporary government of the territory of the U.S. NW of the River Ohio."

9. See Chapter 9

10. These provisions included: 1. A more elaborate provision for intestate succession than had existed in the September 1786 draft. (314) This was a preoccupation of the Virginians. 2. Permission for the French and Canadian inhabitants of Kaskaskias and Post Vincent and former Virginians in nearby villages, to use their own laws of descent and conveyance, rather than those laid out in the ordinance, as required in the Virginia deed of cession. 3. A restatement of the "compact" concept found in Jefferson's 1784 ordinance and King's 1785 bill, which would assure that the elements in the ordinance were carried forward into state constitutions. "It is hereby ordained and declared by the authority aforesaid that the following articles shall be considered as articles of compact between the original states and the people and states in the said territory, and forever remain unalterable unless by common consent." *JCC* Vol. 32, 339

11. "And for extending [to all parts of the confederacy] the fundamental principles of civil and religious liberty which form the basis whereupon these

republics, their laws and constitutions are erected; to fix and establish those principles as the basis of all laws, constitutions, and governments, which forever hereafter shall be formed in the said territory; to provide also for the establishment of states and permanent government therein; and for their admission to a share in the federal councils on an equal footing with the original states at as early periods as may be consistent with the general interest." These rights were: 1. Protection of religious liberty; 2. Proportionate representation of the people in the legislature. The question of proportional representation had been raised in several states where seaboard interests—including the slave owner interests—had retained political control despite the population shifts to the west. (Nevins, *American States*.) 3. Judicial proceedings according to the course of the common law; 4. Bail for non-capital offenses; no excessive bail or fines, no cruel or unusual punishment; 5. Compensation for property and services taken for the public good 6. No law interfering with bona fide private contracts. Rufus King may have had a hand in this; he apparently squeezed such a clause into the Constitution even though it had not been voted upon before the committee of detail redrafted the document. (See Ernst, *Rufus King*) 7. Promotion of schools and the means of education. This clause may reflect a long standing interest of Richard Henry Lee. In his letter to Col. Martin Pickett, March 5, 1786, Lee wrote: "A popular government cannot flourish without virtue in the people, and...that knowledge is a principal source of virtue; these facts render the establishment of schools, for the instruction of youth, a fundamental concern in all free communities....Such establishments will be the surest means of perpetuating our free forms of government, for, when men are taught to know, and well to understand, the great inherent rights of human nature, they will take care not to suffer the hands of office, of violence, or of ignorance, to rob them of such inestimable blessings." Lee offered to give two aces of land "for the sole use of a public school, or seminary of learning." James Curtis Ballagh, Ed., *The Letters of Richard Henry Lee*, Vol. 2 (MacMillan Co.,1914) 411–12. In its July 9 form, the provision read: "Institutions for the promotion of religion and morality, schools, and the means of education, shall forever be encouraged, and all persons while young shall be taught some useful occupation." The final version read: "Religion, morality, and knowledge being necessary to good government and the happiness of mankind, schools and the means of education shall forever be encouraged." This version eliminated institutional support for religion. Governmental support for religion was, at the time, limited to Massachusetts, Connecticut, and New Hampshire. Ruth H. Bloch, "Battling Infidelity, Heathenism, and Licentiousness; New England Missions on the Post Revolutionary Frontier, 1792–1805," in Frederick D. Williams, Ed., *The Northwest Ordinance: Essays on its Formation, Provisions and Legacy* (Lansing: Michigan State University Press, 1989) 41, 42

The initial draft reflected the New England approach of public support for religion, the final version the Virginia approach of separating church and state. 8. Respect and justice toward and for the Indians; 9. Navigable waters to the Mississippi and St. Lawrence to be "forever free without tax impost or duty." See "Benjamin Hawkins to Governor Richard Caneel of North Carolina," Smith, *Letters of Delegates*, 618, July

10. He reported that the Secretary of the Congress had written to him and to William Blount to return to NY to make a quorum. They did so on the July 4. "Blount to Caneel," Smith, *Letters of Delegates*, 618, July 10. One object of returning was of "securing and preserving our right to the free and common use of the navigation of the Mississippi." This, "which is very interesting to the western citizens of the southern states and regards their peace and welfare, has, at length, from a variety of circumstances unnecessary, as well perhaps as inappropriate to relate, been put in a better situation than heretofore." Smith, *Letters of Delegates*, 618-19. There may be an implication that this language was involved in the willingness of the southern states to adopt the antislavery provision of the Northwest Ordinance. The South had long been interested in access to the Mississippi for the settlers west of the Appalachian. Southerners were adamant about opening the Mississippi, and considered the proposal by Jay to agree with Spain to close it for twenty-five years to be dangerous to the union as it served the Atlantic states at the expense of southern growth. Banning, *Sacred Fire*, 58–70, especially 68.

William Grayson, [VA] on May 25, 1785, moved before the Continental Congress that, "The navigable waters leading into the Mississippi and St. Lawrence, and the carrying places between the same, is, and are hereby declared to be, common highways, and be forever free, as well to the inhabitants of the said territory, as to the citizens of the United States, and those of any other states that may be admitted into the confederation, without any tax, impost, or duty thereof." *JCC*, Vol. IV, 638. The motion was seconded by Rufus King [MA], although the northeastern states were assumed to be willing to accept closing of the Mississippi for commercial advantages which Spain might supply. 10. Three to five states to be carved out of the territory, thus keeping the "balance" of slave and free states in the Senate; 11. Admission as state on equal footing when reach sixty thousand free inhabitants, or sooner if Congress agreed.

12. Smith, Ed., *Letters of Delegates*, Vol. 7, 621–2. From July 6 through July 11, the date the committee bill was reported, the states of MA, NY, NJ, VA, NC, SC, and GA were present. July, 1987, *JCC* Vol. 32, 303-13. Connecticut, New Hampshire, and Rhode Island presumably would have supported the antislavery clause, but they were absent.

13. See Chapter 9

14. Smith, Ed., *Letters of Delegates*, Vol. 7, 621–2. From July 6 through July 11, the date the committee bill was reported, the states of MA, NY, NJ, VA, NC, SC, and GA were present. July, 1987, *JCC* Vol. 32, 303-13

15. Ibid. The provision was taken from King's 1785 proposal, see Chapter 10.

16. This additional period would have allowed slave owners sufficient time to settle the area and become influential. As Madison commented on the twenty-year permission for the importation of slaves at the Convention in Philadelphia later that summer: "Twenty years will produce all the mischief that can be apprehended from the liberty to import slaves. So long a term will be more dishonorable to the national character than to say nothing about it in the Constitution." Farrand, *Records*, Vol. II, 415, Aug. 15, 1787.

17. See Chapter 9

18. See "Bartholomew Tardiveau to Governor St. Clair, June 30, 1789," in William Henry Smith, Ed., *The St. Clair Papers* II, (New York: Da Capo

Press, 1971) 117–19. As it turned out, Governor St. Clair interpreted the clause as not applicable to existing slaves. Carter, *Territorial Papers*, Vol. II 332–33. St. Clair had become the first governor of the territory after Manasseh Cutler had withdrawn his support from Parsons at the behest of his "southern friends" and shifted his support to St. Clair. Not for the first, nor the last, time has the selection of an administrator influenced the interpretation of a statute. Nevertheless, the slave interests complained to Congress that the clause was causing slave owners to go to Missouri instead of Illinois. The slave interests came close to securing repeal of the antislavery state constitutional provision in Illinois in 1823. See Chapter 13, the Edward Coles story.

19. Finkelman, "Slavery and Bondage" in Williams, *Northwest Ordinance*; MacLeod, *Slavery, Race* 49–56. Governor St. Clair later interpreted it as applying to slaves subsequently brought into the territory, rather than as freeing those already there. But even this interpretation deprived slave owners of some rights they had previously, most particularly, the right to the labor of children born of slave mothers.

20. *JCC* Vol. 32, 343

21. Maryland had voted no in 1784, did not vote in 1787.

22. *JCC* Vol. 26, 247

23 *JCC* Vol. 28, 165

24. *JCC* Vol. 32, 343

25. Carrington carried the amendment to the Virginia cession agreement required by the ordinance through the Virginia legislature in 1788. His opinion in *Pleasants v. Pleasants* supported a broad interpretation of manumission agreements. See Robert Cover, *Justice Accuse: Antislavery and the Judicial Process* (New Haven: Yale University Press, 1975) 69–71

26. William H. Smith, *Life and Public Service of Arthur St. Clair* (Original,1882; Da Capo, 1971) 132, explains the antislavery clause by "the prevalence of antislavery sentiment among the prominent statesmen of Virginia, at that period. It was not until after 1808, the date of the suppression of the slave trade, when Virginia assumed a new relation to the cotton states, that this sentiment became unfashionable in the Old Dominion. In 1784–87, the echo of the Declaration of Independence had not yet died away. Jefferson believed slavery to be an evil, and drafted an article prohibiting it in all territory after 1800."

27. Grayson had pressed the same motion through Congress in 1785 or 1786. William Blount (NC) was "interested" in the Mississippi question. See Collier, *Decision in Philadelphia*, 212–15

28. Smith, *Letters of Delegates*, Vol. 8, 621–2

29. Dane wrote to Rufus King on August 12, Smith, *Letters of Delegates*, Vol. 8, 636–37, discussing appointments of officers for the territory, and the timing of elections. "Much will depend on the directions given to the first settlements in my opinion, and as the eastern states for the sake of doing away the temporary governments, etc., established in 1784, and for establishing some order in that country gave up as much as could be reasonably expected, I think it will be just and proper for them to establish as far as they can consistently, eastern politics in it, especially in the state adjoining Pennsylvania. You are informed, I presume, of the terms of the Ohio contract. All circumstances considered I think they are advantageous to the public."

Carrington, who was chairman of the committee which reported the Ordinance, wrote to Monroe on Aug. 7th: "We have at last made a break into the western lands....This...will be a means of introducing into the country, in the first instance, a description of men who will fix the character and politics throughout the whole territory, and which will probably endure to the latest period of time. This company is formed of the best men in Connecticut and Massachusetts, and they will move out immediately. I am about to join them with a few shares; what think you of such an adventure?" Smith, *Letters of Delegates*, Vol. 8, 631

Manasseh Cutler, the lobbyist for the Ohio Company, emphasized this point in pressing the Congress for the land contract. After threatening to walk out on the proposed deal and buy land from the states instead of Congress, Cutler said "At length, told them that if Congress would accede to the terms I had proposed, I would extend the purchase to the tenth township from the Ohio, and to the Scioto inclusively, by which Congress would pay near four millions of the national debt; that our intention was an actual, a large, and an immediate settlement of the most robust and industrious people in America; and that it would be made systematically, which must instantly enhance the value of federal lands, and prove an important acquisition to Congress. On these terms I would renew the negotiations, if Congress was disposed to take the matter up again." Cutler, life, p. 296.

30. Manasseh Cutler saw that persuading the southerners, not the northerners, was the way to secure vast land grants to the Ohio Company. He paved the way with extensive correspondence with southern figures, then made his celebrated trip to New York, spending three days there, before journeying to Philadelphia, where he spent his time largely with southern representatives.

31. MacLeod, *Slavery, Race*, 44. Both MacLeod (54) and Finkelman, "Slavery and Bondage" in Williams, *Northwest Ordinance*, 74–7 overstate the importance of "enforcement" of fundamental rights, particularly in the period after the adoption of the ordinance. There was no enforcement mechanism at all for any purpose in most of the northwest territory at that time. "Ambiguous" overestimates the importance of "enforcement" of fundamental rights, particularly in the early period of our history.

32. Robinson, *Structure of American Politics*, 382, states that the territory south of the Ohio " was tacitly set aside for future consideration." David Brion Davis, *Problem of Slavery*, 155: "The Northwest Ordinance tacitly implied that there would be no opposition to the extension of slavery south of the Ohio." Peter J. Parish, *Slavery: History and Historians* (Harper & Row, 1995) 18: "In 1787, the framers of the Constitution employed various circumlocutions to avoid using the actual word 'slavery,' but they gave the institution tacit recognition and protection where it already existed." Lynd, "Compromise," in Williams, *Northwest Ordinance*.

Fehrenbacher, *Dred Scott Case*, 86–87, suggests that the two policies concerning slavery were not intended. "Without being entirely conscious of doing so, perhaps, it officially adopted a policy of having two policies regarding slavery in the western territories. North of the Ohio, slavery was forbidden....South of the Ohio, Congress did not establish or protect slavery in federal territory. It merely refrained from prohibiting the

institution or exercising any kind of authority over it." He disagrees with
the "tacit sanction of slavery" theory as a "perspective distorted by hind-
sight," because the decision to limit the ordinance to the northwest was
made before the antislavery clause was introduced.(79) But the decisions
to exclude slavery from the northwest and to repeal the 1784 ordinance to
the extent it was inconsistent were taken at the same time and together
divided the nation in two. Fehrenbacher erroneously assumed that the
Northwest Ordinance repealed the 1784 ordinance in its entirety. (79)
Feherenbacher does not address the probability that, because the colonies
that ceded their land claims to the United States—particularly Virginia—
had explicitly permitted slavery, that institution remained lawful until
Congress acted against it. See Chapter 9.

Paul Finkelman, a major student of the Northwest Ordinance, has
concluded, "The vigorous defense of slavery by the Deep South delegates
to the Convention stands in contrast to the adoption of Article VI of the
ordinance, if that article is seen as 'antislavery.' However, it is likely that
the Deep South delegates in Congress thought that the Article would protect slavery where it was and allow it to spread to the southwest; thus
they may have seen the article as pro-slavery, or at least as protective of
slavery." But he agrees that the "chain of events [leading to its adoption]
remains a puzzle." Finkelman, "Slavery and Bondage" in Williams,
*Northwest Ordinance*, 88n4, 67

33. See Chapter 8, note 29
34. Clarence W. Alvord, *Governor Edward Coles*, 394-395; "Coles' History of
the Ordinance of 1787, read before the Historical Society of Pennsylvania,
June 9, 1856."
35. "Grayson to James Monroe, Aug. 8, 1787," Smith, *Letters of Delegates*,
631–2. "Since my last, Congress has passed the ordinance for the government of the western country, in a manner something different from the
one which you drew, though I expect the departure is not so essential but
that it will meet your approbation. You will observe that the consent of
Virginia is necessary to entitle the people to certain rights, as also that the
former act is repealed absolutely; I am satisfied, therefore, you will do
every thing in your power to get the state to alter her act of cession in
such a manner, as will square with the ordinance: It seems that the subject was not taken up last year. The clause respecting slavery was agreed
to by the southern members for the purpose of preventing tobacco and
indigo from being made on the N.W. side of the Ohio, as well as for sev'l
other political reasons." There follows a discussion of how the Ohio Company has purchased lands and proposed to "settle the country very thick
and without delay; of course the adjacent lands will become very valuable...from the great number of inhabitants in the eastern states, and in
the Jerseys, I should not be surprised to see them in a very few years
extend themselves by additional purchases quite to the Mississippi,
thereby form a complete barrier for our state [Virginia], at the same [time]
greatly validating the lands on the Virginia side of the Ohio."

This and other letters have given rise to speculation concerning the
reasons for the southern switch. Lynd has extensive discussion on the
issue at 180–8 of "Compromise."

36. See Grayson's letter, note supra. His reference to "several other political reasons" carries on the southern tradition of avoiding public or written discussion of slavery considerations at that period. At the Virginia ratifying convention, Grayson expressed concern about northern domination of the new government, and possible northern oppression of southern slave interests by taxing slaves. See Banning, *Sacred Fire*, 254. See also Mason's concerns, expressed in Frederic Bancroft, *Slave Trading in the Old South* (University of SC Press, 1996) 7–8

37. See Chapter 10 for a discussion of the legality of slavery in the territory between 1783 and 1787.

38. Lynd, *Class Conflict*, 185–213

39. Lynd, *Class Conflict*, 185-213. Davis, *Problem of Slavery*, 154n75, doubts this thesis because evidence of such a deal would have come out in later debates. But this is unlikely because the later debates at the Convention did not involve the repudiation of the Northwest Ordinance.

    Lynd believed that discussions between delegates to New York and Philadelphia may have fashioned a compromise which took account of the uncertainties as to whether the northwest or the southwest would be developed more rapidly and what effect this would have on control of the Congress under the Constitution which was in the process of formulation.

    His view is that the expected southern opposition to the antislavery provision in the ordinance was tempered by three factors: (1) the northwest states might support southern policies in Congress without slavery, (2) the ordinance might have been viewed as tacit endorsement of slavery in the southwest, and (3) there may have been an agreement to speed admission of the new states in the northwest by lowering population requirements for admission.

40. See Chapter 9.

41. Farrand, *Records*, Vol. I, 589-99

42. It did not appear in the draft of July 11. Lynd, *Class Conflict*, 208

43. Farrand, *Records*, Vol. II, 13-19

44. Paul Finkelman, "Slavery and the Constitutional Convention." The "liberation" of a quarter of the slaves in the South during the war both demonstrated the necessity of slavery and contributed to southern nervousness about their personal security. On the effect of the loss of slaves during the war on slave holders at the end of the Revolution, see Frey, 237–8, 243. See also, Paul Finkelman, *Imperfect Union*, 28, 36

    "General Pinckney, August 21," Farrand, *Records*, Vol. II, 364 (Madison) "South Carolina can never receive the plan if its prohibits the slave trade. In every proposed extension of the powers of Congress, that state has expressly and watchfully excepted that of meddling with the importation of Negroes."

    Rutledge, On August 21, in arguing against a prohibition or tax on the import of slaves, Farrand, *Records*, Vol. II, 364 "The true question at present is whether the southern states shall or shall not be parties to the Union. If the northern states consult their interest, they will not oppose the increase of slaves which will increase the commodities of which they will become the carriers."

    The next day, Farrand, *Records*, Vol. II, 373, he said: "If the Convention thinks that North Carolina, South Carolina, and Georgia will ever agree to the plan, unless their right to import slaves be untouched, the expectation is vain. The people of those states will never be such fools as to give up so important an interest."

Madison, at the Virginia ratifying convention: The southern states would not have entered into the union of America, without the temporary permission of that [slave] trade. Farrand, *Records*, Vol. III, 325–26

Pinckney, In S. C. House of Representatives, Farrand, *Records*, Vol. III, 252–5, describes the bargain to continue the slave trade for twenty years. "Show us some period," said the members from the eastern states, "when it may be in our power to put a stop, if we please, to the importation of this weakness [slaves] and we will endeavor, for your convenience, to restrain the religious and political prejudices of our people."

Farrand, *Records*, Vol. III, 165, "all good men wish the entire abolition of slavery as soon as it can take place with safety to the public, and for the lasting good of the present race of slaves. The only possible step that could be taken toward it by the convention was to fix a period after which they should not be imported."

James Wilson in Pennsylvania Convention, Farrand, *Records*, Vol. III, 160–61. "I consider this as laying the foundation for banishing slavery out of this country; and the period is more distant than I wish, yet it will produce the same kind of gradual change that was pursued in Pennsylvania."

Madison to Jefferson, Farrand, *Records*, Vol. III, 131, 135, "Some contended for an unlimited power over trade, including exports as well as imports, and over slaves, as well as other imports."

45. Freehling, *Road to Disunion*, 147–53. Additional influence of the three-fifths rule is outlined in Dumond, *Antislavery*, 69–75

46. If the "supermajority" principle had been adopted and applied to the commerce power, it would have prevented the adoption of antislavery legislation of any type. See George Mason's explanation, Farrand, *Records*, Vol. III, 211–13. Charles Cotesworth Pinckney had moved to require a two-thirds vote on statutes regulating interstate and foreign commerce (navigation acts). He believed that the different interests of the northern states would lead them to adopt laws which disfavored the South. But his colleague, General Charles Pinckney, disagreed. He viewed the grant of power to regulate foreign commerce as a "pure concession" on the part of the southern states, whose "true interest" was to have no regulation of commerce, "but considering the loss brought on the commerce of the eastern states by the Revolution, their liberal conduct toward the views of South Carolina, [Farrand says this means the permission to import slaves. He considered this debate an expression of the "understanding on the two subjects of navigation and slavery"] and the interests the weak southern states had in being united with the strong eastern states," he thought it proper that no fetters should be imposed on the power of making commercial regulations, and that his constituents, though prejudiced against the eastern states, would be reconciled to this liberality. He had himself, he said, prejudices against the eastern states before he came here, but would acknowledge that he had found them as liberal and candid as any men whatever. Immediately after the proposal for a two-thirds vote on regulation of congress was defeated, Delegate Butler moved the adoption of the fugitive slave clause, and it was approved unanimously without

debate (Farrand, *Records*, Vol. II, 446, 453) suggesting that it was indeed a part of a compromise reached off of the convention floor.

47. Paul Finkelman, "Slavery and the Constitutional Convention," 188–225, 190–192, lists five clauses directly supporting slavery and ten clauses which do so indirectly in addition to restraints arising from the limited powers of the federal government.

48. General Pinckney explained the self interest of Virginia, Farrand, *Records*, Vol. II, 371–72. "General Pinckney declared it to be his firm opinion that if himself & all his colleagues were to sign the Constitution & use their personal influence, it would be of no avail toward obtaining the assent of their constituents. S. Carolina & Georgia cannot do without slaves. He contended that the importation of slaves would be fore the interest of the whole Union. The more slaves, the more produce to employ the carrying trade. The more consumption also, and the more of this, the more of revenue for the common treasury."

49. Thomas P. Abernathy, *Western Lands and the American Revolution*, (New York: Russell and Russell, 1937)

50. See Monroe's report, Chapter 9

51. Finkelman, "Slavery and Bondage" in Williams, *Northwest Ordinance*, 88n4

52. Charles A. Beard, *An Economic Interpretation of the Constitution* (New York: MacMillan Co., 1913) 29. Beard's list of considerations included, "the South had many men who were rich in property other than slaves, and it was this type, rather than the slave-holding planter as such which was represented at the convention" (at 30). This point was factually incorrect. See Nevins, *American States*. Beard incorrectly assumed that the wealth of the southern political leadership was not based on slavery, nor did he explain that the "overbalancing considerations" included protection of slavery in the southwestern territories. In addition Beard disregarded the fact that slaves increased land values thus enhancing the wealth of the southern economy. Henretta, "Wealth and Social Structure"

53. Jensen, *Articles of Confederation*, 111–24, discusses the extensive migration south during this period.

54. Morgan, *American Slavery*, 309. "No white person was killed in a slave rebellion in colonial Virginia"

55. Ibid. 265

56. Ibid. 250–70

57. Jack P. Greene, "The Constitution of 1787 and the Question of Southern Distinctiveness," in Robert J. Haws, Ed., *The South's Role in the Creation of the Bill of Rights* (Jackson: University Press of MS, 1991) 28

58. The French government resolved the student unrest which had ground Paris to a halt in 1968, by designating a university—Vincennes—to emphasize the concerns of the "radicals." They flocked to "their" university, thereby leaving the rest of the universities without a radical presence.

59. Thus both Dane and Carrington reported proudly that the Northwest Ordinance would send Massachusetts and Connecticut men to the west, and provide a buffer for the northern lands of Virginia. MacLeod, *Slavery, Race*, 144–45, notes that more than one thousand Quakers from South Carolina left for Ohio between 1805 and 1819.

60. Lynd, "Compromise," in *Class Conflict*, 212, comes close to this point at the close of his essay. "Finally, why did the Congress and the Convention act

so differently? The evidence suggests that the motives which moved men in making ordinance and constitution were essentially the same. The drafters at Philadelphia were troubled about slavery, as were the legislators in New York. But in Congress, southerners who sought to guarantee slave prospect and to make possible a stronger southern voice in Congress saw northwest settlement, even without slavery, as a means to these ends."

61. Monroe, Writings, Vol. III, p. 253, June 15, 1801

62. Jefferson, "Letter to J. Monroe, Nov. 24, 1801," in Ford, *Works*, Vol. 9, 317. Jefferson urged consideration of the West Indies and Africa, rather than the west.

63. "At present however, St. Louis is the most flourishing village of the Spaniards in the upper part of the Mississippi, and it has been greatly advanced by the people who abandoned the American side: to that they were induced partly by the oppression they suffered, and partly by the fear of losing their slaves, which they had been taught to believe would be all set free on the establishment of the American government....Much pains had indeed been taken to inculcate that belief (particularly by a Mr. Morgan from New Jersey), and a general desertion of the country had like to have been the consequence. The construction that was given to that part of the ordinance which declares there shall be neither slavery nor involuntary servitude was that it did not go to the emancipation of the slaves they were in possession of, and had obtained under the laws by which they had formerly been governed, but was intended simply to prevent the introduction of others. In this construction I hope the intentions of Congress have not been misunderstood, and the apprehensions of the people were quieted by it; but the circumstances that slaves cannot be introduced, will prevent many people from returning who earnestly wish to return, both from a dislike to the Spanish government, and that the country itself is much less desirable than on the American side—could they be allowed to bring back with them, all those who retired from that cause would return to a man." "Report of Governor St. Clair to the Secretary of State, Feb. 10, 1791," Carter, *Territorial Papers*, Vol. II 332–33

64. Fehrenbacher, *Slaveholding Republic*, 424n11

65. Melancton Smith was the third member of the committee, which recommended the Northwest Ordinance, who was credited by Dane with bringing new ideas to bear on the issue. Smith, *Letters of Delegates*, Vol. 8, 621–2. Smith's experience in the next year in securing the ratification of the constitution in New York, by adding a condition subsequent seeking a bill of rights, illustrates a competence at working through conflicting polycentric problems to achieve a goal of stable government. See Robin Brooks, "Alexander Hamilton, Melancton Smith, and the Ratification of the Constitution in New York," in Kermit Hall, Ed., *The Formation and Ratification of the Constitution* (Garland, 1987) 93–112. On the general approach of the Federalists to ratification, see Rakove, *Original Meanings*, 94–130

66. The Northwest Ordinance constituted a trial of many provisions which were later incorporated into the Bill of Rights, which tended to protect southern interests. The South Carolinians failed, however, in their effort to limit federal powers by including the word "expressly" in the tenth amendment. This proposal would have further protected slavery. See

James W. Ely Jr., "The Good Old Cause: The Ratification of the Constitution and Bill of Rights in South Carolina" in Robert J. Haws, Ed., *The South's Role in the Creation of the Bill of Rights* (Jackson: University Press of MS, 1991) 101–124

67. Some southern delegates may have harbored the hope that the antislavery provision of the Northwest Ordinance was unconstitutional, although there was no practical mechanism under the Articles to test the issue Madison, in the *Federalist* 38, 248–9), described the Northwest Ordinance and other actions, "All this has been done; and without the least color of constitutional authority."

68. "John Adams to Colonel Smith, Dec. 26, 1787," John P. Kaminski and Gaspare J. Saldino, Eds., XVI *The Documentary History of the Ratification of the Constitution: Commentaries on the Constitution, Public and Private*, Vol. 4, 1 February–31 March, 1788 (State Historical Society of Wisconsin, 1986). In the nineteenth century, the same view of the ordinance and the Constitution was held in the northwest territory. Onuf, *Statehood and Union*, 133–41. Daniel Webster, in his defense of the Fugitive Slave Act of 1850, stated that the sentiments of both North and South underlying both the Constitution and the ordinance were the same. John C. Rives, Ed., "Appendix" *The Congressional Globe*, Vol. 22, 1849-1850, (Washington, D.C., 1854–73) 271.

## CHAPTER 12
## CEMENTING THE BARGAIN: RATIFICATION BY VIRGINIA AND THE FIRST CONGRESS

1. If it were urgent, the trip could be completed more quickly. In 1775, news of the battles at Lexington and Concord, which opened the Revolutionary War, took seventeen hours to travel from New York to Philadelphia, arriving at 10 a.m. on April 21. David Hackett Fischer, *Paul Revere's Ride* (Oxford University Press, 1994) 271

2. Bowen, *Miracle at Philadelphia*, 186; Forrest McDonald, *E Pluribus Unum: The Formation of the American Republic 1776 through 1790* (Indianapolis: Liberty Fund Inc., 1979) 285, mentions the weather but does not give it the influence that Bowen suggests. Farrand, *The Framing of the Constitution*, 104, also spent a paragraph about how the weather changed on July 12. Hutson, *Supplement to Farrand*, 325 amassed considerable detail about the weather during the convention.

3. Farrand, *Records*, Vol. II, 8

4. Ibid. 13–14

5. Massachusetts was divided, and New York was absent

6. Farrand, *Records*, Vol. II, 18

7. Ibid.

8. Ibid.

9. Ibid. 19

10. Ibid.

11. Ibid. at 19–20, July 16. "On the morning following, before the hour of the Convention, a number of the members from the larger states, by common agreement, met for the purpose of consulting on the proper steps to be taken in consequence of the vote in favor of an equal representation in the Senate, and the apparent inflexibility of the smaller states on that

point—several members from the latter states also attended. The time
was wasted in vague conversation on the subject, without any specific
proposition or agreement. It appeared indeed that the opinion of the
members who disliked the equality of votes differed so much as to the
importance of that point, and as to the policy of risking a failure of any
general act of the Convention by inflexibly opposing it. Several of them
supposing that no good government could or would be built on that foundation, and that as a division of the Convention into two opinions was
unavoidable, it would be better that the side comprising the principal
states and a majority of the people of America should propose a scheme
of government to the states, than that a scheme should be proposed by
the other side, would have concurred in a firm opposition to the smaller
states, and in a separate recommendation, if eventually necessary. Others
seemed more inclined to yield to the smaller states, and to concur in such
an act however imperfect and exceptionable, as might be agreed on by
the Convention as a body, though decided by a bare majority of states
and by a minority of the people of the United States. It is probable that
the result of this consultation satisfied the smaller states that they had
nothing to apprehend from a Union of the larger, in any plan whatever
against the equality of votes in the Senate."

12. Banning, *Sacred Fire*, 157
13. Bowen, *Miracle at Philadelphia*, 200–204, neatly summarizes the discus-
    sions of slavery. See also, Wiecek, *Antislavery Constitutionalism*, 62–83;
    Fehrenbacher, *Slaveholding Republic*, 29–37
14. Farrand, *Records*, Vol. II, 364
15. Ibid.
16. Ibid.
17. Ibid.
18. Farrand, *Records*, Vol. II, 369–70
19. Mason, Elsworth, and Pinckney comments Ibid. 370-1
20. Ibid. 374–5
21. Ibid. 400
22. Ibid. 409
23. Ibid. 415
24. Ibid. 443
25. This was the anti-*Somerset* provision discussed in Chapter 8.
26. Farrand, *Records*, Vol. II, 443. See Finkelman, *Imperfect Union*, 9–40.
    Finkelman's explanation——that pro-slavery delegates believed the issue
    was already decided in their favor—seems unlikely in light of their sensi-
    tivity to the question, which he discusses fully at 28–32, 34–36, 40
27. Art. IV, Sec. 2
28. Madison's notes, Farrand, *Records*, Vol. II, 443
    "Art. XIV was taken up. (reading 'The citizens of each state shall be
    entitled to all privileges and immunities of citizens in the several states.')
    Gen. Pinckney was not satisfied with it. He seemed to wish some provi-
    sion should be included in favor of property in slaves. On the question,
    Ayes 9, Noes 1 (SC), divided 1 (Geo.)" This exchange suggests that to
    Pinckney, the "stripped down" privileges and immunities clause did
    deprive the citizens of the slave states of the right to take their slave
    property to non-slave states and to take them home again. George Mason

of Virginia noted that the protections for "removing their property" of Article 4 of the Confederation had been taken away by the Constitution, Farrand, *Records*, Vol. II, 637

The Confederate Constitution corrected this "error" by reestablishing the privileges and immunities clause from the Articles, and strengthening the fugitive slave clause. Finkelman, *Imperfect Union*, 21. The Confederacy was fighting Somerset's ghost as late as 1861, ninety years after Lord Mansfield's decision.

29. Farrand, *Records*, Vol. II, 443
30. Ibid. 446. Madison, in debate in VA convention, June 17, 1788, Farrand, *Records*, Vol. III, 324–5, regarding Art. 1, Sec. 9: "I should conceive this clause to be impolitic, if it were one of those things which could be excluded without encountering greater evils. The southern states would not have entered into the union of America without the temporary permission of that trade. And if they were excluded from the union, the consequences might be dreadful to them and to us....No power is given to the general government to interpose with respect to the property in slaves now held by the states....They cannot prevent the importation of slaves for twenty years; but after that period they can. The gentlemen from South Carolina and Georgia argued in this manner: 'We have now liberty to import this species of property, and much of the property now possessed has been purchased or otherwise acquired in contemplation of improving it by the assistance of imported slaves. What would be the consequence of hindering us from it? The slaves of Virginia would rise in value, and we would be obliged to go to your markets.'"
31. Farrand, *Records*, Vol. II, 454. Butler's initial motion included the word "justly." That was later removed.
32. Art. IV, Sec. 2
33. "Madison's speech to the Virginia ratifying convention, June 17, 1788," Farrand, *Records*, Vol. III, 325: "Another clause secures to us that property which we now possess. At present, if any slave elopes to any of those states where slaves are free, he becomes emancipated by their laws. For the laws of the states are uncharitable to one another in this respect. But [the fugitive slave clause] was expressly inserted to enable owners of slaves to reclaim them. This is a better security than any that now exist."
34. See Wiecek, *Antislavery Constitutionalism*, 54, quoting New Jersey Statute of 1786, which prohibited the foreign slave trade, both to discontinue "the barbarous custom of bringing the unoffending Africans from their native country and connections into a state of slavery," and, "to afford ample support to such of the community as depend upon their labour for their daily subsistence," the state should not increase the pool of slave labor. Owners seeking to emancipate slaves in NJ were required to guarantee that they would not become public charges.
35. Finkelman, *Imperfect Union*, 146–180
36. Farrand, *Records*, Vol. II, 559. No one mentioned that the concept of an "unamendable" provision in the Constitution was inconsistent with the principle of the Declaration of Independence concerning the right of the people to "alter or abolish" a form of government that no longer served their interests.
37. His diary is highly detailed about some matters as befits a scientific

approach of one who also had a eye for beautiful and engaging women, but he was vague about his role with respect to the Northwest Ordinance. He left New York on the evening of July 10, en route to Philadelphia. After reporting a dinner with fifteen different sorts of wine, he added this paragraph: "As Congress was now engaging in settling the form of government for the federal territory, for which a bill had been prepared, and a copy sent to me, with leave to make remarks and propose amendments, and which I had taken the liberty to remark upon, and to propose several amendments, I thought this the most favorable opportunity to go on to Philadelphia. Accordingly, after I had returned the bill with my observations, I set out at seven o'clock." Cutler, *Journals*, 242

Barrett, *Evolution of the Ordinance*, 71, questioned which bill Cutler saw; the May 10 version as amended by July 9, or the version introduced on July 11, which contained significant changes and additions? On this turns part of the claim that Cutler was responsible for the antislavery article. His second diary entry discussed below, makes clear that he did not see the July 11 version.

Cutler returned to New York on the evening of July 17, on July 18 renewed his negotiations with Congress, and on July 19 called on some members very early in the morning (Cutler, *Journals*, 292–3) and: "Was furnished with the ordinance establishing a government in the western federal territory. It is in a degree new modeled. The amendments I proposed have all been made except one, and that is better qualified. It was that we should not be subject to continental taxation until we were entitled to full representation in Congress. This could not be fully obtained, for it was considered in Congress as offering a premium to emigrants. They have granted us representation, with right of debating, but not of voting, upon our being first subject to taxation."

The language which accomplished this appears in the document which was presented by the committee on July 11. This document had not been seen by Cutler, or he would not have remarked on the new provision regarding non-voting-delegate status. The provision for a non-voting delegate appears in Jefferson's 1784 land ordinance. Even if Cutler saw the ordinance as introduced on July 11, the day after he left, it would not have contained the antislavery provision. Dane had decided not to include it in the July 11 presentation. William Frederick Poole, *The Ordinance of 1787 and Dr. Manasseh Cutler as an Agent in its Formation* (Cambridge University Press, 1876) 26–7. For a similar conclusion, see Finkelman, "Slavery and Bondage" in Williams, *Northwest Ordinance*, 68–70. Cutler's second entry also suggests that his proposed amendments were "technical" in nature, rather than philosophical, as befits a person preparing to open the wilderness. Several amendments fit this suggestion, but not the antislavery provision. Given the extensive detail about many matters in Cutler's diary—including a description of how he "leaned on" the Congress to grant the Ohio Company's requests by threatening to buy land still held by some of the northern states instead—it is inconceivable that he would not have discussed his proposed amendments more fully if they had encompassed the massive changes which appear in the July 11 document, even aside from the antislavery clause. Cutler, *Journals*, Vol. 2, 295–305

38. Smith, *Life and Public Services of Arthur Sinclair*, Vol. 1,128–30. Citing and quoting Cutler.
39. Lynd concludes that this shows that the makers of both the ordinance and Constitution were ready to compromise the concept that all men are equal. Lynd, "Compromise," in *Class Conflict*, 213. But that principle had been compromised in 1774. In August of 1788, at the last session of the Continental Congress, a committee of Hamilton, Sedwick, and Madison reported on efforts to persuade Spain to return fugitive slaves who had escaped from Georgia. The report was acted upon on August 26. *JCC* Vol. XXIV, 188n3; *Secret Journals of Congress* IV, 439–42 (1937). The matter appeared to be handled as a routine diplomatic problem.
40. See the discussion in Chapter 9
41. Smith, *Letters of Delegates*, Vol. 8, 660
42. Carter, *Territorial Papers*, Vol. II 172–73
43. In the debates surrounding the Missouri Compromise in 1820, the actions of the Virginia legislature in supporting the Northwest Ordinance and its antislavery character were embarrassing to southern supporters of states' rights. On January 28, 1820, Rep. Smythe of Virginia discussed the ordinance, noting that although the South had voted for the ordinance in 1787, it had voted against the antislavery clause in both 1784 and 1785. He did not mention that Virginia had accepted the Northwest Ordinance by changing the deed of cession to conform to its terms. Annals of the 16th Congress, Jan. 28, 1820, 1002
44. Justice Curtis would make a point of this ratification in his dissent in *Dred Scott*, fifty-eight years later.
45. 1 Stat. L. 123 (May 26, 1790.), 2 Annals of Congress 2226–7.
46. 1 Annals of Congress, 2208
47. 1 Annals of Congress, 2211. The obscurity may have led historian David Brion Davis to an incomplete statement in *Problem of Slavery*, 153: "In 1790, Congress omitted any mention of slavery when it enacted provisions for the territorial government of the southwest." The incorporation by reference to the acceptance of the deed of session may not constitute a "mention" of slavery, but it had the same effect.
48. 1 Annals of Congress, 1477
49. Wiecek, *Antislavery Constitutionalism*, 94–5
50. Freehling, *Road to Disunion*, 536–65
51. The land area of the United States in 1790 was 864,746 square miles.

CHAPTER 13
HOW THEN SHOULD WE VIEW THE FOUNDING FATHERS?
1. Onuf, *Statehood and Union*, 133–52
2. On narrow enforcement, See Fehrenbacher, *Slaveholding Republic*, 256–8; Finkelman, "Slavery and Bondage" in Williams, *Northwest Ordinance*, 61; Wiecek, *Antislavery Constitutionalism*, 108–109. In 1857, Chief Justice Taney, thinking he would resolve an impending conflict between North and South, held in *Dred Scott v. Sanford* that the Northwest Ordinance had no effect on slaves who had entered the territory with their masters, and that blacks had no rights that federal law recognized. See Ferenbacher, *Dred Scott Case*, 322–34
3. Washburne, *Sketch of Edward Coles*

4. See Eugene Berwanger, *The Frontier Against Slavery: Western Anti-Negro Prejudice and the Slavery Extension Controversy*, (University of Illinois Press, 1967) 8; Roger L. Ransom, *Conflict and Compromise: The Political Economy of Slavery, and the American Civil War* (Cambridge University Press)22–27. See also, Dumond, *Antislavery*

5. See David Herbert Donald, *Lincoln* (New York: Simon and Schuster, 1995) 23–4

6. E. B. Washburne, *Sketch of Edward Coles*, 21–31

7. Alexis de Tocqueville, *Democracy in America*, Vol. 1 (New York: Vintage Books, 1990) 361

8. *Dred Scott v. Sandford*, 60 U.S. 691, 15 L. Ed. 691(1857). For a full discussion, see Fehrenbacher, *Dred Scott Case*

9. *Dred Scott v. Sandford*, 60 U.S. 691, 15 L. Ed. 691 at 701-02(1857).

10. Associate Justices Campbell and Daniel supporting Taney's opinion, did refer to *Somerset* in a dismissive tone. See Fehrenbacher, *Dred Scott Case*, 396–400

11. Freehling. *Road to Disunion*, Part VI

12. Swayne Wagner, *The Ordinance of 1787 and the War of 1861* (New York: C. B. Burgoyne, 1892) 79. Address before the New York Commandery of the Military Order of the Loyal Legion

13. Alan T. Nolan, *The Iron Brigade: A Military History* (Bloomington: Indiana University Press, 1961). James M. McPherson, *Battle Cry of Freedom: The Civil War Era* (New York: Ballantine Books,1988) 654–63; James M. McPherson, *What They Fought For: 1861–1865* (New York: Doubleday, 1995)

14. Richard Moe, *The Last Full Measure: The Life and Death of the First Minnesota Volunteers* (New York: Henry Holt & Co, 1993) 258–97; James J. McPherson, *Battle Cry of Freedom: The Civil War Era* (New York: Ballentine Books, 1988) 660

15. Edward C. Longacre, *Custer and His Wolverines: The Michigan Cavalry Brigade, 1861–1865* (Conshohocken, PA: Combined Pub. Co., 1997) 151–3

16. Jean Edward Smith, *Grant*, (New York: Simon & Schuster, 2001) 21–2

17. http://americancivilwar.com/colored/histofcoloredtroops.html

18. Hubert H. Humphrey, *The Education of a Public Man* (Doubleday, 1976) 459. The speech was given to the Democratic Party Convention in Chicago, July 14, 1948 (458). This was 161 years and one day after the adoption of the Northwest Ordinance, and the 159th anniversary of the fall of the Bastille in Paris.

19. Charles Whalen and Barbara Whalen, *The Longest Debate: A Legislative History of the 1964 Civil Rights Act* (Washington, DC: Seven Locks Press, 1985).

20. *Griggs v. Duke Power Co.*, 401 U.S. 424, 429-430 (1971). The Chief Justice held that "The objective of Congress in the enactment of Title VII is plain from the language of the statute. It was to achieve equality of employment opportunities and remove barriers that have operated in the past to favor an identifiable group of white employees over other employees. Under the Act, practices, procedures, or tests neutral on their face, and even neutral in terms of intent, cannot be maintained if they operate to 'freeze' the status quo of prior discriminatory employment practices."

21. The plan reads: Philadelphia, 26 October, 1789. A Plan for improving the condition of the Free Blacks. The business relative to Free Blacks shall be transacted by a committee of twenty-four persons, annually elected by ballot, at the meeting of this society in the month called April; and in order to perform the different services, with expedition, regularity, and energy, this committee shall resolve itself into the following sub-committees, viz. I.) A committee of inspection, who shall superintend the morals, general conduct, and ordinary situation of the Free Negroes, and afford them advice and instruction, protection from wrongs, and other friendly offices. II.) A committee of guardians, who shall place out children and young people with suitable persons, that they may (during a moderate time of apprenticeship, or servitude) learn some trade or other business of subsistence. The committee may effect this partly by a persuasive influence on parents, and the persons concerned; and partly by cooperating with the laws which are, or may be enacted for this, and similar purposes; in forming contracts on these occasions, the committee shall secure to the society, as far as may be practicable, the right of guardianship, over the persons so bound. III.) A committee of education, who shall superintend the school-instruction of the children, and youth of the Free Blacks; they may either influence them to attend regularly the schools already established in this city, or form others with this view; they shall in either case provide that the pupils may receive such learning as is necessary for their future situation in life; and especially a deep impression of the most important, and generally acknowledged, moral and religious principles. They shall also procure and preserve a regular record of the marriages, births, and manumissions of all Free Blacks. IV.) A committee of employ, who shall endeavour to procure constant employment for those Free Negroes who are able to work, as the want of this would occasion poverty, idleness, and many vicious habits. This committee will, by sedulous enquiry, be enabled to find common labour for a great number; they will also provide that such as indicate proper talents may learn various trades, which may be done by prevailing upon them to bind themselves for such a term of years as shall compensate their masters for the expense and trouble of instruction and maintenance. The committee may attempt the institution of some useful and simple manufacturers, which require but little skill, and also may assist in commencing business, such as appear to be qualified for it.

22. Nash, *Race and Revolution*, 28–30

23. Finkelman, "Slavery and the Constitutional Convention"

24. Freehling, *Road to Disunion*, 121–31

25. Leviticus 19:34, 24:22

26. Hubert Humphrey anguished before he made his speech to the Democratic Convention which split the Democratic Party over the race issue. Hubert H. Humphrey, *The Education of a Public Man* (Doubleday, 1976) 112–13.

27. "Jefferson to John Holmes, April 22, 1820," in Foner, *Basic Writings of Thomas Jefferson*, XV 248-50

28. "Jefferson to Roger C. Weightman, June 24, 1826," Andrew Lipscomb and Albert Bergh, Eds., *Writings of Thomas Jefferson* Vol. XVI (Washington, DC: Publisher, 1903) 181–82. The source of this phrasing is discussed in Ellis, *American Sphinx*, 289, and Maier, *American Scripture*, 125

28. Commager, *Documents of American History*, 488–9
29. Lincoln's speech to the Republican Convention in June, 1858. www.nation-alcenter.org/HouseDivided.html
   The phrase derives from "If a house be divided against itself, that house cannot stand" (Mark 3:25).
30. Madison, *Federalist* 14
31. http://www.lbjlib.utexas.edu
32. *Metro Broadcasting v. FCC*, 497 U.S. 547, 612 (1990)
33. A statistical study of intentional job discrimination found that eight million minorities and women had benefited from the equality principle in employment between 1975–1999, beyond that which would have occurred under the employment patterns of 1975, and that two million minorities and women were affected by intentional job discrimination in 1999. Alfred W. Blumrosen and Ruth G. Blumrosen, *The Realities of Intentional Job Discrimination in Metropolitan America*. 1999, at EEO1.com and at http://law.newark.rutgers.edu/blumrosen-eeo.html;  Alfred W. Blumrosen and Ruth G. Blumrosen, "Intentional Job Discrimination: New Tools for Our Oldest Problem," 37 *University of Michigan Journal of Law Reform* (2004) 681–703

# Index

# F

# G

# H

# R

Rakove, Jack, 94, 99
Randolph, Edmund, 172-173, 186, 227-228
Randolph, Peyton, 49, 87
Reid, John Phillip, 110
Repugnancy clauses in colonial charters, 21, 58, 70
Robinson, Donald, 40, 88, 94
Rush, Dr. Benjamin, 76, 89, 117
Rutledge, John, 81, 102-104, 147-149, 228-229, 230, 236

# S

Sharp, Granville, 5, 7
Shays's Rebellion, 160, 171-172, 187, 218
Slavery
  declared "odious" by Lord Mansfield, See Mansfield
  distinguished from slave trade, 44, 46-8
  former slaves in Union army in Civil War, 251-2
  impact on white wages, 26, 158, 160, 183-4, 213, 226-7
  lawful in colonies until legislative or judicial change, 163-4
  legality confused in England before *Somerset*, 6-8
  unlawful in Northwest Ordinance, 207-8
Smith, Melancton, 204
*Somerset* decision, 12
  in colonial papers, 15-16
  colonial slaves' awareness, 24
  impact on the colonies, 27, 48, 142, 151-155
  London papers, 12
  prohibited under Articles of Confederation, 145-155
  see Lord Mansfield
  viewed as freeing slaves in England, 12-14
Somerset, James, 1-14
Stamp Act, 17, 30, 48, 50
Stewart, Charles, 1-3, 5-6, 9
Strong, Jonathan, 5
Sutton, Robert, 194